KANT'S MORAL RELIGION

KANT'S MORAL RELIGION

ALLEN W. WOOD

Cornell University Press » « *Ithaca and London*

First published 1970

Standard Book Number 8014-0548-3
Library of Congress Catalog Card Number 71-99100

PRINTED IN THE UNITED STATES OF AMERICA
BY VAIL-BALLOU PRESS, INC.

To the Memory of
Daniel L. Deegan

Preface

Kant's philosophical thought about religious faith has frequently been treated as a weak point in his philosophy. Even Kant's most ardent admirers have often felt it necessary to reject and to apologize for his "moral arguments" in favor of belief in God and immortality, to admit that these arguments are beneath the high standards of the critical philosophy, and even to claim that they are incompatible with the fundamental principles of Kant's philosophy itself. The present study was undertaken in the conviction that this common estimate of Kant's doctrine of moral faith is altogether wrong. I have attempted to show not only that Kant's doctrine of moral faith is consistent with his best critical thinking, but also that a full understanding of this doctrine is necessary for any genuine appreciation of the outlook of the critical philosophy as a whole.

My defense of Kant's doctrine of moral faith remains at all times within the scope of the critical philosophy itself. Yet this scope is broad enough for the results obtained to have important philosophical consequences in their own right. If the thesis of the present essay is correct, Kant's philosophical thought about religion represents a great philosopher's solution to difficult problems that must be confronted by all of us. An achievement of this magnitude cannot be ignored, and, indeed, Kant's doctrine of moral faith may serve us well as a guide or model in any attempt to deal *rationally* with questions of religion, and to apply to them that universal communicability among men which Kant considered the essence of reason and rationality. This choice to remain within the critical philosophy in this study, then, is not motivated by any belief that Kant's thought itself is infallible, but rather by the conviction that his thought does form a coherent and plausible whole which ought to be viewed as such if proper use is to be made of it, and which ought to be appreciated.

Among those who in one way or another have been of aid to me in the preparation of this book, I wish particularly to thank my friend and teacher George Schrader, John D. Glenn, Jr., Ronald Jager, and Max Black. I also wish to express most affectionate thanks to my wife, Rega, for her courage in withstanding personal hardships and the strain not only of her own work but of mine as well.

Quotations from Immanuel Kant: *Critique of Practical Reason*, translated by Lewis White Beck, copyright © 1956 by the Liberal Arts Press, Inc., are reprinted by permission of the Liberal Arts Press Division of the Bobbs-Merrill Company, Inc.; quotations from Immanuel Kant: *Religion Within the Limits of Reason Alone*, translated by T. M. Greene and H. Hudson, are printed by permission of The Open Court Publishing Co., La Salle, Illinois.

A. W. W.

Ithaca, New York
June 1969

Contents

Abbreviations Used
in Citing Works of Kant

A . . . = B . . .	*Critique of Pure Reason*
Anthro	*Anthropology from a Pragmatic Standpoint*
EaD	*The End of All Things*
EF	*Perpetual Peace*
G	*Foundations of the Metaphysic of Morals*
IAG	*Idea for a Universal History from a Cosmopolitan Point of View*
IKU	First Introduction to the *Critique of Judgment*
KpV	*Critique of Practical Reason*
KU	*Critique of Judgment*
Log	*Logic*
MT	*Concerning the Failure of All Philosophical Attempts at Theodicy*
NVT	*Concerning a Recently Extolled Noble Fashion in Philosophy*
OP	*Opus Postumum*
P	*Education*
Prol	*Prolegomena to Any Future Metaphysics*
Rel	*Religion within the Limits of Reason Alone*
RL	*Metaphysic of Morals:* Preface, Introduction, and First Part: The Metaphysical Elements of Justice
RR	*Reflections on the Philosophy of Religion*
SF	*The Conflict of the Faculties*

TL   *Metaphysic of Morals:* Second Part: The Doctrine of Virtue

TP   *Concerning the Common Saying: That May Be Correct in Theory, but Does Not Work in Practice*

VE   *Lectures on Ethics*

VpR   *Lectures on Philosophical Theology*

WA   *What Is Enlightenment?*

Wh   *What Does It Mean to Orient Oneself in Thought?*

KANT'S MORAL RELIGION

Introduction

Kant is a philosopher whose thought is understood far more often in its details than in its general import. Much careful and fruitful labor has been devoted to the analysis of the subtle argumentation of Kant's epistemology and moral philosophy; but his philosophical outlook as a whole, his view of the world and man's place in it, is often grotesquely caricatured, or dismissed through the hasty use of names like "rationalism," "pietism," "the Aufklärung," "idealism," "the protestant world-view," or even "the teutonic outlook." Relatively few have, like Richard Kroner, succeeded in uniting an interest in "Kant's *Weltanschauung*" with a responsible reading of his philosophy. To some extent, this is understandable. Kant is hardly an approachable philosopher, and he is usually far too concerned with the detail and integrity of his philosophical arguments to make concessions to popular intelligibility. But there is an area of Kant's philosophical thought—itself badly neglected by responsible scholarship—which though no less demanding on the reader than most of his writing, does give us a more or less direct access to Kant's outlook as a whole. Here Kant has attempted to focus the results of his philosophical inquiry on man's situation as such, and to ask and answer questions of universal human concern and significance. This area of thought is Kant's investigation of rational religious faith. In his justification of moral faith and religion, Kant exhibits the critical philosophy itself as a *religious* outlook, a profound conception of the human condition as a whole, and of man's proper response to that condition.

The foundation for this outlook can be found in the character of "criticism" itself. The critical philosophy, true to the Socratic tradition, is a philosophy of human self-knowledge. Kant describes the task of a "critique of pure reason" as "the most difficult of all [reason's] tasks, namely, that of self-knowledge".[1] For Kant, this self-knowledge takes the form of a *critique* of man's highest faculty (reason) by that faculty itself. This critique is described as a "tribunal" whose purpose is to discover the "sources, extent and limits" of human reason.

The critical enterprise, so conceived, has two contrasting aspects. Its aim is to investigate human *capabilities*, to make man aware of what he is able to do and know. As such, the critical philosophy is a philosophy of "enlightenment," a philosophy which exhorts man to have the courage to use his own reason.[2] But the critical philosophy also has the task of making man aware of his *limitations*, and of avoiding the errors brought about by attempts to transgress these limits. It is the twofold nature of "criticism" itself which has given rise to most of the interpretations of Kant's conception of human nature as "dualistic."[3] Most of these interpretations, however, have misunderstood the nature of this "dualism"—if this is even a proper word for it—and attribute to Kant a view of man as having "two irreconcilable natures,"[4] as though Kant were maintaining a kind of manichaean view of man. Properly understood, however, the roots of this "dualism" are to be found in the nature of the critical project of human self-knowledge.

The "dualism" in Kant's view of human nature arises because human activity in all its forms is at once subject to the necessary principles of man's *reason* and to the inevitable limitations of his *finitude*. Humanity for Kant is not composed of "two irreconcilable natures," but there does appear throughout the critical philosophy a kind of irreconcilable *tension* between man's rational destination and the finitude within which his reason is destined to operate. This tension, in Kant's view, is the destiny of man as such, and defines the problems which confront human existence. It is, indeed, even impossible to say whether Kant's "dualism" is based on a conception of human nature or on the critical method of inquiry itself. This is so because Kant's critical method is directed toward self-knowledge, and it is impossible to separate the results of self-knowledge from the activity of human reason whereby this knowledge is obtained.

This fundamental posture of the critical method determines the philosophical place of two of Kant's most important notions: sensibility and reason. That man is a *finite* being is expressed by Kant when he says that man is subject, both theoretically and practically, to the conditions of *sensibility*. Heidegger, in his own way, makes this point concerning Kant's conception of sensible intuition:

If human intuition as finite is receptive and if the possibility of its receiving something "given" presupposes affection, then organs capable of being affected—the organs of "sense"—are necessary. Human intuition, therefore, is not "sensible" because its affection takes place through "sense" organs. Rather, the converse is the case: it is because our Dasein is finite—existing in the midst of the essent which already is and to which our Dasein is abandoned—that it must of necessity receive the essent. . . . Kant was the first to arrive at an ontological, non-sensuous concept of sensibility.[5]

Kant's empiricism in epistemology is founded on a conception of man's nature, of his capabilities and limitations, and not simply on the dogmatic claim that the immediate deliverances of sense are the only possible things deserving the name "knowledge." A similar conception of man's *moral* nature underlies Kant's practical philosophy. Man as he can and must know himself is a *living* being, and this alone accounts for the nature of the human will as a faculty of desire, determinable by reason or by inclination. As such a being, man is subject to the impulses of the life-force (*Lebenskraft*) which incline him to fulfill his natural needs as a finite being. Again, man's sensibility is not for Kant the reason we call man a "being of needs." [6] Rather, it is man's *finitude* which gives *transcendental* significance to the sensible factors in human volition:

To be happy is necessarily the desire of every rational but finite being, and thus it is an unavoidable determinant of its faculty of desire. Contentment with our existence is not as it were an inborn possession or a bliss, which would presuppose a consciousness of our self-sufficiency; it is rather a problem imposed upon us by our own finite nature as a being of needs. [7]

Man's finite and hence sensibly affected will is a condition for the possibility of the moral life, in Kant's view. If man were not subject to inclinations (if he possessed a divine holy will), obligation would not be the necessary feature of the moral life that it is. The very concept of a *holy* being excludes the possibility of obligation, for such a being would by its own inner nature follow the law, and would not need the *constraint* which the concept of obligation presupposes. A holy being could not be "autonomous," since an "autocracy" of reason would necessarily govern all its willing. Such a being would no longer be subject even to moral *imperatives*. [8] Human sensibility is thus a condition for the possibility of our moral life, as well as of our empirical knowledge.

Sensibility, then, both in intuition and inclination, is an essential feature of that nature through which man can and must know himself. But although man does know himself as a finite being, limited through his sensibility, he is possessed also of a faculty of *reason*, which points him beyond his limitations, and provides him at once with the measure and the means of his striving. Reason is man's highest faculty of knowledge in the theoretical realm, the sole source of obligation and autonomy in the practical. This highest of all human faculties constitutes the possibility, even the necessity, of man's extension of his strivings beyond his limitations, and is the means whereby the necessary limitations of his nature can first be recognized as such.

Reason is described in the first critique as "a faculty of principles strictly so called"—that is, "the faculty which secures the unity of the rules of understanding under principles." [9] It is in this office of seeking unity under principles that reason is said to seek the *unconditioned* for any series of conditions given by the understanding. A *unity* of any set of rules of the understanding may be achieved only by a synthesis uniting them as *conditions* in a *totality*:

The transcendental concept of reason is, therefore, none other than the concept of the *totality* of the *conditions* for any given conditioned. Now since it is the *unconditioned* alone which makes possible the totality of conditions, and, conversely, the totality of conditions itself is always unconditioned, a pure concept of reason can in general be explained by the concept of the unconditioned, conceived as containing the ground of the synthesis of the conditioned. [10]

This abstract argument is best understood in the context of the first critique by means of Kant's own examples of the dialectical employment of reason. We cannot engage in a detailed discussion of the difficult matters involved in Kant's dialectic without straying far off our path. But it will clarify Kant's concept of "reason" for us to note the *outcome* of this dialectic. The unconditioned, as we have just seen, is a pure concept of reason, a concept whose object can never be met within finite and conditioned human experiences. And yet reason, as a faculty of inferring according to principles, *seeks* the unconditioned in order to unify the conditions given by its sensible knowledge. Such inferences, however, since they purport to give *knowledge* of objects to which no sensible intuition can correspond, are dialectical and produce only illusion. This outcome has two important consequences for Kant:

> The outcome of all dialectical attempts of pure reason does not merely confirm . . . that all those conclusions of ours which profess to lead us beyond the field of possible experience are deceptive and without foundation; it likewise teaches us this further lesson, that human reason has a natural tendency to transgress its limits, and that transcendental ideas are just as natural to it as the categories are to the understanding—though with this difference, that while the categories lead to truth . . . the ideas produce what, though mere illusion, is nonetheless irresistible, and the harmful influence of which we can barely succeed in neutralizing even by means of the severest criticism.[11]

"Criticism," then, is man's self-knowledge of the capacities and limitations of his reason. But because man's capacities and his limitations are seen by Kant as resulting in a conflict, a tension, human nature itself is "dialectical." By this term Kant refers to the natural tendency of human reason to extend itself beyond the limits set by man's finitude for the legitimate employment of reason. A "criticism" of this dialectic is man's own self-knowledge of his tendency to fall into these illusions, and hence his self-knowledge of his own limitations themselves. The tension, the problematical condition in which man finds himself, is thus a result not of "two irreconcilable natures" in man but of the natural conflict between man's finite limitations and his rational tendency to attempt to overcome them. Critical self-knowledge thus reveals human nature not as "dualistic" but as *dialectical*.

The dialectical tension in which man finds himself poses problems for human existence which are a permanent part of man's condition. The limitations of his nature are inescapable; he can never pretend by a "dialectical progression" to reach beyond them. But neither can he preserve his rational nature without a constant encounter with these limitations, a constant temptation and tendency to transgress them. Just as dialectical illusions can never be transformed into knowledge, so they can never be dismissed once and for all as if they were mere blunders. Dialectical illusions, says Kant,

are sophistries not of men but of pure reason itself. Even the wisest of men cannot free himself from them. After long effort he perhaps succeeds in guarding himself against actual error; but he will never be able to free himself from the illusion, which unceasingly mocks and torments him.[12]

The dialectic which leads to moral faith is a dialectic not of theoretical but of practical reason. It results not from our limitations as regards knowledge, but rather from our limitations in the pursuit of our unconditioned and final moral end. Yet in both the theoretical and the practical dialectic, the permanent tension in human existence between man's finite limitations and his rational aspirations is crucially exhibited. In both these dialectical problems, man is seen by Kant as a limited being, a being of needs. And yet at the same time he is a being possessed of a capacity to think and to will which points him beyond these limitations. Rooted in man's condition is an awareness of his own limitation and dependence, his inability by himself to fulfill all the aspirations which are necessary and proper for him. Were it not for the tendency of man's reason

to transgress his limitations, the latter would never have been
experienced by him *as* limitations. But equally, if a critical examination of human reason did not reveal its finitude, the true
awesomeness of man's aspirations would never have become
apparent. The critical philosophy, then, views it as essential to
the human condition for man to be concerned with the awesomeness and nobility of his rational destiny, and yet to be
aware of his finitude, his inability ever to gain a firm hold on
that which his reason proposes as his destiny.

Socratic self-knowledge does not end, of course, with a
mere recognition of man's situation, but rather functions as
part of man's higher aspirations themselves. Likewise, critical
self-knowledge does not consist only in an awareness of the
problematic and dialectical character of human existence, but
involves also an appropriate *response* of a rational and active
being to the condition in which he finds himself. Criticism
makes man aware of the irresolvability of the tension within
which he exists, but also addresses itself to the task of supply-
ing a *rational* means whereby meaningful inquiry and action
may be undertaken in man's state of dialectical tension. Theoretically, this task is the *regulative* employment of the transcendental ideas. Practically, it is the task of *rational religious
faith*. The former shows man how he may employ the transcendental ideas in his theoretical inquiry without falling into
illusion and contradiction. The latter guides man in his rational pursuit of his unconditioned final *end*, showing him
how he may view the world of his moral action so as not to
be led astray by the illusion of moral despair which threatens
his pursuit of his lofty practical destination. Moral faith is for
Kant the rational response of the finite being to the dialectical
perplexities which belong essentially to the pursuit of the
highest purpose of his existence. To understand this faith,
then, will give us access to the critical *Weltanschauung*, to

Kant's most fundamental conception of man's place in the world and of his proper response to the condition in which he, by means of critical self-knowledge, recognizes as his own.

In this book, I shall examine Kant's defense of moral faith, by rethinking it from its foundations in the critical philosophy. I believe it can be shown in this way that Kant's moral arguments, along with the moral faith they justify, constitute an integral part of the critical philosophy. We will see also, I think, that Kant's doctrine of moral faith exhibits a fully rational yet profoundly sensitive religious outlook on the world, which deserves to be counted among the greatest of Kant's philosophical contributions.

1. Kant's Moral Arguments

Kant's moral arguments for God, freedom, and immortality represent an abiding concern throughout his critical works. We find attempts of greater or less clarity and detail to state these arguments in no fewer than eleven of Kant's critical writings,[1] and innumerable allusions to them throughout these writings. Not many of Kant's doctrines were defended more often or at greater length than his doctrine of moral faith. Yet for all of Kant's attention to this subject, and indeed perhaps because of it, we find it extremely difficult to extract from his works any single and coherent account of the line of reasoning with which he attempted to justify moral faith. Very few of Kant's readers seem to have even tried to formulate for themselves in a precise way just what Kant is attempting to show in the moral arguments, and to state clearly just how he tried to show it. And those who do seem to have attempted formulations of this kind appear also to have for the most part concluded that no really valid argument for moral faith can be extracted from Kant's works.[2] But I do not believe that a clear account of the moral arguments is necessarily inaccessible to the patient reader of Kant, and I do think that once a clear account has been arrived at, we shall see that these arguments possess a far greater degree of insight and plausibility than has usually been accorded them.

Before beginning our consideration of the arguments themselves, however, attention must be paid to an important issue in Kant scholarship which relates to our investigation. Erich Adickes, in his pioneering work in editing and interpreting Kant's *Opus Postumum*, concluded that Kant repudiated the moral arguments of his critical period in the *Opus Postumum*, and that he had replaced them with a more "personal" and "subjective" faith in God based on a "subjective awareness" (*subjectives Erleben*) of God in the recognition of the categorical imperative.³ Adickes' conclusion on this point has been accepted as authoritative by many of Kant's commentators since without their realizing—as I believe Adickes did—how problematic any interpretation of the scattered and enigmatic remarks the *Opus Postumum* must be and how much any such interpretation must be based on a particular reading of Kant's published and relatively clearer works. And Adickes' conclusion—valid or not—has all too frequently been *misused* by Kant's interpreters to suggest that Kant himself might have endorsed their own less than sympathetic readings of the moral arguments, or to explain away their inability to understand these arguments by the claim that they are not a genuine and valid part of the critical philosophy anyway.

More recently, however, Adickes' conclusion itself has been cogently challenged by Schrader and, following him, by Silber.⁴ Schrader argues that Adickes' conclusion is based on insufficient evidence from the *Opus Postumum* itself and is rendered plausible only by Adickes' own highly dubious and highly unsympathetic reading of the moral arguments as they appear throughout Kant's published works. It will not be our task here, happily, to attempt an interpretation of the *Opus Postumum*, or to attempt any direct assessment of Adickes' conclusion or Schrader's response. But I think it can be seen quite simply how the argument of the present essay, if it is correct, does contribute to this discussion.

Even Adickes can find no positive "repudiation" of the moral arguments anywhere in any of Kant's works, including the *Opus Postumum*. Thus he says only that in the *Opus Postumum* the moral arguments "*sind so gut wie vollig verschwunden.*" [5] (Schrader, however, contests even this claim. [6]) It seems to me that the absence of a detailed restatement of the moral arguments in the *Opus Postumum* must be conceded to be a conspicuous one, but by itself it can hardly be conclusive evidence that Kant had repudiated these arguments. And it is plain that Adickes' other grounds for his conclusion rest largely on his own claim that the moral arguments always were incompatible with the critical philosophy, that they undermined the "subjective" character of faith, that they constituted speculative demonstrations of the existence of God and of immortality, and that they represent a "hedonistic intrusion" into Kant's ethics. These, quite clearly, are not claims about the *Opus Postumum* at all, and to assess them requires only a careful examination of Kant's own statements of the moral arguments and of his moral philosophy. Of course, if Kants' moral arguments are as clearly unsound, as obviously incompatible with the critical philosophy, and as inimical to Kant's ethics as Adickes and others have believed, then it would be no wonder if Kant had repudiated them at *some* point in his career. The only puzzling thing in this case is that Kant continued to state and restate these arguments time and time again throughout his critical writings, and to defend them at every turn. The puzzling thing then is only that Kant did not repudiate the moral arguments long before the *Opus Postumum*, and that he did not give a more unequivocal repudiation there.

But if, on the other hand, a closer examination of the moral arguments themselves reveals that they are in fact not incompatible with Kant's philosophy, that they are the natural and proper consequence of his ethics, and that they are as sound and perceptive as anything in his philosophy, then it would be surprising indeed if Kant had ever repudiated them; and we could not in this case take his failure to restate the arguments in the *Opus Postumum* as conclusive evidence that Kant had rejected, for no apparent reason, an important part of his philosophical contribution. We should not expect to find Kant repudiating arguments which are sound and perceptive, and we surely ought not to take such repudiations (even if we were to find them) as Kant's best thinking unless they were supported by even stronger considerations. Now it is clear that, whatever we may say about the *Opus Postumum*, all of the reasoning in favor of *our* rejecting the moral arguments, of *our* regarding them as inimical to Kant's ethics and incompatible with his philosophy, come not from Kant but from the critics of the moral arguments. How sound their reasoning is, we will have some occasion to consider in the present essay.

Knowledge and Belief

Kant asserts in many places that his moral arguments are not like the three traditional arguments for God's existence, or any of the speculative arguments for freedom and immortality. He maintains that the arguments he is presenting differ essentially from the traditional ones and, indeed, from any possible speculative or metaphysical arguments. In spite of these assertions, however, the moral arguments are commonly criticized as being "theoretical" in character. Thus Kemp Smith holds the moral arguments to be "illegitimately theoretical" in character and Lewis White Beck claims to have discovered as their "hidden sense" a form of natural theology.[7] It is not uncommon to see Kant as having only deceived himself into thinking that he had formulated an argument which was unlike the traditional ones. Adickes thus bases his claim that

Kant "repudiated" the moral arguments in his later life largely
on the supposed fact that Kant had finally seen through his
own deception:

Yet it always held for him that he must deny knowledge
[*Wissen*] in order to make room for faith [*Glaube*] (B xxx); only
now the earlier practical arguments for God were also counted as
knowledge and as such were rejected.[8]

Adickes must have realized, of course, that passages like B xxx
were intended by Kant to distinguish the moral arguments (in
justification of *faith*) from the traditional speculative ones
(which had promised *knowledge* of God). The question,
then, is not whether Kant's own views on the relation of faith
and knowledge ever underwent any change, but is simply
whether the moral arguments *are* in fact (what Kant said they
were) justifications of *faith* rather than claims to *knowledge*.
    Kant frequently contrasts the moral faith or belief
(*Glaube*) which the moral arguments justify with the knowledge or cognition (*Wissen, Erkenntnis*) at which the traditional speculative arguments had aimed. From what Kant says
about "faith" and "knowledge" it is evident that they possess
both important similarities and crucial differences. Both faith
and knowledge are spoken of as ways of "holding" (*Fürwahr-
halten*) judgments.[9] Both are also said to be ways of holding
judgments which are "valid for everyone" and hence are both
justified or "sufficient" (*zureichendes*) ways of holding
judgments.[10] Both, that is, are judgments held on account of
some good and genuinely "sufficient" reason or ground for
holding them. And since they are justified in this way by a
"sufficient" ground for holding them to be true, both faith
and knowledge are described by Kant as forms of "conviction" (*Überzeugung*) rather than of mere "persuasion" (*Über-
redung*), and both are opposed to mere "opinion" (*Mei-

nung), which is the "insufficient" (*unzureichendes*) holding of a judgment.[11] Both faith and knowledge allow us to "assert" (*behaupten*) the judgments which are known or believed true. These judgments presumably are, or may be, *theoretical* judgments in both cases, and this is why Kant says that "theoretical reason," or the *Erkenntnistriebe*, assumes or presupposes the existence of a God and a future life on the basis of the moral arguments.[12] But this does not imply that the arguments themselves are "theoretical" or that they make claims to "knowledge" of any kind.

The crucial difference between "knowledge" and "faith" is the way in which each is regarded as "sufficient":

> If our holding of the judgment be only subjectively sufficient, and is at the same time taken as being objectively insufficient, we have what is termed *believing* [*glauben*]. . . . When the holding of a thing to be true is sufficient both subjectively and objectively, it is *knowledge* [*Wissen*].[13]

Unfortunately, Kant does not draw the distinction between "subjective" and "objective" sufficiency with the clarity we might wish. In several places, he seems to identify "objective sufficiency" with "being valid for everyone," and suggests that only "objective sufficiency" can give rise to a true "conviction" (*Überzeugung*).[14] But he also asserts that moral faith is "subjectively . . . sufficient absolutely and for everyone" and that it is a form of justified conviction.[15]

A clue to Kant's meaning seems to be provided by his statement that "from a practical point of view the theoretically insufficient holding of a thing to be true can be termed believing."[16] This suggests that Kant does not mean by "objectively sufficient" in this context "valid for everyone," but rather that he means by this term "*theoretically* sufficient." Kant is thus entertaining the possibility that there might be a form of justified conviction which is not held on theoretical grounds, but is somehow justified "absolutely and for everyone" on other grounds which are completely "sufficient" but "subjective" in character. If this is so, then it seems to me that what Kant intends to say is something like this: the holding of a judgment is "objectively sufficient" if the grounds for holding that judgment consist in knowledge of, evidence concerning, or reasoning about the *object* (or objects) with which the judgment deals. Such knowledge, evidence, or reasoning dealing with the existence and characteristics of objects is included for Kant in the province of *theoretical* reason. Thus for instance to hold the judgment that God exists on the grounds that one knows, has evidence, or can demonstrate that God exists, would be to hold this judgment in an "objectively sufficient" way, and to have *theoretical* grounds for this judgment. It would also be *knowledge* (*Wissen, Erkenntnis*) that God exists, and not a faith or belief (*Glaube*) in God. Faith, in Kant's view, is essentially different from knowledge, and no theoretical demonstration or even any evidences (*Zeugnisse*) can be presented in support of judgments which are held in this way.[17] Faith, instead, presupposes that the believer be *conscious* of the "objective insufficiency" of the judgment he holds.[18] Kant anticipates at this point the famous remark of Kierkegaard in the *Concluding Unscientific Postscript*:

If I am capable of grasping God objectively, I do not believe, but precisely because I cannot do this I must believe. If I wish to preserve myself in faith I must constantly be intent upon holding fast to the objective uncertainty, so as to remain out upon the deep, over seventy thousand fathoms of water, still preserving my faith.[19]

Faith for Kant, as for Kierkegaard, is a personal and "subjective" matter. Kant expresses this character of faith when he says that as a result of the moral arguments, no one, indeed, will be able to boast that he *knows* that there is a God and a future life. . . . No, my conviction is not logical but *moral* certainty; I must not even say, *It is* certain that there is a God, etc., but only *I am* morally certain etc.[20]

Yet it must not be concluded that faith for Kant is "illogical" or irrational. The moral arguments are intended by him to justify a conviction which is "subjectively . . . sufficient absolutely and for everyone," to show that this conviction is "the most reasonable one for us men" to hold.[21] The moral arguments, then, will not demonstrate *that* there is a God or a future life, nor will they add a single shred of *evidence* in favor of their existence (thus Ewing's comment that Kant's arguments are of "some probability value"[22] could not be more wrong); and yet, on the basis of practical considerations holding for each man personally as a moral agent, Kant proposes to justify and even rationally to require of each man the personal conviction that there exist a God and a future life.

Pragmatic Belief

We may well wonder at this point how Kant can possibly hope to justify the holding of a judgment without attempting in any way to offer evidence in favor of its truth. Is such a "subjectively sufficient" holding of a judgment even possible? How can I be required to believe something if no shred of evidence for its truth is set before me? And if I can be so required, why can't I then be "justified" in believing propositions true which I *know* are false? But isn't this absurd? "No indeed," we may be tempted to say, "there can be no such thing as a 'subjectively justified' faith."

Before we content ourselves with this hasty judgment, however, let us at least consider the manner in which Kant himself proposes to justify moral faith. Let us first ask what sorts of "objectively insufficient" beliefs admit of a "subjective" justi-

fication. Kant is clearly not trying to justify belief in propositions which are *known* to be false. Nor does moral faith
apply, in Kant's view, to judgments which are *known* to be
true. If I *know* a proposition to be true, all other considerations relating to my holding it are irrelevant; if I *know* it to
be false, no other consideration can possibly justify believing
it. Thus belief (*Glaube*) is justifiable as such "only . . . if
the insufficiency of [theoretical demonstration] is fully
conceded." [23] Kant denies, in fact, that moral faith can apply
to *any* judgment which *admits* of theoretical knowledge as to
its truth or falsity. In the case of such judgments (e.g., historical judgments) there is no "faith" (*Glaube*) but only "credul-
ity" (*Leichtgläubigkeit*).[24] In the moral arguments, Kant is
attempting to justify belief in *transcendent* objects. Objective
uncertainty, the inability to demonstrate or give evidence either for or against the existence of these objects, is in this case
forced upon us by a conceptual necessity relating to the limitations of our powers of theoretical cognition. A form of justified belief, different from moral faith, can occur, however,
also in cases where our objective uncertainty is based only on
an insufficiency of empirical evidence. This belief, which
Kant calls *pragmatic belief* (*pragmatische Glaube*), is used in
the first critique to elucidate the concept of moral belief in an
insightful way. Kant describes pragmatic belief as a "contingent belief, which yet forms the ground for the actual employment of means to certain actions." As an example of this
kind of belief, Kant gives the following: "The physician must
do something for a patient in danger, but does not know the
nature of the illness. He observes the symptoms and if he can
find no more likely alternative he judges it to be a case of
phthisis." [25]

Pragmatic belief, it should be noted, is not itself a means to
an end, but a "ground for the . . . employment of means."

But it may be strongly objected that this example does not offer us any unique way of justifying beliefs. The only justification for the physician's belief here is the actual evidence in favor of the patient's having phthisis, and his belief is justified only insofar as evidence to this effect is present. Or, indeed, it might be urged (in a vein reminiscent of the intellectual puritanism of W. K. Clifford) that in such a case *belief* is a dangerous luxury on the physician's part, a luxury which he cannot in good faith afford. Such a "belief" may prejudice his evaluation of new evidence and prevent his impartial weighing of the facts. In good conscience he must simply treat the patient as best he can and suspend judgment about matters of which he has no sufficient objective grounds for belief.

But whatever the merits of this line of reasoning, it quite misses the point of Kant's example. For what concerns Kant in his discussion of pragmatic belief is not the relation between belief (or action) and the evidence which justifies it, but rather a *relation between belief and action themselves*, considered apart from whatever evidence justifies them. Let us consider this point further. Suppose our physician were to announce his intentions to cure a certain patient, and that he were to tell us that he is treating the patient for phthisis. And then suppose that we were to ask him (rather moronically perhaps) whether he *believes* that the patient has phthisis. Now Kant's point is that no matter how much or how little evidence he has for believing the patient to have phthisis, he cannot reasonably give a *completely* negative answer to our question. He might, to be sure, give us some sobering information about how uncertain the situation was, he might say that he didn't *know* or wasn't *sure*. For, as Kant says, "even in his own estimation his belief is contingent only; another observer might perhaps come to a sounder conclusion." [26] But unless he is giving a silly answer to a silly question, he cannot reasonably say simply that he does not believe the patient to have phthisis at all. Not only could he not reasonably tell us that he did believe the patient to have some other disease; but it would also be unreasonable for him to tell us that he had decided to avoid the risk of error by a judicious "suspense of judgment." He incurs the risk of error by his *action*, and he cannot pretend to avoid it by disavowing the belief on which his action is rationally based. Indeed, his "suspense of judgment" would be the most unreasonable attitude of all. For we might imagine a case where the physician had a (perhaps quite strong and objectively well-founded) belief that his patient had a minor ailment, but treated him for a more serious one as a precaution. But of course he could not in such a case disavow *all* claims that the patient might have the more serious disease, and would thus maintain a "contingent" belief in this possibility.

Kant's point here is of course not merely that we may *predict* from the physician's actions and his expressions of intention that he will be found to hold certain beliefs. The point is not that (as a sort of general psychological fact) we find that people who act in certain ways *do* actually hold appropriate beliefs as grounds for the employment of means to the ends they seek. The importance of the relation between belief and action for Kant is that it is a *rational* relation. Kant's point is that a finite rational being acting purposively in a situation always "presupposes," "implies," or "commits himself to" certain beliefs about his situation which form the "ground for the employment of means" to the ends which he has set himself. Much as, according to Moore, a person who asserts that he went to the pictures last Tuesday *implies* that he believes he did; and as, according to Strawson, a person who uses a uniquely referring expression *presupposes* that (in the context of his use of that expression) there is one and only one thing to which the expression applies; so similarly, according to Kant, when a person announces his intentions to pursue a certain end, and undertakes a certain kind of action in pursuit of that end, he *presupposes, implies* or *commits himself* to a belief that the end in question is at least *possible* of attainment through the action he is taking toward it.

It might appear that this relation between belief and action does not apply to every case, or at least that a counterexample to it can be imagined. Suppose, for instance, that I am playing a chess game with the chess champion of the world. I am a novice at chess, and it would not be excessive humility for me to admit that I have absolutely *no* chance of beating the champion, that it is quite *impossible* in fact for me to win (not *logically* impossible, of course, but still quite impossible enough). But even conceding this, I might continue to play as best I can and play to all appearances with the goal of *winning* (I will protect my king, attempt to take my opponent's pieces, and so on). Now here it seems reasonable to describe my behavior by saying, "He is trying to beat the champion, although he knows it is impossible for him to do so." Moreover, it also seems that it is not in the least irrational for me to play against the champion in this way. But here I am, with perfect rationality, pursuing an end (winning the game) while firmly believing that it is quite impossible for me to attain this end, and this would seem to be ruled out by what Kant has said.[27]

It seems to me, however, that this proposed counterexample is mistaken, for the following reasons. In playing chess, I am following a kind of procedure which *might* have any one of a number of purposes. The most obvious one, of course, is to win the game. But if my goal in playing the chess champion were not to *win* but to *draw*, or even just to last more than ten moves, my procedure would be the same—namely, to play as best I can. In many cases of this kind, people perform actions without any clear end in view (which is not to say that they have *no* end). They follow a procedure which leads them in a certain *direction*, but are quite willing to leave how *far* they go in that direction more or less indefinite. It would probably be best to say, then, that in playing the champion, my end is simply to do as well against him as I can. But in cases like this, where no *specific* end has been adopted, of course no *specific* belief can be presupposed as a ground for the employment of means to that end. But this does not show that in those cases where one's end *is* specific, that no such belief is presupposed. Thus if I were to announce that I did actually intend to *beat* the chess champion of the world (and not merely to last ten moves, or to do "as well against him as I can") I *would* have committed myself to the belief that it is possible for me to do so.

There are various accounts which one might give of this relation between belief and action. I do not propose to consider this question in detail, but will try to state what seem to me the two most plausible alternatives, without trying to decide which of them is the more plausible. (Each of them seems to have some support from Kant's texts, but there is no *conclusive* evidence, it seems to me, that he favored either of them.) We might say, on the one hand, that a person who pursued an end E but did not believe E was possible of attainment was acting "irrationally," involving himself in a "practical contradiction" of some sort. We would be saying, on this account, that by pursuing E he had adopted a *commitment* to hold some belief about his situation such that E would be possible of attainment according to this belief, but that by not holding that belief he had failed in some way to meet this commitment. We would also say, then, that according to his own beliefs he *should* (in a logical, rather than a moral sense of "should") stop pursuing E.

But we might, on the other hand, view the relation between belief and action in a different way. We could say that the behavior of a person could not even be called "purposive action" unless he believed the end of his action to be possible of attainment. For this reason, we could say that a person who expressed his intention to pursue an end E *implies* or *presupposes* that he actually does believe E to be possible of attainment. And indeed on this account we would regard a remark like "Jones is pursuing E but does not believe that it is possible of attainment" as self-defeating, or even as a misuse of language. Hence if a person claims to be pursuing some end E, but does not believe E to be possible of attainment, we will not say merely that he has failed to meet a commitment; rather, we will say that by failing to believe E possible of attainment, he has admitted that he cannot really be pursuing E *at all* and is just confused or even hypocritical if he thinks he is. Thus on this second account an agent's commitment to hold a belief about his situation such as to make his end possible of attainment will proceed from a requirement imposed on any attempt to give a coherent description of his own behavior as purposive action toward the end in question.

In either case, however, it is clear that the commitment of which we speak is not to be regarded as a "moral commitment" or a *duty*. Neither pragmatic belief nor moral faith is a duty in Kant's view, and he regards it as immoral that beliefs of any kind should be imposed on free men as duties.[28] The "belief" of which Kant speaks is rather a *condition* for purposive volition, or for the rationality of that volition, be it moral or immoral.

We are now ready to see how Kant moves from "contingent" pragmatic belief to moral belief, which is said to be "necessary." In contrast to the "contingency" of pragmatic belief, moral belief is "necessary" in two separate and distinct ways:

[1] The practical point of view is either in reference to *skill* or in reference to *morality*, the former being concerned with optional and contingent ends, the latter with ends which are absolutely necessary. [2] Once an end is accepted, the conditions of its attainment are hypothetically necessary. This necessity is subjectively but still only comparatively sufficient if I know of no other conditions under which an end can be attained. On the other hand, it is sufficient, absolutely and for everyone, if I know with certainty that no one can have knowledge of any other conditions which lead to the proposed end. In the former case, it is merely *contingent* belief; in the latter, it is *necessary* belief.[29]

"Pragmatic belief," as illustrated by Kant's example, is "contingent" in both these ways. The physician is not necessarily acting in obedience to a moral imperative in seeking to cure his patient, so his ends are "optional" and "contingent" in the example. If he finds that it is impossible to cure the patient, he can with perfect rationality abandon his pursuit of this end, and turn his attention to curing another patient, or to relieving the suffering of the doomed man. His belief that the patient has phthisis is also only one possible belief which might be the condition for the employment of means to his end; another physician might judge the patient to have bronchitis, or yet some other ailment, and adopt an altogether different means. The physician's belief is "subjectively but only comparatively sufficient," because it is merely the *best* practical hypothesis *he* can come up with.

Moral faith, according to Kant, is by contrast "necessary" on *both* counts. Our physician might give up his attempt to cure the patient, in which case he would no longer be committing himself to any beliefs about the patient's condition.

But, according to Kant, there is one end, called the "highest good," which is "an a priori necessary object of our will and is inseparably related to the moral law." [30] We cannot abandon the pursuit of this end without ceasing to obey the moral law altogether, and this end is therefore *morally* "necessary." The second "necessity" of moral belief involves the conditions under which this end can be thought as attainable. In the case of the physician, many diagnoses were possible, and many different beliefs might have grounded his purposive action. But, Kant claims, in the case of the pursuit of the highest good, only one set of conditions for the practical possibility of this end is thinkable by a finite rational being: and these conditions involve the existence of a God and a future life.

The necessity of moral belief, then, is made to rest on two claims which are taken by Kant from the critical philosophy. Clearly both these claims are open to question, and both will receive careful attention in subsequent chapters. My first task, however, will be to see how Kant employs these claims in his defense of moral faith.

The *Absurdum Practicum*

In the Antinomy of Practical Reason, Kant claims that if the highest good is not possible of attainment (as the argument at that point threatens to prove), "then the moral law which commands that it be furthered must be fantastic, directed to empty imaginary ends, and consequently inherently false." [31] Now this statement suggests one possible way in which Kant's two claims may be employed in an argument for "necessary belief" in God and immortality, an argument which would be based on the following principle: If in order to obey a command, I must pursue an end which I cannot conceive possible of attainment, then that command is invalid or "false" and I am under no obligation to obey it. According to this principle we may reason as follows: Suppose I deny either the existence of God or of a future life. Now if I deny either of these, I cannot conceive the highest good as possible of attainment. But if I am to obey the moral law, then I must pursue the highest good. Thus the moral law requires me to pursue an end which I cannot conceive possible of attainment. Therefore, the moral law is "false" and I am under no obligation to obey it. In Kant's view this must lead to an "antimomy," since we have already seen (if we have read the Analytic of the second critique) that the moral law is the condition for all obligation and that this law is unconditionally binding on me.

Beck seems to support this reading of Kant's argument when he says, "In the Dialectic's discussion of the postulates . . . we come to the following situation: Given a practical proposition, Kant argues that it can be valid, even for practice, only if a theoretical proposition is assumed and if this theoretical proposition is known to be neither demonstrable nor refutable as such." [32]

Viewed in this way, the moral arguments can be seen to be *reductiones ad absurdum*, which may be stated thus: If I deny the existence of a God or of a future life, I can be made to deny the validity of the moral law. But I know the moral law to be valid. Therefore, if I am to avoid this contradiction, I must not deny the existence of a God and a future life. But if we view them *precisely* in this way, I think it can also be shown that they are extremely inadequate. For consider: I am told on the one hand that a command is *invalid* if in obeying it one must pursue ends which he cannot conceive possible of attainment; and I am told, on the other hand, that the moral law has been shown in the Analytic of the second critique to be *valid*. Now from this I ought to be able to infer that in the Analytic of the second critique it was shown that all the ends one must pursue in obeying the moral law are ends which he can conceive possible of attainment. But one such end (the most important one in fact, the highest good) was not even discussed in the Analytic and in fact discussion of it was explicitly postponed until the Dialectic.[33] And no attempt whatever was made in the Analytic to remove this threat to the validity of the moral law. Hence if I really take seriously what Kant says, it follows not that I must believe in a God and a future life, but rather that the argument of the Analytic was *incomplete*, and that the moral law may very well be invalid. As Cohen correctly remarks, the moral law itself would in this case be merely a "postulate." [34]

But it is evident from what Kant says in numerous passages that he does not mean the argument of the antinomy to prove (even as an "illusion") that the moral law is "false" or *invalid*. In the second critique itself, he says: "Duty is based upon an apodictic law, the moral law, which is independent of . . . and needs no support from theoretical opinions . . . in order to bind us completely to actions unconditionally conformable [to it]." [35] And again in the third critique, he asserts that the moral arguments "do *not* say: it is as necessary to assume the existence of God as to recognize the validity of the moral law, and consequently he who cannot convince himself of the first can judge himself to be free of the second." [36]

Kant's misleading way of stating the moral arguments in the second critique seems to me to have been the result of his attempt to state the antinomy of practical reason after the form of the theoretical antinomies in the first critique. the natural dialectic of theoretical reason results from a misemployment of a priori principles, but it never calls these principles into question. And yet it does result in paralogisms, antinomies, unwarranted and contradictory assertions, in *theoretical* errors. Kant seems to have been trying to produce in the antinomy of the second critique also a contradiction between the "truth" of the moral law, proved in the Analytic, and its alleged "falsity." As a contradiction between two assertions, this would constitute also a *theoretical* error. But is the practical dialectic as Kant presents it really a theoretical illusion, a theoretical error? Beck seems unhesitating in his reply to this question:

The illusions are theoretical illusions about *morality*, not *moral illusions.* . . . Because the illusions to be exposed are theoretical, we cannot expect so much novelty here or advance beyond the first critique as we found in the Analytic. Most of the problems have already been discussed in the Dialectic of the earlier critique, though to some degree with a different outcome.[37]

If what Kant intends to do in the Dialectic of the second critique is to justify belief in God and immortality, then it would seem that a great deal of "novelty" *is* to be expected here. Moreover, Kant's own descriptions of the results of the practical dialectic do not seem to bear out Beck's claim that its errors are only "theoretical" ones. If I were to deny that I can conceive the highest good as possible of attainment, says Kant, then "my moral principles would themselves be overthrown, and I cannot disclaim them without becoming abhorrent in my own eyes."[38] And in the *Foundations*, though Kant speaks in a rather indefinite way about the "dialectic of practical reason," it is evident that such a dialectic does not result in mere theoretical error, but in subjective moral sophistries which "adapt moral laws to our wishes and inclinations" and "pervert their very foundations and destroy their whole dignity."[39]

Kant's clearest statement of the nature of this dialectic, and of the strategy of the moral arguments as a whole is to be found in his *Lectures on Philosophical Theology*, where he says:

Our moral faith is a practical postulate, through which anyone who denies it can be brought *ad absurdum practicum*. An *absurdum logicum* is an inconsistency in judgments. There is an *absurdum practicum*, however, when it is shown that if I deny this or that I would have to be a scoundrel [*Bösewicht*].[40]

A moral argument is, then, a *reductio ad absurdum*. But it is not a *reductio ad absurdum logicum*, an argument leading to an unwelcome inconsistency in judgments. Rather, it is a *reductio ad absurdum practicum*, an argument leading to an unwelcome conclusion about the person himself as a moral agent.

In order to see how Kant constructs such a *reductio ad absurdum practicum*, we must return to the rational relation between belief and action which we observed in the case of pragmatic belief. We saw that a person who acts in pursuit of an end *E* presupposes, implies, or commits himself to a belief that *E* is at least possible of attainment. Now from this it follows also that anyone who denies that a certain end *E* is possible of attainment thereby presupposes, or implies, that he himself will not pursue *E*, or commits himself not to pursue *E*, so long as he denies that *E* is attainable.

Using this result, we may state Kant's *reductio ad absurdum practicum* as follows: Assume that I deny either the existence of God or of a future life. Now if I deny either of these, then I cannot conceive the highest good to be possible of attainment. If I deny that I can conceive the highest good to be possible of attainment, then I presuppose or imply that I will not pursue the highest good, or commit myself not to pursue it. But if I do not pursue the highest good, then I cannot act in obedience to the moral law. Therefore, by denying the existence of a God and a future life, I have presupposed or implied that I will not obey the moral law, or have committed myself not to obey it. But if I do not obey the moral law, I am a *Bösewicht,* and presumably this is an unwelcome conclusion about myself, and one that I cannot tolerate. I might of course try to say that I will obey the moral law, but just not meet my "commitment" to believe the highest good to be possible of attainment. But in this case I will have to admit that I am acting "irrationally" and that according to my own beliefs I *should* (in a logical, but not a moral sense of "should") give up my pursuit of the highest good and my obedience to the moral law, and *become* a *Bösewicht.* So in either case, my denial of the existence of a God or a future life has led me to an *absurdum practicum.*

In the arguments as we have just stated it, it has been the "denial" of the existence of God and a future life which has led us to an *absurdum practicum.* It might be wondered whether this would satisfy Kant, and whether he might not also want to exclude religious "doubt" as well as "denial." And it might be questioned whether Kant's argument *could* legitimately exclude such doubt, even if Kant would wish it to. There can be no simple answer to these questions, but we will do well to give them some careful consideration. Kant's argument, it might be said, does exclude the *denial* of the existence of God and a future life; but that this is not the same thing at all as requiring or even justifying a positive *belief* in God and immortality. For if we do not deny the existence of God and a future life, it does not follow that we will affirm their existence. And if we do not deny that the highest good is possible, we need not affirm positively that it is possible either. We might have no opinion as to whether the highest good is possible or not, or indeed we might never have given the matter any thought. And this is at least not so incompatible with pursuing the highest good as would be our positive denial that it is possible. But then we might also have no opinion about whether there exist a God and a future life, or just not think about this question either, and our attitude would not have to lead us to an *absurdum practicum.*

To a certain extent, Kant would agree with this line of reasoning. As a champion of religious toleration, he is more concerned with justifying a proper kind of religious faith than with condemning those who do not believe. There is no doubt, of course, that Kant believes a *dogmatic* atheism to be quite incompatible with obedience to the moral law.[41] But the question of religious *skepticism* is more complex. Kant says in several places that the "minimum" theology it is necessary to have is a belief that God is at least *possible.* This minimum, says Kant, "may . . . serve as *negative* belief, which may not, indeed, give rise to morality and good sentiments, but may still give rise to an analogon of these, namely, a powerful check on the outbreak of evil sentiments." [42]

Religious skepticism, then, is in Kant's view morally tolerable. But it is far from the most tenable of positions. According to Kant, morality requires that we positively pursue the highest good, that we concern ourselves about its attainment and establishment, that we "promote it with all our strength." [43] Now our having "no opinion" or giving "no thought" to the possibility of the highest good may be in a minimal way compatible with pursuing this end; at least such an attitude does not straightforwardly commit us *not* to pursue it. But an attitude of deliberate aloofness, which prefers to have "no opinion" about the possibility of an end, or which never gives the matter any thought, seems to go very badly with "promoting that end with all one's strength." Such aloofness tempts us to accuse the person who adopts it of hypocrisy in saying that his end—of whose very possibility he has no opinion and to which he gives no thought—is an end whose attainment is of vital concern to him. Thus although skepticism may be in a minimal way compatible with pursuit of the highest good, it is far from the most appropriate and rational attitude for the moral man to hold. It is far better—and more honest—for him to recognize the positive commitment he has adopted in choosing to pursue the highest good, and to maintain a genuine belief in God and a future life as conditions for the conceivability of this end as a practical possibility.

The question of religious doubt, however, has another aspect. While Kant does say that the moral arguments justify a *"zweifellosen Glauben,"* he also admits that a truly honest faith may "waver." [44] Kant seems well aware that a faith which is "consciously objectively insufficient," which holds fast to objective uncertainty and preserves itself over seventy thousand fathoms, that such a faith is not, as Tillich has put it, the opposite of doubt, but rather that doubt is an "element" of faith itself.[45] Thus Kant praises a faith which has the courage to cry "Lord, I believe! Help thou mine unbelief." [46] "Doubt" is not a simple concept. The sentence "I doubt it" may be uttered in as many different ways and under as many different circumstances as the sentence "I am afraid." [47] The doubt which is an element of faith is clearly different from the deliberate, habitual, and complacent doubt of the aloof religious skeptic; and the former sort of doubt is clearly compatible with a constant, concernful and devoted pursuit of the highest good in a way that the latter is not.

Now that we have attempted—with some success, I believe —to state the moral arguments in a fairly precise and plausible way, let us return to the question of the personal and "subjective" character of the faith justified by them. Kant of course realizes that a rational *defense* of faith cannot substitute for faith itself, nor can it exhaust the emotional and personal character of faith. The moral arguments aim at justifying not simply the assent to certain speculative propositions, but more

fundamentally the adoption of an outlook on the world of
moral action itself. The arguments themselves cannot fully describe or present this outlook, but can only show that it is justified and point to its general features. If we do not see this,
we will, like C. C. J. Webb, conclude that although Kant's arguments are "consistent," they are "artificial" and "produce
no conviction." [48] In Chapter 5, after I have given the arguments themselves a thorough treatment, I will try to describe
the outlook of moral faith more concretely. For the present,
however, we can see how the moral arguments themselves justify only a faith which is subjective and personal in character.

The moral arguments depend for whatever force they may
have on my regarding the conclusion that I am (or am committed to be) a scoundrel as an unwelcome and unacceptable
conclusion, and *absurdum practicum*. If I am willing to tolerate this conclusion, if I candidly admit that I am a ruthless villain, concerned wholly with my own private welfare and un-
concerned with the furtherance of justice or the improvement
of my moral character, then Kant's arguments are powerless
to persuade me of anything. Kant recognizes this fact, and
notes that moral faith is adopted "freely" and "voluntarily,"
and that the moral arguments are binding "only for moral
beings." [49] For it is only if I freely choose to lead a life in
conformity with the moral law, and to pursue the ends it sets
for me, that I can be threatened by the practical absurdity of
the conclusion that I am a scoundrel. In this way, the moral
arguments depend for their impact upon my personal moral
decision and can justify and require moral faith only if I
allow them to do so by choosing to act in conformity with
my duty. Their "sufficiency absolutely and for everyone" depends upon the universal validity of the command of duty itself, but does not in any way alter the fact that it is only the

personal decision to *do* one's duty which makes a subjective justification of faith possible.* The moral arguments, then, do justify a "subjective" faith, in that they are founded not on objective proof or evidence but on a personal, but rationally commanded, decision to adopt a morally upright course of life.

The Moral Argument for Freedom

Thus far in our discussion, we have neglected Kant's moral argument for freedom, and have spoken only of the arguments for God and immortality. Since the postulate of freedom is not properly part of Kant's philosophy of religion as such, we will not be dealing with it in as much detail as we will deal with the other two postulates. But freedom is closely associated with the postulates of God and immortality, and therefore deserves our consideration also. Kant himself, indeed, accords the postulate of freedom fundamental importance, and even bases the other postulates on it:

The concept of freedom, insofar as its reality is proved by an apodictic law of practical reason, is the keystone of the whole architecture of the system of pure reason and even of speculative reason. All the other concepts (those of God and immortality) which . . . are unsupported by anything in speculative reason now attach themselves to the concept of freedom and gain, with it and through it, stability and objective reality. That is, their

---

* But we must not, with Adler, identify the "subjectivity" of the moral arguments with the "subjective a priori" of the third critique, the "sensible subjective" which we must "presuppose in all men" in the case of aesthetic judgments (*KU* 290g 132e; Adler, *Das Soziologische in Kants Erkenntniskritik*, 203ff). For the latter there can be no "ground of proof," nor is it "determinable by concepts or precepts" (*KU* 283g 125e). But the moral arguments do make use of conceptual reasoning and, if valid, do offer a genuine (moral) ground for belief.

possibility is proved by the fact that there really is freedom, for
this idea is revealed by the moral law.[50]

This passage might tempt us to think that our belief that we
are free is somehow certified in a stronger way than our belief
in God and immortality. We might think that freedom is
known as the "fact of pure reason" which Kant speaks of in
the second critique and elsewhere. And we might even be
tempted to think that freedom is known "directly" by a special kind of experience, perhaps by means of a *"subjectives
Erleben,"* as Adickes claims we are aware of God according
to the *Opus Postumum.*[51] Kant of course never uses such language, either in the *Opus Postumum* or anywhere else.[52] But
it would also be fundamentally un-Kantian to think that we
could be aware of freedom in this way. For even if there
were an *"Immanenz Gottes im Menschengeist"* [53] or an *Erleben* of free will, we could not know these queer feelings to be
evidences of God or freedom without an intellectual intuition;
but at no time in his critical period did Kant hold that we are
capable of knowledge of this kind.

A look at Kant's texts on the "fact of pure reason"—whatever he may mean by that expression—shows that this "fact"
is not usually freedom at all but rather the moral law, or our
rational awareness of it.[54] Kant does say sometimes that freedom and the moral law are "identical," and this seems to be
the reason why he places freedom in the category of *res facti*
in the third critique (and Kant is careful to emphasize the
uniqueness and the nontheoretical character of this "fact").[55]
But if these remarks are intended to express anything more
than that "freedom and the moral law reciprocally imply each
other," then Kant never substantiates this further claim.[56]

The moral argument for freedom must rest, then, on the
way in which it "reciprocally implies" the moral law. But
Kant can no more hold that the *validity* of the moral law de-

pends on the objective reality of freedom than he could hold
that it depends on the objective reality of God or immortality:

The question . . . is whether our *knowledge* of the unconditionally practical takes its inception from freedom or from the practical law. It cannot start from freedom, for we neither know this
immediately, . . . nor infer it from experience. . . . Had not the
moral law already been distinctly thought in our reason, we
would never have been justified in assuming anything like
freedom.[57]

The moral law, as has been said, and as we shall see later,
commands us to pursue the highest good. But more fundamentally than this, it commands us to *will* in a certain way. It
commands us to will *autonomously*, to *determine* our will by
the legislative form of its maxim, rather than by the end we
adopt. But, says Kant, "the conception of this form as a determining ground of the will is distinct from all determining
grounds of events in nature according to the law of causality." [58] Therefore, moral volition in general can be conceived possible only in the case of a being whose will can be
determined by grounds which are *not* events in nature. But
this kind of will is a *free* will.[59] Freedom is then the condition which must be assumed, presupposed, and believed of our
own will if moral volition in general is to be conceived as a
possibility for us. The postulate of freedom thus gives "stability and objective reality" to the ideas of God and immortality
in the sense that only a will which is free can will autonomously and thus make the highest good its end. Thus the furtherance of this end in obedience to the moral law presupposes a kind of volition which can be conceived possible only
if freedom is postulated.

Kant's argument for freedom can thus be stated analo-
gously to the moral arguments for God and immortality: Suppose I deny that my will is free. If I deny this, I must deny

that I can conceive the possibility of my willing autonomously. But in order to obey the moral law, I must will autonomously. Therefore, if I deny that my will is free, I am committed to deny that I do (or even can) obey the moral law. But I am rationally aware that I am unconditionally obligated to obey the law. Thus if I deny that I am free, I am committed to deny that I can do what I am unconditionally obligated to do. This conclusion is presumably an *absurdum practicum*, a conclusion about myself as a moral agent which I cannot tolerate. Therefore, I postulate and believe that I am free, even though I can neither demonstrate that I am free nor produce evidence that I am free. The moral argument for freedom is thus also a *reductio ad absurdum practicum*, and is essentially similar to the moral arguments for God and immortality. It differs from them, however, in that it does not require the doctrine of the highest good, which is crucial for the *absurdum practicum* arguments both for God and for a future life.

2. Finite Rational Volition

We have seen that Kant's moral arguments require two important—and as yet unexamined—premises. The first is that obedience to the moral law commits the finite rational being to make the highest good his end, and the second is that the highest good can be conceived practically possible by him only if he admits the existence of a God and a future life. In this chapter and the next, I shall examine the first of these two premises and seek a foundation for it in Kant's ethics.

Nearly all critics of Kant's moral arguments seem sooner or later to alight on the doctrine of the highest good as the weak point in Kant's defense of moral faith. This doctrine, indeed, is often charged not only with philosophical inadequacy, but also with moral blame. Erich Adickes' conclusion that Kant "repudiated" the moral arguments in the *Opus Postumum* is based in large part on his view that the doctrine of the highest good represents an intrusion of hedonism into Kant's ethics which Kant himself at last found intolerable.[1] Hermann Cohen concluded that the doctrine of the highest good must be completely rejected if Kant's fundamental principles are to be maintained.[2] Kant's introduction of happiness into the moral ideal renders the second critique, according to Fredrich Paulsen, "internally inconsistent" in a way so blatant that it "is probably not to be met with again in the history of philo-

sophical thought." [3] Criticisms of the doctrine of the highest
good as "inconsistent" and "incompatible" with Kant's fundamental moral principles are to be found throughout the Kant
literature. This doctrine is described as "inconsistent with
Kant's moral principles, and highly detrimental to them," and
as "disastrous both from a moral and a religious point of
view." [4]

These criticisms cannot be taken lightly; they represent a
large body of scholarly opinion, and address themselves to
fundamental issues in the critical moral philosophy. The "inconsistency" with which Kant is charged at this point, however, is seldom stated with the clarity one would wish. The
doctrine of the highest good is more often treated with indignant rejection than with reasoned refutation. The clearest criticisms usually maintain that Kant's doctrine of the highest
good contradicts his ethic of "duty for duty's sake," by introducing a "corrupt" motive for moral volition, and motivating
moral action by the promise of rewards rather than respect
for the moral law. It is sometimes noted, of course, that Kant
gives frequent and strenuous denials that his doctrine of the
highest good makes happiness a motive for moral volition. But
such protestations have not fooled Kant's wily critics. If Kant
has not blatantly contradicted himself, still the doctrine of the
highest good is held to be a supreme example of clandestine
moral corruption. In Schopenhauer's picturesque language,
happiness may be detected in the highest good, "like a secret
article, the presence of which makes all else only a sham contract. It is not really the reward of virtue, but yet is a voluntary gift, for which virtue, after work accomplished, stealthily
holds its hand open." [5]

Kant himself regarded the highest good as extremely important in the articulation of the critical philosophy. He even regarded the formulation and pursuit of this ideal as the "chief

goal" of all philosophy and the concept of the highest good itself as representing "the world morality would create." [6]
Hence if this concept is actually inconsistent with his moral
principles, or "corrupt" as judged by them, it follows that in
formulating it Kant himself suffered from a fundamental misunderstanding of the intent of his entire moral philosophy. In
view of this, it seems plausible to think that it may be Kant's
critics, and not Kant himself, who have been guilty of a fundamental misunderstanding of Kant's ethics. I think that this is
the case, and that a brief examination of some of the concepts
employed by Kant in moral philosophy can show that Kant
was quite justified in regarding his concept of the highest
good as "the unconditioned totality of the object of pure
practical reason." [7] In order to see this, we must turn first to
the conception of finite rational volition which underlies
Kant's critique of moral reasoning.

Motives, Ends, and Maxims

In the Introduction we observed that the critical philosophy, both in its theoretical and its practical aspects, is a philosophy of self-knowledge. In a critique of theoretical reason,
this self-knowledge takes the form of discovering the source,
extent, and limits of man's capacity for knowledge. In the
practical sphere, it takes the form of a specification of the
practical concepts proper to our reasoning about moral action
from the point of view of a finite rational agent. The human
will is subject to the moral law as an *imperative;* it stands
under the law which it imposes on itself as *duty.* The concepts of "imperative" and "duty" are fundamental ones for
understanding the nature of finite rational volition. But
equally important are three other concepts to which close attention must be paid. These are "motive," "end," and
"maxim."

The finite rational will always acts according to a *motive,* or determining ground (*Bestimmungsgrund, Bewegungsgrund*), and it is the nature of this practical ground which distinguishes the good, the autonomous will, from the will which is heteronomous or morally bad. Hence there are fundamentally two kinds of motives for human action. Kant distinguishes these in various ways, but it is the same distinction which is being expressed in all of them. The good will is determined by "reason," "the moral law," "respect for the law," "the legislative form of its maxim." The heteronomous, evil, or impure will is determined by "inclination," "self-love," "the principle of one's own happiness," "the matter of its maxim." Kant expresses this point in the *Religion* and in the *Metaphysic of Morals* by saying that the will, or power of choice (*Willkür*), is determined either by the rational will (*Wille*) or by inclination (*Neigung*), depending on which incentive (*Triebfeder*) the agent incorporates into his maxim.[8]

Equally, the finite rational will always has an *end* (*Zweck*) or object (*Object, Gegenstand*).[9] It is for this reason that Kant also calls the will a "faculty of desire" (*Begehrungsvermögen*) or "faculty of ends" (*Zweckenvermögen*).[10] Human action, from a practical point of view, is thus both *motivated* and *purposive.* The same, however, can be said for willing in general. For Kant, the very concept "will" in some way involves both motivation (determination) and purposiveness. This point can be illustrated by comparing the concept of the finite rational will to that of the divine will. The divine will, though infinite, all-sufficient, and totally free from the conditions of sensibility and subjective inclination, is spoken of by Kant as having motives and also as proceeding toward ends—"for no will can be entirely without an end." [11]

The concept of a divine holy will is the concept of a will

necessarily determined solely and exclusively by the objectively practical. Kant sometimes speaks of such a will as standing "under objective laws," though not as imperatives.[12] This
is, however, a misleading way of stating his view. Just as God,
whose understanding is intuitive, needs no "faculty of principles" to obtain cognition of all things, so a being whose will
or faculty of desire consists only in the fact that "the divine
understanding determines its activity to the production of
those objects which it represents"—such a being needs no
laws to determine its will. The motives of the divine will can
be only the objective good of the object of its understanding,
and its purposiveness consists only in the well-pleasedness
(*Wohlgefallenheit*) which God takes in the immediate products of his intuitive understanding.[13]

The concept of a divine will is the concept of a will whose
determining ground, necessary, unique, and unopposed by
need or inclination, is always *absolute* and not merely *unconditioned* as in the case of the human will. God's *Wahl* is no
Auswahl.[14] The finite rational will is subject to the moral law
as an imperative only because *both* duty and inclination are
naturally adopted into his maxim, and form a necessary part
of the practical concepts of finite rational action.[15] This is
what Kant means when he says that happiness "is necessarily
the desire of every rational but finite being, and thus it is an
unavoidable determinant of its faculty of desire." [16] The difference between good and evil in the human will thus cannot
consist in the presence or absence of any incentives (for in
this case man would always be *both* good and evil); rather it
consists in the *subordination* of one incentive to another, "i.e.
which of the two incentives he makes the condition of the
other." [17]

The purposiveness of the human will is also different from
that of the divine will. God never *adopts* ends, or "makes an

object his end," for the same reason that he never chooses *between* motives of action. But in addition, God never is thought of as *striving* for an end. He is all-sufficient (*allgenugsam*). The divine understanding is immediately effective in producing its object. Therefore, God has no "needs" of any kind and no "interest" in objects.[18] God has no ends which are unrealized, which are made the objects of purposive *effort*. But man's finitude—the limitations on his powers, his worldly condition—imposes on him the burden of action *toward* an end.

The distinctive character of finite rational volition is to be found by investigating the relation of motives and ends to its action in terms of *maxims*. Kant distinguishes maxims as "subjective practical principles" from "objective practical principles" or "practical laws":

A *maxim* is a subjective principle of action and must be distinguished from an *objective principle*—namely, a practical law. The former contains a practical rule determined by reason in accordance with the conditions of the subject (often his ignorance or his inclinations): it is thus a principle on which the subject *acts*. A law, on the other hand, is an objective principle valid for every rational being; and it is a principle on which we *ought to act*—that is, an imperative.[19]

Maxims manifest both man's reason and his finitude, both his freedom and his subjection to the conditions of sensibility. They are "determined by reason" but "in accordance with the conditions of the subject." The former feature of maxims distinguishes the human will from subrational animal will, and the latter feature distinguishes it from the divine holy will. Kant puts this otherwise by distinguishing in maxims a "form" and a "matter." The form of a maxim consists in its character as a principle or rule, in its *generality*. Human action always is performed according to a rule; by its nature it has this measure of rationality. If I should decide to go to a lecture on philosophy tonight, this decision is prompted to be sure by a number of particular circumstances. Do I have enough time? Will the lecturer be interesting? Is the subject one which interests me? The particular answers to all of these questions will play an important part in my decision. But even so, my decision will consider the particular facts, and be a decision "determined by reason" in accordance with them, only insofar as I recognize in my decision a rule or policy to act in this way (to attend a lecture) when certain relevant facts stand as they do. This rule may indeed be difficult to formulate in many instances, but it is not often necessary to formulate it in a precise fashion. Still, it is Kant's insight that such a rule must be in use whenever I engage in a conscious and intentional action.

It is one of the inescapable limitations of man and of his faculty of practical reason (a limitation, perhaps, of all other worldly beings as well) to have regard, in every action, to the consequence thereof, in order to discover therein what could serve him as an end. . .—which consequence, though last in practice (*nexu effectivo*) is yet first in representation and intention (*nexu finali*).[20]

A maxim must also have a "matter," or "material" (*Materie*). The matter of any maxim is an end or object of the faculty of desire adopted by the will acting according to that maxim. In virtue of this, the end adopted by the will is also called by Kant the "material of the faculty of desire." Such an end must be present in the maxim if the will is to be determined purposively by it. As we have seen, every will (even the divine holy will) must have an end or purpose. In man, this end is represented in the maxim of his action, and is necessary for the determination of his powers to an action.

Man's finitude imposes on him the task of *representing* ends in all his action, of *striving* for the attainment of his ends. It is man's calling to labor and struggle in the world for the attainment of his ends, and it is his finitude which imposes this task upon him. The representation of ends of action is an essential part of the subjectivity of the finite rational will, and of the life of conscious, intentional action. Men never seek money, or power, or justice, or self-respect, simply in the abstract. They aim at gaining profit from a particular venture, or power in a given social order by means of a particular stratagem. They intend to correct particular injustices, or at any rate address themselves to the reform of a social order with a particular material existence. They represent their ends *amid* the sensible world of which they are a part.

In the maxim of any finite rational volition, both freedom and nature, both the formal and the material aspects of human action, are given at once. Human action is purposive, and each human act has a particular end represented for it. But this representation of an end is made by means of a maxim, a rule. The will always chooses in accordance with rules, and never chooses *only* particular acts.[21] Action in terms of a maxim is always finite rational action, action determined by reason under the conditions of finite material existence. A maxim is not an abstract principle concocted in thought, but a principle embodied in human action, "a principle on which the subject *acts*." Human habits (*Gewohnheiten*) consist for Kant of *rules* of the subject's action, and are therefore the embodiment of maxims.[22]

Maxims and Autonomy

All human action, whether good or evil, autonomous or heteronomous, takes place according to maxims. The maxim of any act is, for morality, the practical concept or rule under which it falls. Hence it is only after we understand the nature of maxims and their fundamental importance for finite rational volition, that we can have an adequate understanding of the nature of the *good* will, or the difference between autonomous and heteronomous volition. Kant's ethical theory is based on the claim that a will is *good* if and only if its maxim has a universal or *legislative* form, and if the will is determined or motivated by this legislative form rather than by the matter of the maxim. Maxims which are adopted and followed on account of their legislative form are called "formal principles," and as such represent an obedience of the subject to objective practical law.[23] In contrast, a "material principle" is one which motivates the will by means of the end or matter of its maxim, and which presupposes such an end as a motive for the adoption of the maxim. Since principles of this latter sort presuppose an immediate relation to an object (or end) as the determining ground of the will, and since all such relations of a finite rational being can be given only through sensibility (intuition), material principles are "without exception empirical and can furnish no practical laws." [24] Volition according to such principles is thus "sensibly determined" or "sensibly conditioned."

The crucial difference between autonomy and heteronomy for Kant therefore lies in the *motivation* of the will, and in the formal universality of its maxim. Every maxim, to be sure, has a matter, and represents an end which the subject actually desires and labors to attain. But this matter need not and *ought* not to be the *motive* for the adoption of the maxim, and hence not the motive for its own attainment. Consider the following case. A man, living in a slum, puts forth effort to correct the unjust and indecent housing conditions to which he and those around him are being subjected. After years of effort and labor, laws are passed and civil agencies instituted to enforce minimum housing standards in his community, thanks to this man and others like him. As a result of his action, and certainly an intentional result of it, his own housing conditions have improved. Now let us ask what moral credit accrues to such a reformer. Many of his neighbors did nothing, put forth no effort, and would have been content to remain oppressed by an unjust housing system. But this man was not. Now it may be that he and his more passive neighbors differed only in their respective tastes, in what they preferred. It may be that for this man improved housing conditions gave him sufficient pleasure and personal satisfaction to make it worth many years of effort to attain them, whereas his neighbors did not think the effects of social justice on them were worth the price in time and labor. If this is so, then in Kant's view no moral credit must go to our reformer, any more than we credit his neighbors. To be sure, his maxim of action may be a universalizable one, such as the principle of correcting a social injustice. But if this maxim is adopted on account of the increment of his own welfare, or even the welfare of those for whom he feels a natural compassion, then his action has in Kant's terms mere "legality" and is not of moral worth.

Of course, it is unlikely that such a man would undertake so difficult and uncertain a project, a project rewarding so great an effort with only a minimum of satisfaction, for the sake of his own welfare. It is more likely, indeed, that the hardest labor would not be done for such reasons, but would require some motive other than his own happiness. And his action would have true moral worth if it were motivated not by what he would in fact obtain by it, but rather by the fact that the principle of his action, his maxim, is one which is sanctioned by the command of moral reason. The *reason why* injustice should be corrected is that he as a finite rational being cannot will a system in which injustice prevails. And his action is of moral worth, in Kant's view, only insofar as it is done for *this* reason, the *objective* reason that it *should* be done.

Let us, then, suppose that our reformer *is* motivated by the legislative form of his maxim. This being the case, his action is of moral worth and constitutes obedience to the moral law. Now his maxim involves as its matter the improvement of housing conditions in his community, including, no doubt, the conditions in which he himself lives. His action has moral worth, and he himself will achieve a certain "intellectual satisfaction" or "self-contentment" in realizing this; [25] but such an awareness will not of itself get housing conditions improved, which is after all the end he has set for himself. And it will not in any way *substitute* for the attainment of this end, for his moral contentment with his action can continue with justification only so long as he continues to *act* from the maxim of correcting unjust housing conditions. His self-contentment is justified, that is, only so long as he continues to desire and labor toward the end which is the matter of this maxim—namely, the actual correction of injustice.[26] This awareness and self-contentment is no more than an intellectual recognition of the fact that his action has moral worth. It is clear that it is *not* intended by Kant to *substitute* for action toward a moral goal, as though what Kant were recommending were not moral striving but a self-righteous and hypocritical moral lethargy.

But let us now turn to the reformer's relation to his end itself. Suppose his end to be attained and that after years of labor the housing conditions of his community have been improved. From this it is to be expected that he himself will be somewhat better off, and certainly he has been conscious of this from the start. But he has not been *motivated* by his own welfare, nor by any other aspect of the *end* of his action.

Hence there is nothing immoral or "heteronomous" about his actually improving his own lot. Indeed, it is just such a person who *deserves* to have his material condition improved.

I think now that we can see what Schopenhauer's criticism, given at the outset of this chapter, amounts to. It would have to be Schopenhauer's claim that in our example the fact that the reformer's own welfare was part of the end of his action "reduces all else to a sham contract," and that there is something "stealthy" in his enjoyment of the benefits accruing to him from the success of his moral enterprise. Now of course this might actually *be* the case, and our reformer might have convinced others (and even himself) that he was motivated by morality when in fact it was his own happiness all along which motivated him. But if, as Kant claims, pure reason of itself *can* be practical, and *can* motivate the will without any consideration whatever of the consequences of one's actions, then this *need* not have occurred. For Kant, there is nothing "stealthy" about desire, granted that the motivation of one's volition is pure. Neither is there anything "cunning" about reason, which knows perfectly well the distinction between right and wrong, and does not take credit for what it has not done.

Many similar criticisms of Kant's doctrine of the highest good rest precisely on the confusion of the *motive* of action with its *end*. The remarks of Theodore M. Greene on this topic are in many ways typical:

Morality is said to be the concern of a purely autonomous rational will. Kant's introduction of happiness into this scheme is therefore inconsistent with his own principles and highly detrimental to them. . . .

The attempt has been made to defend Kant by saying that he intends the individual to seek virtue for himself, happiness only for others. But even if this were Kant's meaning his position would be no more defensible. For he never tired of insisting that *any* appeal to empirical motives, such as happiness, is a pollution of morality and a vitiation of the good will. And if happiness is never to be the motive of action, why should an exception be made with regard to the happiness of others? . . . If the moral law is really to be kept pure it must have nothing to do with happiness, whether my happiness or that of others. How can it be right for me to promote in others what I must strenuously avoid seeking for myself? [27]

In view of the frequency of such criticisms of Kant's doctrine of the highest good, it is interesting to note that Kant himself replied to one such criticism in a 1793 essay, "Concerning the Common Saying: That Might Be Correct in Theory, but Does Not Work in Practice." Here Kant defends himself against the objections of Christian Garve, who was probably the first to note the "inconsistency" between Kant's ethics and his doctrine of the highest good. Garve, like Greene and others, had assumed that if happiness constitutes part of the unconditioned object (end) of pure practical reason, then it must somehow have worked its way into moral motivation and become the *"Halt und Festigkeit"* of duty. Kant points out to Garve that the highest good is not in any case to be regarded as a motive or incentive (*Triebfeder*) of the moral will, but is its ideal *Object*.[28] * It is plain that in the

---

* Beck (pp. 242ff) argues at length that the only sense in which Kant may legitimately say that the highest good is a determining ground of the will is that the obedience to the moral law (the supreme condition of the highest good) is such a ground (*KpV* 110g 114e). His arguments are for the most part correct, though they do not in any way show that the highest good is not—as Kant claims—the unconditioned totality of the object of pure practical reason. Miller (Chap. IV) and Hägerstrom (pp. 515ff), however, seem to believe that it is necessary to take the highest good as a determining ground of the will, and have set about elaborate justifications of this claim. Miller holds that the highest good may be included in the mo-

above passage, Greene too has confused the *ends* of moral action with its motives. Greene refers to Kant's inclusion of happiness in the highest good by the phrase "the introduction of
happiness into this scheme." But such a phrase is ambiguous.
For as we saw above, happiness (the happiness of our reformer or his neighbors) may be "introduced into the
scheme" as an *end* or object of action, without implying that
it is "introduced into the scheme" as a *motive* of action. Now
Kant has specified that the highest good is an end, and not a
motive or incentive of moral action. And yet Greene, finding
happiness "introduced into the scheme," concludes that this
must be a recourse to "empirical motives." Again, Greene says
that the moral law "must have nothing to do with happiness."
This phrase too is ambiguous. Kant's theory holds that a will
is good if it is motivated or determined by the legislative form
of its maxim, rather than by its matter. Thus happiness (or
any other end, for that matter), if made the motive of the
will, results in heteronomous action. Thus happiness must
have "nothing to do" with the *motivation* of the will. But this
clearly does *not* say that happiness must have "nothing to do"
with the ends or objects the morally good man sets for himself in obedience to the law.

Garve, like Greene, interprets Kant as saying that the mor-

---

tive for moral action by an "extended determination of the will," and
Hägerstrom argues that although happiness is not an "objective" determinant of the will, it is legitimately regarded as a "subjective"
one. These defenses are not only themselves mistaken, but they are
also quite unnecessary, since Kant himself wishes only to maintain
that the highest good is a necessary *object* of the will, and he neither
can nor needs to make any further claim (*KpV* 109g 113e). The purpose of the passage in which Kant speaks of the highest good as the
"determining ground" of the will is meant only to establish that since
the supreme condition of the highest good is the motivation of the
will by the moral law, the highest good is the necessary *object* of
any will so motivated.

ally good man must renounce (*entsagen*) or "strenuously avoid seeking" happiness. Thus Garve characterizes Kant's view in the following words: "The virtuous man strives to follow unceasingly those principles whose consequence is to make him worthy of happiness, but never, *in so far* as he is virtuous, those which make him happy." [29] Kant himself notes the ambiguity of Garve's statement, and replies that

the term "in so far" contains an ambiguity here, which must be resolved. It can mean: "*In the act* by which he, as a virtuous man, subjects himself to his duty; and then it absolutely agrees with my theory. Or: [it may mean] only, "if he is in general virtuous," and thus [says that] even where nothing depends on duty or contradicts it, the virtuous man should take no thought of his happiness. And this contradicts my assertions entirely.[30]

Kant makes this point even clearer when he explains that his ethics does *not* say of man that

he ought, if it is a matter of following duty, to *renounce* his natural end, happiness; for he, like any finite rational being, cannot do this. Rather he must abstract from this consideration whenever the command of duty enters. He must not make it a condition of his obedience to the law prescribed to him by reason.[31]

For Kant, the crucial moral question is one of motivation; what must be "strenuously avoided" in his view is making *any* empirical object or material consideration (whether this be one's own happiness, or anything else) the unconditioned motive of the will. Of course, all willing is purposive, and all finite willing represents an end to itself. But such an end need not, and indeed *should* not, become the motive of the will.

"Happiness" and Rational Volition

A critical approach to human volition shows all such volition to be motivated and purposive, and to embody both its *motive* and its *end* in its *maxim*. Further, Kant's moral theory hold that autonomous volition, obedience to the moral law, consists in willing according to a maxim with a legislative form, on account of (motivated by) that form. Our task here, that of seeking a foundation for Kant's doctrine of the highest good, must now proceed by way of elucidating the relation between the special character of autonomous volition and the purposiveness of finite rational volition in general. Man's finite nature imposes upon him certain natural needs, or "natural ends." These needs make themselves felt in man's inclinations. From these natural ends, reason creates an idea in which "all inclinations are combined into a total sum." This idea is called by Kant "happiness" (*Glückseligkeit*).[32]

Since "happiness" has for so long played the role of villain in treatments of Kant's ethics, it will be well to note a few thing about the place of this conception in Kant's moral theory. First, happiness is an *idea*, and thus requires reason for its formulation. Happiness is not to be equated even with conscious inclination as such, much less with blind natural impulse. Second, happiness is an idea formed as the maximum of all natural ends, as "complete well-being and contentment with one's state." [33] Any being who has such ends, and who is capable of forming an idea of their totality, thereby has happiness as a natural end. This is what Kant means when he points out that "to be happy is necessarily the desire of every rational but finite being." [34] Of course, if we are to form a definite conception of what happiness is for some particular person, we must have empirical knowledge of that person's inclinations, temperament, and so on. Happiness is the totality of ends given by experience, the needs and desires of any finite creature. No determinate concept of it can be formed a priori. It can be said a priori, however, that every being who is both rational and finite has the totality of his natural ends as a necessary object of his faculty of desire. Thus, while it is always an empirical question whether any given state of affairs will make a given person happy, we do not need any experience to tell us that a finite rational being has happiness as his natural end. This is, if not a transcendental proposition, at least an a priori "metaphysical" one.[35]

But although finite rational beings necessarily have "happiness" as a natural end, an end given to them by their finite nature as beings of need, such beings also have a higher calling, and are capable of giving themselves ends.

Certainly our weal and woe are very important in the estimation of our practical reason. . . . Man is a being of needs . . . and to this extent his reason certainly has an inescapable responsibility from the side of his sensuous nature to attend to its interest and to form practical maxims with a view to . . . happiness. . . . But . . . that he has reason does not in the least raise him in worth above mere animality if reason only serves the purposes which, among animals, are taken care of by instinct. . . . But he has reason for a yet higher purpose.[36]

It is these two ways of specifying the ends of action which distinguish objects of practical reason from those of pure practical reason. Man's rationality inevitably and properly aids him in the pursuit of his natural ends, both by advising him as to the means of his action, and by formulating the idea of happiness. But this merely "practical reason" is not *pure*, because it requires that ends of action be given in advance, that it might find the means to achieve them, or form an idea of their totality. Moral reason, however, is "pure practical reason," because it and it alone is capable of giving a priori principles according to which ends *should* be adopted. Practical reason is "prudential" reason; only pure practical reason is specifically moral, capable of an autonomous determination of the ends of action.

Now if, as we have seen, it is not Kant's view that happiness is to be excluded from the ends of morality, from the objects of pure practical reason, and if, moreover, happiness is to form part of the unconditioned object of pure practical reason, then there must be a systematic way in which natural ends, the ends given by man's finite needs, can be included within the ends of morality, the objects of pure practical reason. Clearly the housing reformer in our example had as his end the welfare and happiness of many people, himself included. Our problem is now to see how Kant's moral theory takes account of this aspect of his purposive action.

To begin with, we must recall that for Kant the good will is characterised by its motive, it ground for adopting and following its maxims. Obedience to the moral law consists in the motivation of the will by the legislative form of its maxim. It is obvious but important that obedience to the law must have the subjectivity characteristic of all finite rational volition. Obedience to the law, that is, consists in following a maxim of a legislative form on account of its form. Thus the "pure reason" which is practical is the *agent's* reason, and is expressed in the formal universality of his maxim itself. The lawfulness of my volition is to be found in the subjective act of following the maxim I have chosen in obedience to the law. The importance of this observation consists in the crucial role of the agent's maxim, the principle on which he acts, in his obedience to the law. For it is in such principles that man's rationality and his finitude, his motives and his ends, are embodied. And it is in terms of such principles that the *motives* which constitute the autonomy of volition, and the *ends* characteristic of autonomous volition, will be related to one another.

Whenever I follow a maxim on account of its legislative form, I thereby make the matter of that maxim (whatever it may be) my end. If I engage in the correction of unjust housing conditions, the ends I pursue will involve the actual betterment of such conditions for given persons (perhaps including myself). An object of pure practical reason is, therefore, the *matter* of a maxim which possesses a legislative form, and is followed by the agent on account of that form. Kant notes this when he replies to Garve that "in itself duty is nothing but the *limitation* of the will by the condition of universal law-giving through the maxim it assumes; its object may be what it will (even happiness)." [37]

It is sometimes thought that one's own happiness cannot be an object of pure practical reason, owing to Kant's assertion that one's own happiness can never be a direct duty.[38] But if we see why Kant asserts this, it will become clear that his view in no way involves the incompatibility of one's own happiness and the pursuit of moral ends. Kant does *not* say that one's own happiness cannot be a direct duty because the pursuit of happiness is regarded as necessarily "corrupt." As we have already seen, only a confusion of motives with ends could give rise to this interpretation of Kant's ethics. Kant's real reason for saying that one's own happiness cannot be a direct duty is quite clear:

Since every man (by virtue of his *natural* impulses) has *his own happiness* as his end, it would be contradictory to consider this an obligatory end. What we will inevitably and spontaneously does not come under the concept of *duty*, which is a *necessitation* to an end we adopt reluctantly.[39]

Happiness is thus not an object of duty because it would be superfluous to command it, and not because it would be "corrupt" to seek it. Man naturally has his own happiness as an end, and does not need to be *constrained* to adopt this as an end. Of course, there is an exception to this rule, and Kant himself takes note of it. Happiness, as we have seen, is an idea formulated by reason, and not an immediate or blind sensuous impulse. Therefore, Kant points out, it may sometimes occur that "a single inclination which is determinate as to what it promises" will "outweigh a wavering Idea." In such cases as these, a man does not have his happiness naturally as an end, and may be constrained to make it his end.[40] Hence it is only insofar as one's own happiness is already conceived to be part of the matter of the maxim of action that it cannot be a duty to promote it.

To sum up: Finite rational volition necessarily has its own happiness (as the sum of all its natural ends) as an end, and this end is necessarily involved in the matter of all its maxims. An object of pure practical reason is the matter of any maxim which has a legislative form and which is followed on account of that form. But since happiness is part of the matter of every maxim of a finite rational being, it must be part of the matter of those maxims whose form is legislative. Therefore, happiness must be part of every object of pure practical reason. Again, of course, this does not imply that happiness must always (or ever) be the motive of finite rational volition. The above argument, however, still leaves us discontented. For while it does tell us in a general way *why* we should expect to find man's natural ends included in his moral ends, it does not show us *how* this comes about. And it is still possible to wonder how the ends given to man by nature (the totality of which constitutes his happiness) become included in the ends which man as rational and autonomous being gives to himself.

The clue to the answer to this question is provided by Kant's statement cited above (and repeated by Kant elsewhere) that duty is the "*limitation* of the will in accordance with the universal form of law-giving." The human will naturally has certain ends given to it by its finite nature, and the totality of these ends is its own happiness. Its higher calling, morality, consists in its self-restraint, its own subjection of it-self to maxims which allow the pursuit of these natural ends only on the condition that such maxims equally allow for the promotion of the same ends for all other finite rational beings. It is this limiting form of universality, applied to the material ends given by man's finite and sensible nature, which consti-tutes the self-constraint of autonomous action. Kant gives an exposition of his fundamental ethical viewpoint on this ques-tion in the second critique:

The mere form of a law, which limits its material, must be a con-dition for adding this material to the will but not presuppose it as the condition of the will. Let the material content be, for exam-ple, my own happiness. If I attribute this to everyone, as in fact I may attribute it to all finite beings, it can become an objective practical law only if I include within it the happiness of others. Therefore, the law that we should further the happiness of others arises . . . from the fact that the form of universality, which reason requires as condition for giving the maxim of self-love the objective validity of law, is itself the determining ground of the will. Therefore not the object, i.e. the happiness of others, was the determining ground of the pure will, but rather the lawful form alone. Through it I restricted my maxim, founded on incli-nation, by giving it the universality of law, thus making it con-formable to the pure practical reason. From this limitation alone, and not from the addition of any external incentive, the concept of obligation arises to extend the maxim of self-love also to the happiness of others.[41]

Here it is plain that the application of the moral law, the ac-tual obedience to it, presupposes the agent's natural and sensi-ble needs and desires. Pure reason conditions and limits his pursuit of his own welfare, but does not prohibit it. On the contrary, since the agent's own needs are presupposed in all applications of the principle of morality which involve the needs of others, these very needs (conditioned by the legislative form of a valid maxim) are systematically and necessarily included as conditioned objects and ends of moral striving. Not to so include them would, in fact, be contrary to the universality required of one's maxim:

I want every other man to be benevolent to me; hence I should also be benevolent to every other man. But since all *other* men with the exception of myself would not be *all* men, and the maxim would then not have the universality of law, . . . the law prescribing the duty of benevolence will include myself as the object of benevolence, in the command of reason.[42]

Hence happiness, both one's own and that of others, the totality of these ends given to finite rational beings by nature, is systematically included also in the ends which such beings give themselves in obedience to the moral law. It is included, however, *conditionally*, limited and conditioned by the universal and legislative form of the maxim of which these ends are the matter.

To make this point more concrete, let us return once again to the case of our housing reformer. He and his neighbors suffer from injustices which cause them suffering and unhappiness, but bring a great deal of much appreciated revenue to a few landlords and their agents. Our reformer recognizes that to allow housing conditions of this sort to continue, and out of laziness to do nothing about them, is a principle which perpetuates a system where some persons obtain great profit by exploiting others. He cannot will the perpetuation of such a system, not simply because it is causing him personal discomfort, but because it is founded on a principle which betters the condition of some persons at the expense of others. He himself understands this through his own suffering, his own desire for a better place to live, and so on. He is acquainted personally with the needs and inclinations which cause suffering to the exploited, and which motivate the exploiter. It is his reason, however, which tells him that the present system is unjust, that it is inequitable, and that it is his duty as a human being and a citizen of that community to make its reform his end. This could not have been told him by his inclinations, for they could only direct him to better his own situation (by whatever means he might) and perhaps also the situations of those whose improved condition caused him some personal satisfaction. But as a reformer, he addresses himself to a difficult task, exposes himself to the reprisals of those whose profits will be threatened by his proposed reforms, and so on. Thus, even though his own happiness is included in a systematic way within the ends of his moral action, it is likely that he will in practice sacrifice much of his own happiness by pursuing his reforms, and that he would not have been prompted to his action out of any concern for his own welfare.

Hence it does not follow that the presupposition and systematic inclusion of one's own happiness in the material of one's maxim will mean that this happiness is the *motive* for action, nor does it follow that one's action will necessarily contribute in the end to one's happiness. Indeed, since the moral law has the effect of limiting and conditioning one's pursuit of his natural ends, it is hardly to be expected that moral action should of itself add to that happiness. But by the same token, one's own happiness, thus limited and conditioned, is necessarily included within the ends pursued by the finite rational being in obedience to the moral law.

The Unconditioned Good

Autonomous action, as we have seen, is action motivated by the legislative form of the agent's maxim, rather than its matter.

In virtue of this fact, the autonomous agent himself rationally determines the matter of his maxim, and gives himself ends, rather than merely receiving his ends from nature. We have just noted that this fact by no means excludes man's natural ends from those ends he will give to himself as an autonomous agent, but, on the contrary, that his natural ends will be systematically included as a component of objects of pure practical reason. And yet we have seen that these ends are included only as limited or conditioned by the formal universality of a morally legislative maxim. Hence it follows that man's natural ends have only a conditioned worth, and human happiness is not to be considered valuable *as such* or *in itself*. This is the meaning of the famous statement with which Kant begins the *Foundations:* "It is impossible to conceive anything at all in the world, or even out of it, which can be taken as good without qualification, except a *good will*." [43] Or, as he elsewhere expresses it, "If something is to be, or is held to be, absolutely good . . . in all respects and without qualification, it could not be a thing but only the manner of acting, i.e. it could be only the maxim of the will." [44]

The goodness of an act depends not on its end, but on its motive. Hence an end may be good, may be an object of pure practical reason, only if it is the matter of a maxim of action which is in conformity with the moral law. It is, then, this maxim, this principle on which the subject wills and acts, which is the *condition* for all good objects. It is by means of the law that the "form [of good objects] is determined a priori." [45] Hence, as the *formal condition* of all good ends, the good will has an "inner unconditioned worth," and is the "highest good" in the sense of being "the condition for all the rest." [46] At the same time, the good will is not the "sole and complete good." It *conditions* all ends, which are thus good in a "conditioned" (*bedingt*), "qualified" (*eingeschränkt*) way.

Hence an act of beneficence or justice is not good in Kant's view because of the human happiness or well-being which is obtained or intended by it. Rather, the happiness or welfare is good, is an object of pure practical reason, only because it is the matter of a maxim whose form is legislative, and thus is the end which the beneficent or just man sets for himself in obedience to the moral law. The natural ends furthered by this act, the welfare of human beings, are good, are objects of pure practical reason, only on the condition that they be part of the ends of an agent whose will is good.

Many critics of Kant's doctrine of the highest good have held that Kant's moral philosophy takes the good will to be the *only* true object of pure practical reason. Clearly this view is implicit in the interpretations of Kant advanced by Garve and Greene, for they hold that other objects (human happiness, for instance), must be renounced in the name of morality. But it might be thought that one could take a milder version of this interpretation. Lewis White Beck seems to be doing this when he holds that in Kant's view "devotion to the moral good does not require renunciation of other goods," and "some desires are compatible with devotion to the good or can be made compatible with it," but maintains that for Kant "the only purpose of moral action as such is to secure the reign of law." For this reason, he holds that "we have no moral duty to promote" the highest good, but only a duty "as determined by the form and not the content or object of the moral law." [47] * Human happiness for Beck is thus "compatible" with the ends of morality, but never a *part* of those ends.

* Of course, Kant never held that our duty to promote the highest good is different from our duty "as determined by the form" of the moral law. Rather, the duty to promote the highest good, to make it our end, *is* just our duty as determined by the formal requirements of the law, and expressed materially as the idea of an unconditioned totality of the object of pure practical reason.

This interpretation of Kant, if it were accurate, would be most unflattering. Although Kant would not be a brutal ascetic, as Greene's reading would make him, still he would not be recommending an altogether appealing life for the moral man. For if moral action as such is not concerned with the realization of actual ends in the world, but only with the "reign of law," Kant would seem to be recommending an indifference to human welfare, and a smug, introverted preoccupation with the purity of one's own intentions. The moral man "as such" would not be concerned with the realization of moral ends, with the practical betterment of mankind, but would be satisfied instead merely with the "inner glow" of his own virtue. Kant has sometimes been criticized for advocating this sort of position, though it is in fact very far from what he held. It is true, of course, that Kant accords "unqualified worth" to moral virtue, and emphasizes that its value is not diminished or changed in any way be its results. But this does not mean that the morally good man is *indifferent* to the results of his action, or that moral action does not express a concern with the attainment of actual results. A good will is "not a mere wish, but the straining of every means in our control" to attain good results in the world.[48]

There is something which strikes us as hypocritical about a person who is concerned solely with his own "virtue," and Kant's theory itself allows us to see very clearly what is wrong with such a preoccupation. Finite rational volition, for Kant, is purposive. The maxims of action always have a matter, they represent an end which the agent strives and labors to attain. The good will, like any finite rational volition, has its end, which it represents to itself and labors to attain by adopting and following a formally legislative maxim. Now the finite rational agent *has* a good will only so long as he *acts* according to this maxim, only so long, therefore, as he directs

effort, and "strains every means in his control" to attain the
end represented for him in his maxim. The man who is concerned only with his own virtue is concerned only with the
formal validity of his maxims; but he is not actually *virtuous*,
for to be so he would have to *act* on valid maxims, and hence
labor to attain the ends represented to him as the matter of
such maxims. For Kant it is of course proper in moral reasoning to be concerned first and foremost with the moral validity
of one's maxims. But if such maxims remain only abstract
rules, and never become "principles on which the subject
acts," then no claim can be made that one deserves any moral
credit for this concern. Beck has failed to see that for Kant all
action essentially involves a concernful pursuit of material
ends, and that there can be no "reign of law" without a pur-
poseful relation to the world of action and a genuine attempt
to transform that world in accordance with the law of morality.

   This "moral criticism" of the interpretation advanced by
Beck is related to serious problems involved in the interpretation itself. Beck's interpretation seems to oscillate between
two equally untenable and mutually incompatible alternatives.
On the one hand, he asserts that for Kant "the object of pure
practical reason is not an effect of action, but the action itself;
the good will has itself as object." [49] It is, of course, perfectly
true to say that the good will aims at having a good will, both
in the sense that its maxim is self-consistent and in the sense
that the good will itself is the formal condition of all good objects or ends. But it cannot be said that the good will has *only*
itself as object. For what, after all, *is* the good will? It is the
will which acts according to a formally legislative maxim.
The goodness of the good will consists, as we have seen, in its
maxim.[50] The maxim of finite rational volition, however, always has a matter, and action according to a maxim makes

this matter the end or object of the finite rational agent. It might be thought that in the case of morally valid maxims, the matter would be identical with the form, thus avoiding the problem.* But this is not possible. Man is a "being of needs" and these needs, his natural needs, are always "directed to the material of the faculty of desire." [51] Man is a sensible being, who must represent ends to himself, and who is given natural ends by his finite nature. His maxim has a distinct "form" and "matter" only because the practical concept "maxim" expresses both the formal-rational and the material-sensible aspects of his finite rationality. The good will, like any finite rational will, must represent ends to itself within its finite rational situation. Its own natural needs are presupposed, as we have seen, throughout moral reasoning, and these needs always give a sensible and material content to the ends of finite rational volition. It is this fact which burdens finite rational volition with the task of representing ends and laboring to attain them. The unqualified goodness of the good will presupposes equally these natural needs of man, which are included as qualified goods in the object of pure practical reason.

Beck himself recognizes, too, that the unqualified goodness of a good will presupposes a qualified object, when he says,

* Beck seems to suggest this view when he says, "The form and the object, so far as the object is moral good, of the maxim coincide" (p. 134). This interpretation of Kant is also the basis for an interesting (if not entirely accurate) comparison between Kant's ethics and the Karmayoga of the Baghavad Gita by Gauchwal (Gauchwal, "The Moral Religion of Kant and the Karmayoga of the Gita," 394ff). Gauchwal refers, for example, to the "unity of ends and means," where it is clear that "means" is to be taken in the sense of "maxim" or "the act itself in its formal determination by reason" rather than in the usual Kantian sense. This comparison might have been well taken if Spinoza or even Nietzsche had been used instead of Kant, but if the Karmayoga of the Gita is taken as Gauchwal expounds it here, it differs significantly from Kant's views concerning the purposiveness of finite rational volition.

quite accurately, that "Every volition has an object, though the object need not itself be an unqualified good. . . . The categorical imperative . . . always presupposes maxims which have a material, and which it controls." [52] Thus Beck seems not always to hold that the sole end of moral action is the unqualified goodness of the good will, but seems to say that there are other ends, included in the material of a formally legislative maxim, which are "compatible" with the object of pure practical reason, but not *part* of it. This position, however, is equally untenable. For if the object of pure practical reason *is* just the material of a formally legislative maxim (or, as Beck himself so quaintly puts it, "the material of a non-material principle" [53]) then it is impossible that there should be anything included in the material of a formally legislative maxim which is not an object of pure practical reason.

Beck bases his interpretation of Kant's conception of the object of pure practical reason on Chapter II of the second critique, which is devoted to the definition of the concept of such an object. Here Kant distinguishes the Good and the Evil (*Gut und Böse*) from Well-being and Ill (*Wohl und Übel*), and points out that only the former pair are objects of pure practical reason, the Good being an object of *desire* and the Evil an object of *aversion*.[54] Now Beck takes Kant to be holding that the Good consists only in the "manner of acting," or in the "maxim of the will"—that is, in the unqualified goodness of the good will. If Kant did hold such a view, it would follow that the unqualified goodness of a good will is the only subject of pure practical reason, since the Good is explicitly used in this chapter to refer to *the object* of pure practical reason. But Kant just does not say, here or anywhere else, that the Good, the object of pure practical reason, is to be simply *identified* either with the unqualified good, or with the manner of acting, or with the good will. He does say that "*Good* or *Evil* always indicates a reference or relation [*Beziehung*] to the will" and that "good and evil are properly related to actions" rather than to "the sensory state of the person." [55] He says this because the goodness of any end is determined and qualified by the goodness of the action whose end it is. Hence the goodness of any object always depends on a *reference* or *relation* to a kind of action. But this is not to say, or to mean, that the goodness of the action is the sole good, or the only object of pure practical reason. Kant does say, too, that if something is "held to be absolutely good or evil in all respects and without qualification" it must be "the manner of acting." [56] But this offers no support whatever to the claim that the manner of acting is the *sole* object of pure practical reason. And in several places, Kant makes it quite clear that the Good spoken of here is not to be identified simply with the unqualified goodness of the good will: "Action in accordance with [the law] is *in itself* good; and a will whose maxims always accord with the law is absolutely and in every respect good and the *supreme condition of all good*." [57] This passage would make no sense if there were no good which was conditioned by this supreme condition. And later in Chapter II, Kant makes it even clearer that he has not identified the object of pure practical reason with the unqualified goodness of the good will. The proper method in moral philosophy, he says, is to seek first "a law which directly determines the will a priori" and only then to seek "the object suitable to it." [58] Now, Kant says, by showing that the concepts of Good and Evil "refer originally not to objects" but to "the category of causality," [59] it has been shown how a will motivated by the law makes possible the a priori determination of an object of pure practical reason:

Only . . . when the moral law has been established by itself and justified as the direct determining ground of the will can this object be presented to the will whose form now is determined a priori. This we shall undertake in the Dialectic of Pure Practical Reason.[60]

The object spoken of here is, of course, the *highest good*.

3. The Highest Good

An end or object of pure practical reason is the material of a formally legislative maxim. As we have just observed, it is possible on the basis of the formal requirement of legislative maxims to see that such ends must have two components, that they must be conditioned by observance to the moral law and that they must include the agent's own natural ends limited and qualified in a systematic way. Kant's concept of the highest good is derived from a further examination of the features of objects or ends of pure practical reason, and from reason's proper fulfillment of its function in setting before itself as an end the unconditioned totality of such ends, as an ideal for deliberate moral labor and striving.

We have already seen the crucial role played by the concept of finite rational volition in the determination of the ends of pure practical reason. It is this crucial role which Kant expresses in simpler and more forceful terms in his claim that finite rational beings are ends in themselves. Proper attention to the meaning and fundamental significance of this claim will make Kant's concept of the highest good much easier for us to grasp.

The moral law, as we have seen, is taken by Kant to determine only a valid *form* for our subjective principles of action. Obedience to the law consists in embodying that form in real purposive action, in giving it a material through a maxim from which the moral subject acts, and by means of which he represents an end of action. Hence any application of the moral law presupposes some material context of action, in the person of an agent whose volitional nature is such that he can, through the maxims of his action, give the form of the law a material embodiment. The existence of beings of this sort is a condition for any autonomous volition, any determination of ends by reason. It is a being possessed of finite rational will, in the form of a human person, who in our experience constitutes this condition. Kant thus says that a being of this kind "constitutes the sole condition under which anything can be an end in itself. Humanity in the person of such a being is possessed of an irreplaceable value, a *dignity*. A person is something "*whose existence* has *in itself* an absolute value, something which as *an end in itself* could be a ground of determinate laws." [1]

The true significance of the phrase "end in itself" in Kant's ethics is just to identify this condition in existence for the autonomous giving of ends, and hence to find the *locus* of all objects of pure practical reason. Such a locus is the finite rational agent. Since it is only the ends of such a being which can in fact be determined autonomously, all objects of pure practical reason have the characteristic of being referable to finite rational volition. All ends of morality are ends of finite rational volition, which is therefore called an *end in itself*. As we focus our attention on the conditioned and the unconditioned objects of pure practical reason, and on the idea of their combination and totality in the highest good, we must constantly keep in view that these objects are to be understood always within the context of finite rational volition and serve as but another form of the moral self-knowledge at which the critical philosophy aims in dealing with the practical sphere.

The Moral Good

The moral law, embodied in the finite rational agent's formally legislative maxim, defines not one but two kinds of ends for the moral agent: one unconditioned and unqualified, the second limited and conditioned by the first. The unqualified good derives from man's moral rationality, his capability of free, autonomous volition. The conditioned good is constituted by those natural ends of men which are systematically and universally included in the material of a formally legislative maxim. Kant sometimes draws a distinction between the "moral good" (*moralisches Gut*) and the "natural good" (*physisches Gut*) which is aimed at clarifying the character of these two components of the object of pure practical reason. An examination of these two concepts and their foundation in Kant's moral theory will enable us to see how the two components of the highest good are to be conceived of and related to one another.

The moral good for Kant is identified with virtue (*Tugend*), and is considered to be the good which limits or qualifies the inclination to well-being (*Wohlleben*).[2] The moral good, the unqualified good of virtue, cannot as we have seen be taken to be identical with "the good for morality"—that is, with the object of pure practical reason. Such an object must include not only this unqualified and unconditioned good, but also the qualified and conditioned ends or objects of the finite rational will.

Thus far, we have identified the moral good, the unconditioned good and the condition for all good, with the good will and with the formally legislative maxim of the will, in virtue of which it is good. This way of treating of the moral good is incomplete, however, and does not allow us properly to consider the moral good as an object or end of purposive action, and as a personal good, whose locus is the person of a finite rational agent. Earlier we cited Kant's important statement in the second critique that what is "absolutely good or evil in all respects and without qualification" could be only "a manner of acting" (*Handlungsart*) or the *maxim* of the will.[3] But to these two ways of characterizing the unconditioned and unqualified good, Kant immediately adds a third, with which we are now prepared to deal. The unqualified good or evil is not only a manner of acting or a maxim of the will, it is also "consequently the acting person himself as a good or evil man."[4] Since both maxims and the "manner of acting" are given in terms of finite rational volition, it is to the acting person himself that all moral good and evil must properly be referred. Hence in Kant's view it *follows* that if the unqualified good is to be located in a kind of maxim, or a manner of acting, then the unqualified good is to be referred to the acting person.

But how is the moral good to be referred to the acting person? To this question we may be tempted to give the answer, "To his maxim, or his manner of acting." This answer, however, is inadequate. It is true, of course, that it is the maxim of any act which determines its morality or immorality, and it is on the basis of their acts that persons are judged morally good or evil. But a person is judged not simply on the basis of his individual acts, but on the basis of the moral character which he exhibits in them. Kant often reserves the term "character" (*Character*) for abilities or qualities of a person (such as self-control or courage) which may be good or evil, depending on how they are used. But he does not always do this. In the *Metaphysic of Morals*, Kant refers to virtue as "the strength of a man's maxims in fulfilling his duty," or simply a "moral strength of will." It is the moral character of a person, or his moral strength, which is the ground for his adoption of good or evil maxims, and thus it is this which constitutes his moral personality (imputability).[5]

In treating of the unqualified good merely as the goodness of the maxim of a given act, we noted that its unqualified or unconditioned goodness followed from the fact that a formally legislative maxim, adopted on account of its form, is the formal condition of all good ends. The moral good, however, is not simply a formal condition, but an *end* which is good without qualification. The moral good is something which one *strives* for. If the moral good regarded as a necessary component of the end of any particular act were taken merely to be the having of a formally legislative maxim *for that act*, then the moral good would have the peculiar quality that one could not even seek it without it following as an analytic proposition that one had completely attained it. For to seek an object of pure practical reason is just to act according to a maxim with a legislative form, motivated by that form. But if one does this, then one has thereby attained the moral good, if the moral good is regarded only as the maxim of the action in question. The moral good, so regarded, cannot be something one strives for, or that one makes progress in attaining. In order, therefore to be in the proper sense an *end* of moral action, the moral good must not refer only to the having of a formally legislative maxim in the case of the particular act in question. Rather, it must refer to something which *can* be striven for, and adopted as an end of action to be promoted and brought about.

Hence the moral good cannot be a mere formal condition of ends, but must consist in an end which is unconditionally and unqualifiedly good, an end whose promotion follows directly from the formal condition of all good ends. This end is virtue, man's moral strength of will, which consists in the perfection of the disposition to make duty (or the legislative

form of his maxim) a sufficient motive of action. Each morally good act *is* good only if it does promote this end by exemplifying this striving in its formally legislative maxim, by
contributing to the "labor of moral reconstruction" and fulfilling every man's duty to increase his own moral
perfection.[6]

Goodness of character, moral virtue, since it is not a mere
formal condition for the adoption of ends but is itself a material end, involves sensibility as well as reason. As an end, it
involves the finite rational being in his moral totality. It is for
this reason that Kant calls man's moral progress "a gradual reform of his sensibility (*Sinnlichkeit*)." The acquisition of a
virtuous character by virtuous action is a continuous "selfovercoming" (*Selbstüberwindung*). Such a character is acquired, according to Kant, by the constant but moderate discipline of one's inclinations, so that by "continuous labor and
growth" the firm resolve to do one's duty becomes a habit.[7]
Also involved in its acquisition is the development of the animal, human, and personal "predispositions to good in human
nature," especially those natural characteristics which constitute "the aesthetic receptiveness of the mind to the concept of
duty." [8]

If the moral good is the unqualified object of pure practical
reason, and applicable to all finite rational beings as ends in
themselves, it would seem evident that our duty to pursue this
good should include not only our own moral good but the
moral good of all men. But Kant himself seems in one passage
to suggest that it is not a man's duty to further the moral
perfection of others.

It is contradictory to say that I make another person's *perfection*
my end and consider myself obligated to promote this. For the
perfection of another man, as a person, consists precisely in *his
own* power to adopt his end in accordance with his own concept

of duty; and it is self-contradictory to demand that I do (make it my duty to do) what only the other person himself can do.[9]

But I do not think that this passage is consistent either with Kant's moral theory, nor with his own moral attitudes as he expressed them in numerous other places in his works. And I wish to hold, contrary to this passage, that the moral good of others is an important component of Kant's conception of the highest good.

Let us first consider the passage itself. Kant is attempting at this point to classify men's duties. He is attempting to base all duties to oneself on "one's own perfection" while basing all duties to others on "the happiness of others." It has been argued that, since one inevitably has one's own happiness as an end, there can be no duty to promote it (an argument we discussed in the previous chapter). But Kant's neat classification scheme will not work, and the desire to preserve it has led him into a serious error at this point. Kant bases his argument on the (quite correct) observation that "it is self-contradictory to demand that I do . . . what only the other person himself can do." From this he wishes to argue that it is contradictory to demand that I promote the perfection of another, which consists in "his own power to adopt his end in accordance with his own concept of duty." Now if what I were being expected to do involved adopting his end for him, Kant's argument would be valid, for this only he could do. But this is *not* what is in question. Rather, what we must decide is whether I can in any way promote his power (*Kraft*) to adopt his ends in accordance with duty. The question is, in other words, whether I can have an effect on the moral character of another.

The consideration of some actual examples may be of help here, and a negative example may, to begin with, be more enlightening than positive ones. Prison officials, or an entire penal system, may utilize cruel and degrading forms of punishment on criminals. And such punishments might commonly and systematically result in continued and more serious crime, increased hostility to basic moral and legal standards, and other vicious or pathological traits of character among the human beings subjected to it. If these effects are the *systematic* result of punishments of this kind, it would be a hypocritical sophistry to argue that the worsened characters of these criminals are due solely to the moral degeneracy of the criminals themselves. To be sure, the criminals themselves are responsible for their continued wrongdoing. They remain free and responsible persons, and it would be an inexcusable indignity to them not to hold them responsible for their own characters and acts. But it cannot be denied that the prison officials, or the penal system, have positively contributed to the moral worsening of the criminals, and must bear partial responsibility so long as it continues to have such effects on those in its charge. Conversely, however, any man who in his public, professional, or personal life helps to educate others and better their lives, and to foster an environment in which the moral characters of other persons became systematically improved, cannot be denied moral credit for promoting the moral good of others.

There are any number of ways—advice, encouragement, example, discipline, education, or social improvement—that I may have a beneficial effect on the moral character of another, on his "power to adopt ends in accordance with his own concept of duty." Kant was perhaps misled here not only by his desire for a neat classificatory scheme, but also by the fear that if he held that I could have an effect on the moral character of another, this would remove from the other the responsibility for his own acts. But this fear can be seen to be groundless, if we keep in mind that the question is not whether or not we can alter the freedom and spontaneity of another, the seat of his moral responsibility, but only whether or not we can effect his "power" to exercise his freedom. Kant's argument would be valid if it were being used to show that the moral good of others cannot be a "perfect" or "narrow" duty (a duty not only to further an end, but actually to attain it). Since the free action of another person is the indispensable condition of his moral good, I could not attain his moral good simply through my own exercise of freedom. But, as Kant makes abundantly clear, even my *own* moral good is not a perfect duty; we have a duty only to strive for perfect virtue, and not a duty to attain it.[10] We could have no duty actually to accomplish the moral betterment of others, but it seems perfectly consistent with Kant's theory to assert that we do have a duty to other men as ends in themselves to aid them insofar as we are able in their own moral progress, and act toward them with a desire that they should fulfill the higher destiny which their rational nature marks out for them. In fact, Kant gives evidence at a number of places in his works that he does believe that men can and should help others in their moral development, and he also indicates that he has given considerable thought to how this can best be done. In both the second critique and the *Metaphysic of Morals*, Kant includes a "Methodology," whose purpose is avowedly to specify "the way in which we can secure to the laws of pure practical reason access to the human mind and an influence on its maxims. That is to say, it is the way we can make objectively practical reason also subjectively practical." [11]

In both accounts of such a "Methodology," Kant deals with the teaching of pupils, and how it may achieve the above end. The subject of moral education was one which profoundly concerned Kant, and he held that such education was a necessary precondition for man's moral improvement, even the sole ground of hope for human moral progress.[12] The most detailed and practical treatment of the topic of moral education is to be found in Kant's treatise *Education*. In the introduction to this work Kant argues that man, as man, is solely a product of education (*Erziehung*) and that the attainment of an individual's moral destiny is impossible without the help of others.[13] Practical Education (*praktische Erziehung*) forms an important part of the educator's task in Kant's view, and Kant offers many observations concerning the best way of developing the moral character of pupils.[14]

Not only the institution of education, but also that of organized religion, in Kant's view, is a systematic means for the mutual moral improvement of men. The rational justification of the necessity for an ecclesiastical organization, in Kant's view, is that such an organization may represent the idea of a People of God (*ein Volk Gottes*) in a "Moral Community" (*ethische gemeine Wesen*), whose "laws are expressly designed to promote the morality of actions." [15] The mutual improvement of men's moral characters through education and religious community play such an important role in Kant's over-all view of the moral destiny of man that it is impossible to take as Kant's best thinking the passage cited in which he denies that one can promote the moral good of others. Rather, it seems altogether proper to regard the critical moral philosophy, along with Kant in his most profound moral convictions, as holding that the moral good of *all* finite rational beings is the unqualified and unconditioned end of the finite rational moral agent.

The Natural Good

In the previous chapter, we saw that for Kant moral reasoning both presupposes and systematically includes men's natural ends in the object of pure practical reason. Kant was seen to argue that reason limits and conditions our pursuit of our own natural ends, and commands the pursuit of the natural ends of others subject to the same condition of universal rational volition. It is from these limited and conditioned natural ends that Kant derives the second, conditioned component of the highest good, which he sometimes calls "the natural good." If we are to have an adequate conception of this conditioned good and its role in defining the concept of the highest good, we must examine further the way in which men's natural ends are qualified by reason and become included in objects of pure practical reason.

Kant argues, as we have seen, that it is a duty for every finite rational being to pursue the natural ends of others, in order to give his own desire for happiness the form of rational universality which morality demands. Thus it seems that Kant is taking the criterion for the inclusion of any natural end in the object of pure practical reason to be the *compatibility* of that natural end with a like pursuit of natural ends by other men. But if this were taken as the sole criterion, or the supreme condition for the objective goodness of a natural end, there would follow the highly repugnant consequence that even if all men sought their own happiness with a selfish single-mindedness, this happiness would be a good in the eyes of morality so long as chance—or perhaps a mysterious "Invisible Hand"—prevented their selfish pursuits from actually interfering with one another. To Kant, this conclusion would be intolerable. Our moral destiny, he says, "is not merely that we should be happy, but that we should make ourselves happy" through rational moral action directed toward a just and benevolent furthering of universal human happiness.[16] A selfish man, acting only with a view to his own profit, renders himself by his conduct unworthy of happiness, even if his conduct does not in fact succeed in actually harming anyone else. It is for this reason that Kant says that

a rational and impartial spectator can never feel approval in contemplating the uninterrupted prosperity of a being graced by no touch of pure and good will, and . . . consequently a good will seems to constitute the indispensable condition of our very worthiness to be happy.[17]

We should recall that in arguing that furthering the happiness of others is a duty, Kant dealt constantly with the maxim of action, and the rational universality of my own natural ends as the material of this maxim. Hence even here the condition for the inclusion of a natural end in an object of pure practical reason was not simply the compatibility of this end with the pursuit of like ends by others. Rather, it was such a compatibility exhibited in the maxim of my action. The condition for the inclusion of natural ends in the object of pure practical reason was thus action from a maxim which subjects every natural end to the condition of rational universality, and includes these ends in its object only if they are the ends of a valid *kind* of action. It is therefore a kind of action, and hence a moral condition of some person, which is the supreme condition of the inclusion of natural ends in an object of pure practical reason, the "indispensable condition of our very worthiness to be happy."

The formal condition for *all* objects of pure practical reason is the moral validity of a man's maxim, and hence the moral goodness of his person. The moral good is thus not only the unconditioned good, but it is also the supreme condition of all else which is good. It is in this role of providing the condition for the goodness and moral validity of men's natural ends that Kant calls virtue, the moral good, the condition of our worthiness to be happy.[18]

Every finite being is a being of needs, a being which by its very nature has inclinations and sensuous desires. These desires provide a finite rational being with natural ends, ends which he can be presumed to have prior to any determination of his will by reason. These ends, we should recall, are unified by reason as prudence into an idea of *happiness*. In forming this idea, reason limits and conditions man's natural ends by one another, so that the pursuit of one such end does not interfere with the pursuit of other ends. Reason balances and weighs the pursuit of natural ends, forming an idea of a stable whole. Such an idea does not come about from mere impulse, but is based on reason. The judgment that the pursuit of some end is conducive to my own happiness, or natural good, is thus not merely a judgment of feeling, but is in Kant's view a judgment of *reason*.

An example may make this clearer. A man has access to large amounts of money in his work, and is tempted to embezzle. Now he might, in response to this temptation, simply slip a roll of large bills into his pocket on the spur of the moment and leave the office. But he is more rational than this. Before he rashly gives in to such a momentary impulse, he will consider whether his embezzlement would in the long run serve his own happiness, and be conducive to his personal desires as a whole. That is, even if he does not consider the morality of his action, he will contemplate his action rationally from the point of view of *prudence*. He will consider whether and how he can escape detection in his theft. He will realize that if he is to escape with the money he will have to leave the city in which he lives and give up his job and the stability of the life he has led thus far. He will either have to confront his wife and family with his theft, or he will have to leave them as well. If our tempted embezzler is prudent, he will weigh all these considerations carefully. He will limit his momentary impulse to steal by his desires to maintain a stable life, to enjoy the respect of his family and friends and the security of the position he has established in his community. It is possible that, after so having weighed matters, he will decide that embezzlement would not, after all, be conducive to his happiness as a whole. Or, on the other hand, he may decide that his job, his family, his stable life, are not so valuable to him and that it is worth the chance he is taking to embezzle a large sum of money and take the first plane to Brazil. But in either case, it will be a careful and prudent weighing of his desires and circumstances which decides the matter for him. His decision will be a rational one.

Reason as prudence, therefore, defines a natural good for man prior to any moral considerations. Insofar as someone weighs the consequences of an act for his own personal happiness or unhappiness, he is not concerned with the morality of his act. Hence although the natural good has a *bonitas pragmatica* determined by reason as prudence, it does not have a *bonitas moralis;* [19] it is not a Good (*Gut*) in the strict sense defined in Chapter II of the Analytic of the second critique. It is not an object of pure practical reason, of morality, but only an object of practical reason as prudence. The natural good simply as such is not a Good (*Gut*) but well-being (*Wohl*).[20]

Human happiness, well-being, or the natural good in given instances, however, may be either included in the object of pure practical reason, or excluded from it. A man who takes pleasure in his work, or one who enjoys the just fruits of his labor, is clearly deserving of the happiness he enjoys, and that happiness is included in the end of his moral action, as we saw in the case of our housing reformer. The happiness of such a deserving person is a good for morality, something which morality commands us to pursue. On the other hand, the happiess of a ruthless embezzler who, ignoring his obligations to his family and community, steals a large sum of money and lives comfortably in Rio de Janeiro is not a moral good at all. For by his conduct, such a man has rendered himself *unworthy* of happiness, and has removed the necessary condition which must accompany his happiness if it is to have moral worth. His happiness, far from being a moral good, is in fact a moral evil in Kant's view, an object of moral aversion to every impartial spectator, and even to the man himself, should he consider his situation in the light of what his conscience tells him. As a moral being, he cannot fail to recognize the moral evil of his act, and see also that the happiness he might gain from his embezzlement would be a happiness of which he had rendered himself unworthy. In this recognition and limitation of his own pursuit of his happiness, we have for the first time the possibility of his winning for himself a moral happiness (*gesittete Glückseligkeit*), a happiness which can be not only a natural good but an object of pure practical reason as well.[21]

Man's natural inclinations may thus be limited by reason not only in its office as prudence, but also by moral reason. And it is through this latter limitation and condition that natural ends in general are included in the object of pure practical reason. Men's natural ends do not, then, become objects of pure practical reason and components of the highest good simply by being given as objects of sensible inclination, nor do they become such by being limited and qualified by each other through the discipline of reason as prudence. Rather, they are included in the object of pure practical reason insofar as they are limited and conditioned by moral reason, and thus by a virtuous disposition, the worthiness to be happy. The moral worth of happiness, then, is a real but conditioned worth. Happiness apart from this condition remains to be sure a form of well-being, a natural good, and has *bonitas pragmatica*, but it is not an object of pure practical reason, an object of *moral* striving. Kant expresses the conditioned moral value of happiness when he accompanies his inclusion of happiness in the highest good with the following admonition:

Happiness, although something always pleasant to him who possesses it, is not of itself absolutely good in every respect, but always presupposes conduct in accordance with the moral law as its condition.[22]

In a like way, as careful attention to Kant's texts will show, when he identifies the two components of the highest good as "virtue" and "happiness," he is always careful to point out that the second component is a good *for morality* only insofar as it is conditioned by the first. "Happiness, therefore, in exact proportion to the morality of the rational beings who are thereby rendered worthy of it, alone constitutes the supreme good of the world."[23] And again: "The highest natural good possible in the world, to be furthered as a final and as far as we are able, is *happiness* under the objective condition of the harmony of man with the law of *morality* as worthiness to be happy."[24] In the *Lectures on Ethics*, Kant tells us that

morality and happiness are two elements of the Supreme Good, . . . they differ in kind, and . . . whilst they must be kept distinct, they stand in a necessary relation to one another. The moral law . . . tells me that if I conduct myself so as to be worthy of happiness, I may hope for it.[25]

And in the *Religion*, Kant defines the highest good as

an idea of an object which takes the formal condition of all such ends as we *ought* to have (duty) and combines it with whatever is conditioned and in harmony with duty in all the ends we *do* have (happiness proportioned to obedience to duty).[26]

Throughout this discussion of Kant's conception of the highest good, considerable emphasis has been given to this conditional relation between the moral and natural goods, between the legislative form of a maxim and the natural ends which are directed to its material, between virtue as worthiness to be happy and human happiness. We have seen that a formally legislative maxim, and consequently a virtuous disposition, is an unconditioned good, necessarily and unqualifiedly an object of pure practical reason; and that the contentment of a finite rational being with his state, the satisfaction of his natural inclinations and needs, is also a good for morality, but only conditionally, and can be an object of pure practical reason only insofar as it is qualified (*eingeschränkt*) and conditioned (*bedingt*) by the moral worthiness of the finite being to partake in it. This theme deserves considerable stress, since it constitutes the most important single aspect of Kant's moral teleology. It also allows Kant to solve the problem posed by the concept of a single highest good, a single final end for all human moral action. We can see how it does this, if we examine the relation between virtue and happiness from a slightly different viewpoint than we have up to now.

It is clear that for Kant the moral and natural goods, virtue and happiness, are *two* distinct goods, that they "differ in kind." John Silber, following the language of Kant, calls this quite aptly the "heterogeneity of the good." [27] Kant puts this point another way when he denies that the relation between the moral and natural good, between virtue and happiness, is analytic. From the fact that a person is virtuous it does not analytically follow that he is happy; nor does happiness analytically imply moral goodness of character. Kant criticizes the ancient Stoics and Epicureans for attempting "to overcome essential differences in principle, which can never be united, by seeking to translate them into a conflict of words." Kant characterizes the errors of these two schools in this way:

The Stoic asserted virtue to be the entire highest good, and happiness was only the consciousness of this possession as belonging to the state of the subject. The Epicurean stated that happiness was the entire highest good and that virtue was only the form of the maxim by which it could be procured through the rational use of means to it.[28]

Now if either of these positions were correct, it would follow that the maxim of pursuing virtue and the maxim of pursuing one's own happiness would be identical. The fact that I act from either of these maxims would analytically imply that I act from the other. For the Stoic, the principle of morality does not merely provide for the pursuit of one's own happiness, as in Kant's ethics. Rather, since happiness is defined by him to be just the consciousness of virtue, the Stoic makes happiness also an unconditioned good, a good whose existence is identical with the consciousness of virtue, and hence makes the supreme principle of morality identical with the principle of pursuing one's own happiness. In a like manner, the Epicurean identifies these two principles, by defining virtue simply as the kind of action necessary to achieve happiness. Now Kant has shown in the Analytic of the second critique that the principle of morality and the principle of one's own happiness are not identical but contrary to one another.[29] Hence it follows that virtue and happiness cannot be identical, nor can the existence of one follow analytically from the existence of the other as the ancient schools claimed.

The two kinds of good are distinct in yet another sense. The moral and natural goods are separate objects of human desire. They are thus desirable in different ways, they answer to different interests of human nature. A human being, both finite and rational, has both natural ends as regards his physical state and moral ends as regards the perfection of his moral disposition and person. Both ends are included in the object of pure practical reason, founded on the finite rational being as an existing end in himself. The two goods, since they answer to different interests, cannot replace one another with respect to the kinds of needs or demands they satisfy. An excess of happiness cannot go proxy for a good moral character; neither can a man's recognition of his own moral virtue substitute for a just satisfaction of his natural needs. The demand of human nature for each of these two goods is distinct from its demand for the other, so that no common measure or equivalence between the *value* of the two goods is possible.

The heterogeneity of the good poses a problem for Kant in the definition of the highest good, a problem which did not arise for the ancient philosophers. The highest good is the idea of a *single* final end for human moral striving. Since for the ancients there was fundamentally only one object of human desire (be it called virtue or happiness) the sole task for them in defining the highest good is that of *naming* this one end. (This is illustrated also quite clearly by Book I of the *Nichomachean Ethics*, especially in Chapter 7.) For Kant, however, there are two distinct kinds of good, the moral and the natural. Given not one good, but two, how is Kant to form the idea of a single highest object for moral striving?

Let us try to get a clearer view of the problem facing Kant at this point. It is often the case in our everyday decisions that we have to weigh different considerations, balance differing goals which lead us in different directions. For example, a man may want his family to be happy, but also want to advance in his career. Here he has two distinct goals that must be reconciled. But in this case it is quite possible for us to see these ends of his as homogeneous in character, possessed of a single measure according to which the pursuit of one may be harmonized with the pursuit of the other. The man may make a given decision between the demands of his family and those of his career on the basis of *prudence*, weighing his personal concern for and pride in his family's happiness and welfare against his professional ambition, limiting each desire by the other in order to reach the greatest whole in the satisfaction of his own personal desire for happiness. Or he may weigh his moral duty to his family against the duty he owes to his profession, to his co-workers, and to those he serves in his work. Here he "limits one duty by another" as Kant describes in the case of "wide" duties.[30] Here, too, he is concerned with forming the greatest whole of goods which are *homogeneous* in character. In both cases, the interest he has in each of the two goals can be reduced to some common standard which allows him to compensate the lack of one good (one kind of happiness or one duty) with a greater amount of the other.

But Kant cannot adopt this sort of solution in the case of the relation between the moral and natural goods. There is no way that the lack of one good can be compensated for by the attainment of the other, no common measure of their distinct kinds of goodness. The two kinds of good, as Kant says, cannot be "mixed" together.[31]

Kant's problem is that of forming a synthetic unity of two specifically different goods, of systematically unifying two distinct kinds of goodness into a single final moral end. "Two terms necessarily combined in one concept," says Kant, "must be related as ground and consequence."[32] Since there is no common measure of their worth, they can be unified into a single object only if one of them constitutes the ground for the worth of the other, and provides the *condition* for its worth. Any other way of resolving the conflict between two goods differing in kind will be haphazard, will not provide a systematic resolution of this conflict according to a general rule or principle. We will sometimes pursue one good, and sometimes the other, but there will be nothing in this diversity but whim and inconsistency. A conditional relation between the two kinds of good, on the other hand, does provide for a systematic unity of both goods into a single end for action. Both goods are pursued, one unconditionally and unquali- fiedly, the other insofar as it is consistent with and condi- tioned by the pursuit of the first.

Thus when Kant formulates the supreme principle of mo- rality, and applies it in the form of a categorical imperative to the volition of rational but finite beings, beings possessed both of moral reason and of sensuous desires and needs, he is already providing for the systematic unity of the object of pure practical reason in the concept of a highest good which takes finite rational nature as an end in itself. The moral value of the natural ends included in the matter of a maxim is con- ditioned by its legislative form; the moral value of happiness is conditioned by a virtuous character as the worthiness to be happy. Kant's moral philosophy provides for both the moral and sensible aspects of human nature, and defines an object of moral striving which takes both into account:

The two kinds of good, the *natural* and the *moral*, cannot be *mixed* together; for then they would only neutralise each other and not even effect a true happiness. Rather, the inclination to well-being [*Wohlleben*] and virtue together constitute the end of the well-intentioned man, one from his sensible the other from the moral-intellectual side. They do this through a struggle, and the limitation of the principle of the first through that of the second.[33]

The Idea of an Unconditioned Object of Pure
Practical Reason

Kant views himself as restoring to philosophy the concept
of the highest good, first introduced in ancient times.[34] The
ancient philosophers devoted their entire ethical investigations, he says, to the nature of the highest object of human
striving. By defining such an object, they intended to give a
complete account of man's proper conduct. We have already
seen how Kant criticizes the homogeneity of the good, on
which in his view their ethical systems were founded. But
Kant sees in the ancients' various attempts a second common
and equally serious error. By making the concept of a highest
end the subject of their moral inquiry, the ancients rendered
themselves unable to consider the possibility that the supreme
principle of morality, and the proper *motive* for human action,
did not consist in an object or end, but in a formal law. Kant's
argument in the Analytic of the second critique aimed at
showing that only after the supreme principle of morality has
been formulated as a law, can the concept of a highest end be
properly defined. In spite of their shortcomings, however,
Kant has a great respect for the insight shown by the ancient
philosophers in their attempts to define a highest end for man.
But the definition of this concept for practice, says Kant,

is the *doctrine of wisdom* [*Weisheitslehre*] which, as a science, is
philosophy in the sense in which the ancients understood this
word, for whom it meant instruction in the concept wherein the
highest good was to be placed and in the conduct whereby it was
to be attained.[35]

Kant's concept of the highest good defines the role of rational teleology in his ethics, and completes the project of a
critique of reason in its practical employment by defining an
unconditioned end for all moral striving, a final purpose for

human action. Up to this point, we have dealt with the foundations of Kant's ethics in moral motivation, and with the kinds of ends the moral law defines for man. We have regarded an end or object of pure practical reason simply as the material of a formally valid maxim. This is only proper, since it is the moral law, and its formal requirement of the rational universality of maxims which provides the condition for all good ends, all objects of pure practical reason. But once the moral law has been formulated, it is then possible to give a *systematic* treatment of its objects, and to define a final end for human action which parallels the moral law and serves as the idea of the concrete embodiment of its command on the world. Like pure theoretical reason in the first critique, pure practical reason

likewise seeks the unconditioned for the practically conditioned . . . ; and this unconditioned is not only sought as the determining ground of the will, but even when this is given (in the moral law) is also sought as the unconditioned totality of the object of pure practical reason, under the name of the *highest good*.[36]

Any idea of an unconditioned for Kant is an idea formed by reason in its office of securing a unity under principles. The highest good, as such an unconditioned, is a "systematic unity of ends," as the entire object of pure practical reason. But more importantly, the idea of the highest good is an idea of an unconditioned, which "alone makes possible the totality of conditions."[37] Kant expresses this fact about the highest good by calling it a final end (*Endzweck*), "that purpose which needs no other as a condition of its possibility."[38] The highest good is thus conceived of also as the *first* end, the *original* end determined by the moral law, the end from which all others are *derived*. The highest good, then, is not a unity of ends in the sense of a mere aggregate; it exists as an idea prior rationally to every particular end we adopt in obedience to the law, and is thought of as the teleological condition for all objects of pure practical reason.

To see how the concept of the highest good is defined in the critical moral philosophy, we must refer to the moral law itself, as the condition of all good ends. If I accept this law as binding over me, I accept it as my duty to strive to adopt only maxims whose form is legislative for all rational beings. When I will according to any maxim, I thereby make my end whatever object would result from successful employment of means to the ends defined by the matter of maxims of that type. The *final end* for all moral striving, therefore, which it is my duty to adopt, is the unconditioned totality of all those ends which constitute the material of maxims whose form is legislative.

We have seen already in some detail that the material of maxims of this type will consist of two components, the moral good (a virtuous disposition, my own and that of others) and the natural good (happiness proportioned to worthiness to be happy, for myself and for others). The highest good will therefore consist in a complete and total attainment of both of these components. The supreme good, the highest moral good, will consist in the goal of perfect virtue, "the complete fitness of intentions to the moral law." [39] Such is the final goal of all moral progress, and constitutes what Kant calls "holiness of will." This "holiness," however, must not be confused with the holiness of the *divine* will, which consists in an absolute and necessary determination of the will by the objectively practical. Kant describes the holiness which is the unconditioned moral perfection of the finite rational being also as the ideal "Son of God" or the "ideal of humanity well-pleasing to God." The nature of such an ideal is regarded as human in the sense of being encumbed with the very same needs as ourselves, hence the same sorrows; with the very same inclinations, hence with the same temptations to transgress; let it, however, be regarded as superhuman to the degree that his unchanging purity of will, not achieved with effort but innate, makes all transgression on his part utterly impossible.[40]

The second component of the highest good will be happiness, in the proportion to worthiness to be happy—a happiness which will be complete and perfect because conditioned by the holiness of will which constitutes the supreme condition of the highest good.

In some places, usually when Kant is giving a brief account of his moral argument, he speaks of the components of the highest good as if he meant only the virtue and happiness of the particular moral agent. This way of expressing himself has caused Kant to be misunderstood, and has given many the mistaken impression that in Kant's view the moral agent must be preoccupied with its own virtue and—worse yet—with his own happiness, and that he is not concerned with the moral and natural good of others. We have taken some trouble to show that the critical moral philosophy makes the moral and natural good both of ourselves and of others objects of pure practical reason. Why, then, does Kant so often express himself only in terms of the moral agent's own virtue and happiness? [41]

The condition for the giving of all ends of pure practical reason is the existence of a being who is an end in himself, the finite rational person. It is with respect to persons, as we have seen, that all ends of pure practical reason are formulated. All such ends are the (obligatory and permissible) ends *of persons*. Thus Kant in many places adopts the method of formulating the highest good for one person (the agent himself) and extends this ideal to an entire world of such beings, a

Kingdom of Ends. When Kant is hurried in his exposition, he does not always make this extension as he does in the second critique: Inasmuch as virtue and happiness together constitute the possession of the highest good *for one person*, and happiness in proportion to morality . . . constitutes that of a possible *world*, the *highest good* means the *whole*, the *perfect good*, wherein virtue is always the supreme good.[42] Kant also makes this explicit in the *Religion*, in his discussion of the need for a "moral community" of men: "The species [*Gattung*] of rational beings is objectively, in the idea of reason, destined for a social goal [*gemeinschaftlichen Zwecke*], the promotion of the highest good as a social good [*des höchsten als eines gemeinschaftlichen Guts*]." [43]

In recognizing the moral law as binding on him, therefore, the moral agent adopts a commitment to recognize the synthesis of the highest moral good and the natural good as the final end for moral striving. But it is incorrect to say, as Silber does, that Kant regards it as a duty to *attain* the highest good.[44] There is a distinction for Kant between what the law commands us to *do* (to accomplish), and what it commands us to *seek* (to make our end). If the law commanded us to *attain* the highest good, then the highest good would be a "narrow" or "perfect" duty, something we were obligated to *accomplish*. But Kant points out that both components of the highest good involve "imperfect" or "wide" duties, duties to act from a certain maxim, to *adopt* a certain end, but not necessarily to achieve or attain that end.[45] But this is certainly *not* to say that the actual attainment of the highest good is of no concern to morality. For if the agent is commanded to make the highest good his end, he is commanded precisely to seek its attainment. It would be absurd for someone to remain indifferent to the actual attainment of the highest good, and yet maintain that he was properly fulfilling his duty to "promote it with all his strength." The duty to seek (but not necessarily to attain) the highest good may be what Silber has in mind when he speaks of a "regulative obligation to *attain* the highest good." [46] To my knowledge, Kant never uses the phrase "regulative obligation," nor does this phrase make much sense when the two terms in it are employed in the usual Kantian ways. At best, then, this is a rather unclear way of putting a point which is relatively clear in Kant's writings themselves.

Kant's philosophical thought about religion is founded on the relation between obedience to the moral law and the adoption of the highest good as an end. I cannot deny or seriously doubt that this object can be conceived possible without committing myself not to obey the moral law. Hence it is of crucial importance to Kant's *absurdum practicum* argument, and to his religious thought as a whole, that the highest good be viewed as an *end* to which any moral agent commits himself in obeying the moral law.

The highest good, of course, is a *philosophical* conception, and while it may play a role in ordinary rational morality, Kant does not intend to confuse the idea of an unconditioned end of morality with an ordinary "duty of virtue," an end which is also a duty. Beck, however, does seem to fall into this sort of confusion when he denies that the highest good has "any practical consequences" and holds that because it is not listed among the "duties of virtue" in the *Metaphysic of Morals* that our duty to seek the highest good "does not exist." [47] Beck's error here is quite like that of the man who denied that Cambridge University was a real educational institution because he failed to find it housed in any of the buildings on the campus. The highest good is not among our duties, it is the unconditioned totality of all ends of pure practical reason "which, while not multiplying men's duties, yet provides them with a special point of focus for the unification of all ends." [48]

Since the highest good is a philosophical ideal which unifies and conditions all ends of pure practical reason, and is not itself among the duties recognized by ordinary rational morality, it would be absurd to reproach anyone morally for not making the highest good as such the object of his action, so long as he does strive for all those conditioned ends whose furtherance the moral law commands of him. It is no moral duty to engage in a critique of moral reasoning. Nor is it a moral duty for everyone to define the unconditioned object of a moral will. This is a philosopher's task. But this task is relevant to morality in that, if it is properly done, the philosophical ideal of the highest good will be one which will have validity for rational moral action and as such will command the recognition of every rational agent that it is the final end for all his moral striving.

But, it may be urged, how can the highest good command such recognition if it is equivalent, in practice, only to the duties of ordinary rational morality as defined by the categorical imperative? What real practical consequences has this doctrine? Beck expresses this objection forcefully when he denies that the command to seek the highest good exists

as a separate command, independent of the categorical imperative, which is developed without this concept. For suppose that I do all within my power—which is all any moral decree can demand of me—to promote the highest good, what am I to do? Simply act out of respect for the law, which I already knew. I can do absolutely nothing else toward apportioning happiness in accordance with desert—that is the task of a moral governor of the universe, not of a laborer in the vineyard.[49]

Beck fails to note, of course, that in acting out of respect for the moral law, I adopt ends, and labor to bring those ends about in the world, and that this is an essential part of my obedience to the moral law. But there is still weight to his objection. Even granted that the highest good is "the world morality would create," what moral value is there in making *this ideal* my end over and above those particular objects of pure practical reason which I, as a mere "laborer in the vineyard," will make my ends by adopting formally legislative maxims? Why, indeed, should moral action have any final, unconditioned *end* at all? [50] The moral law, in Kant's view, gives us a *rule* according to which we must act, and perhaps we do adopt ends in accordance with this rule which do tend to promote the *ideal* of a world of morally perfect beings all enjoying happiness in proportion to their worthiness to be happy. But why is it necessary for us to make the actual attainment of this beautiful ideal our end? If we adopt ends which tend toward it, we do all that can be expected of us by the law. Just as I may play *my best* against the chess champion without expecting to win, so I may do *my best* morally without expecting the highest moral ideal to be attained through my efforts. Relegating the "highest good" to the status of an "unattainable ideal" will not deprive it of any of its actual moral force, but it will free us from the necessity of believing that this ideal must be actually attainable in the world.

The only satisfactory way of meeting this objection is to recognize the extent to which it expresses an attitude towards rational morality and action which is fundamentally different from Kant's. Kant's reason for introducing the doctrine of the highest good, as we have seen, is that human reason *demands* an unconditioned totality of the object of pure practical reason as its final *end*. As the above objection itself recognizes, this is *not* a trivial demand. Reason, as we noted in our introductory remarks, always "seeks the unconditioned," always seeks to unify its rules under the idea of a totality. In the first

critique, this office of reason gave rise to the dialectical perplexities occasioned by the necessary ideas of reason, transcendental ideas which human reason cannot do without, but
whose objects are altogether inaccessible to human knowledge. We saw above that for Kant this dialectic is *unavoidable;* it is not a mere blunder, but a "sophistry of pure reason itself," by means of which human reason is forced to recognize and to respond to its finite and problematic condition.

It is Kant's project in the Dialectic of Pure Practical Reason
also to exhibit the problematic condition of finite rationality,
to set forth the necessary perplexities and tensions which a
being who is both finite and rational must recognize in the
practical employment of his reason. Just as theoretical reason
framed for itself ideas, whose objects lay beyond its power to
know, so practical reason is led by its pursuit of the unconditioned to frame the idea of its final end, an end which is beyond the power of finite rationality, unaided, to attain. Just as
the ideas of reason in the first critique were necessary, and
could not be simply dismissed as foolish chimeras, so the ideal
end of finite rationality cannot be simply ignored, or rele-
gated to the comfortable status of an "unattainable ideal." Just
as the dialectic of pure theoretical reason produces an illusion
which "unceasingly mocks and torments" us in our pursuit of
knowledge, so the pursuit of the ideal of pure practical reason
will lead us necessarily into the troubled waters of illusion
also, where we will be threatened with the unattainability of
an ideal which we ourselves cannot establish, but with which
we cannot cease to concern ourselves without forsaking the
rationality which is proper to our own nature.

The demand of reason that we make the highest good our
end, is in effect a demand that we find for ourselves a single
purpose for our lives, a final purpose which our reason entitles
us to regard as the ultimate meaning and goal of the entire

world.[51] In Kant's view, no man who is content with a mere aggregate of particular ends and purposes in his life can have exercised his rational capacities fully in relation to the purposes of his action. If this demand which reason makes on itself leads it into dialectical perplexities, these perplexities are not to be resolved by pretending them to be a contingent and trivial sort of folly. We must recognize in them the necessary limitations of our own nature, and respond to them in full realization that the problems and perplexities which face us are an essential part of the tension of finite rationality itself.

4. The Practical Postulates

In Chapter 1 Kant's moral defense of faith was reduced to three important premises. We noted there that Kant's argument was of the form of a *reductio*—in Kant's own words, a *reductio ad absurdum practicum*. We also gave attention in the first chapter to the rational relationship between belief and action which forms one of the three crucial premises of Kant's *absurdum practicum* argument. In Chapters 2 and 3, a second premise of this argument was considered by means of a discussion of Kant's concept of the highest good and its role in the critical moral philosophy. Before rounding out our discussion of Kant's moral arguments by taking up the third crucial premise employed in them, it may be advisable to summarize briefly our findings thus far.

In Kant's view it is a requirement of rational purposive action that anyone who acts in pursuit of an end accepts a commitment to ground his action toward this end on a belief that the end is at least possible of attainment. This belief, moreover, must in Kant's view be something positive and definite, a practical conception of the *situation* of action. From this rational requirement it follows that if anyone should deny (or doubt in a serious, habitual, and deliberate fashion) that some object (or state of affairs) can be conceived possible of attainment by him, he thereby commits himself not to make that ob-

ject an end of purposive action. This commitment forms the
first premise of the *absurdum practicum* argument.

But Kant also holds that there is a final end of all *moral*
striving, which he calls the "highest good" or *summum
bonum*. This end is conceived as the unconditioned object of
pure practical reason, from which all ends set by the moral
agent in obedience to the moral law are derived. In adopting
any end of action in obedience to the moral law, therefore,
the finite rational agent represents an end which rationally
presupposes that the agent has already adopted the highest
good as an end. Hence any finite rational agent commits himself to the pursuit of this final end as a condition of the adoption of any end in obedience to the moral law. But since all
finite rational volition and action is purposive, and requires
the representation of an end, the agent's commitment to pursue the highest good is also a condition for any volition and
action in accordance with the moral law. This second commitment forms the second premise of the *absurdum practicum* argument.

From these two premises it will follow, as was observed earlier in our sketch of the *absurdum practicum* argument, that
anyone who denies (or doubts) that he can conceive the highest good as possible of attainment thereby commits himself
not to make the highest good his end, and thus commits himself also not to act in obedience to the moral law. And it is
this immoral commitment, this morally repugnant conclusion,
which constitutes the *absurdum practicum*.

Kant's *absurdum practicum* becomes a *dialectic* of practical
reason by means of a practical illusion, which makes it appear
necessary for us to deny that the highest good can be conceived possible of attainment. From this illusion results the *absurdum practicum*, the "antinomy of practical reason," whose
resolution results in the practical postulates of God and im-

mortality. The postulates alone, it is argued, render us able to avoid denying that the highest good can be conceived possible as an end for the finite rational agent. And here we find the third and final premise of the *absurdum practicum* argument, involving for the first time the explicit connection between moral and religious concepts. The careful examination of Kant's reasoning through the practical dialectic to its resolution in the postulates of pure practical reason is therefore our first task as we turn to the examination of the third premise of the moral arguments.

Any dialectic of reason is for Kant an "unavoidable illusion" arising "from the application of the totality of conditions (and thus of the unconditioned) to appearances as if they were things in themselves." [1] The "totality of conditions" with respect to the object of pure practical reason is, as we have seen, subsumed in the unconditioned final end of morality, the highest good. The dialectic of practical reason, therefore, results from the illusion occasioned by the "application" of the idea of the highest good "to appearances as if they were things in themselves." Let us try to state Kant's point more concretely. To "apply" the idea of an end of action is simply to represent this end as a possible effect of one's volition and action in the world. To "apply" the idea of the highest good in this sense is, then, to represent the world of one's action in its totality as a possible world ordered by moral laws, and to strive to bring this world into existence. The idea of the highest good is therefore "applied" to the world of moral action, the world which the moral agent makes it his end to transform in accordance with this idea. Now this world may be taken, as Kant indicates, either to be the world of appearances, or the world of things-in-themselves. Ordinarily, of course, the moral man represents the ends of his action in the world of appearances, the sensible world in which he exists as a finite being. His ends concern the persons and things around him, his family, his friends, the society in which he lives, the tools with which he works, the products of his labor.* He represents his ends amid the sensible world, and grounds his expectations of success or failure with respect to particular ends on the natural laws to which the world of appearances is subject.

The dialectic of practical reason arises due to the natural assumption on the part of reason that the highest good, the unconditioned object of pure practical reason, is also to be repre-

* The mention of our sensible knowledge of persons as moral agents is bound to raise in the minds of some the vexed question of the possibility of an empirical (and specifically a moral) psychology in the critical philosophy. The problem facing Kant at this point is often put in a vague and speculative way by saying that Kant had trouble "reconciling" the phenomenal and noumenal realms, or "bringing them together" (England, *Kant's Conception of God*, 208). Having justified freedom as a practical postulate in the supersensible world, Kant did not further inquire into the conditions for the possibility of the empirical judgments we commonly make concerning the morality of the motives, intentions, and purposes of persons in the sensible world. Kant accepted the obvious fact that we do make judgments of this kind, and that we can be quite justified in our assessment of men's (our own and others') motives and intentions. To be sure, he remains cautious concerning such judgments, and points out that we can never make them with "complete certainty" (*G* 407g 74e; *Rel* 20g 16e). It is probably the case that Kant confused his own peculiar epistemological grounds for this uncertainty with that reasonable degree of forbearance in judging the intent of others which is necessary in showing due respect for their own use of their reason and with the avoidance of a self-righteous cocksureness concerning our own motives (see *G* 407fg 75e). And surely in some cases such a blanket caution is absurd. (If a man shoves a gun in my ribs and demands my money, for example, it will not do to say that it is only highly probable that he intends to rob me.) I do not think that Kant's problem at this point is necessarily insoluble within the scope of the critical philosophy, but it is clear that Kant himself did not solve it, and it is in any case beyond the scope of our present discussion to consider it further.

sented as applying merely to the world of appearances. Kant
argues that once we grant this assumption, we cannot escape
the conclusion that the highest good is not possible of attainment, or at least cannot be conceived as attainable. And once
we are forced to this conclusion, we are committed by the
natural dialectic of practical reason, the *reductio ad absurdum
practicum*, not to obey the moral law. In this way, there arises
what Kant calls the "antinomy of practical reason." * In order
to escape this antinomy, it is necessary to deny the natural assumption of reason, that the highest good may be applied as a
practical ideal merely to the world of appearances, and to postulate in the world of things-in-themselves the existence of
conditions which render the possibility of the highest good
conceivable to us. In this way, Kant proposes to justify a *belief*
in a God and a future life which can never become a form of
knowledge, since the world of things-in-themselves remains as
inaccessible as ever to the theoretical powers of cognition of a
finite rational creature.

Before beginning a closer examination of the dialectic of
practical reason, one further preliminary point must be noted.
Kant seems to suggest in sections I and II of the Dialectic of
the second critique that there is a single "antinomy of practical reason" (or *absurdum practicum*). But when we turn to
his arguments for the postulates in sections IV and V, it is evident that he is giving us two separate arguments, each of

* We noted above (Chap. 1, p. 27) that in the second critique Kant
attempts to describe this "antinomy" on the model of a *theoretical*
conflict, claiming that it proves the "falsity" of the moral law. But
as we noted above, the "antinomy" here is not a conflict of judgments, an *absurdum logicum*, but an *absurdum practicum*, a conflict
between a moral obligation and an apparent rational commitment not
to adhere to this obligation. We will therefore use the terms "antinomy of practical reason" and *absurdum practicum* interchangeably,
recognizing that the latter is a more accurate expression of Kant's
meaning.

which alone constitutes a practical dialectic and results in an *absurdum practicum*. Both, indeed, relate to the illusion engendered by our viewing the highest good as a practical ideal applying only to the world of appearances, and this is the central point which Kant is making in sections I and II. But since the antinomies engendered are two, and not one, we must deal with each *reductio ad absurdum practicum* separately, and consider each along with the practical postulate which it is intended to justify.

The First Antinomy of Practical Reason

In the Dialectic of the second critique, Kant applies the same "skeptical method" he used in dealing with the antinomies of theoretical reason. This method consists of three distinct stages (1) Kant provokes the dialectic of practical reason by provisionally admitting the natural assumption that the totality of conditioned ends (and consequently the unconditioned totality of such ends) applies to the world of appearances as if it were the world of things in themselves. He then reasons from this assumption to an antinomy of practical reason, or *absurdum practicum*. (2) Kant critically examines the reasoning he has set forth, exposing its error and indicating the unwarranted assumption which is responsible for it. (3) Finally, Kant guarantees against the errors with which this dialectic threatens us, by formulating practical postulates which guard us against it. Kant intends to follow this method in the Dialectic of the second critique by devoting Section I of Chapter II of the Dialectic to the first of the three stages mentioned above, Section II to the second of these stages, and Sections IV and V to the third. The same pattern is to be noted in Book II, Chapter II, of the Dialectic of the first critique, which is devoted to the antinomies of theoretical reason. Here, Sections 1 and 2 constitute the first stage, Sections 3–7 the second, and Sections 8 and 9, dealing with the regulative employment of the cosmological ideas, correspond to the third stage. In the second critique, however, the detailed presentation of each of the two antinomies of practical reason is given in the section dealing with the corresponding practical postulate (Sections IV and V).

From this brief summary of the skeptical method used by Kant in the Dialectic of the second critique, it is clear that the argument for each practical postulate arises from the resolution of an antinomy of practical reason. Since the postulates are justified as the necessary means of *avoiding* dialectical error, the arguments for them are, as we noted earlier, *reductiones ad absurdum*. Further, each of the two practical postulates arises from the resolution of a separate antinomy, a separate dialectical argument threatening the practical possibility of the highest good. We should recall that for any given person the possession of the highest good consists of complete moral perfection, or holiness of will, combined with the enjoyment of happiness insofar as this happiness is compatible with and conditioned by the worthiness to be happy. Hence the attainment of the highest good, for one person or for a world of persons, requires that two distinct states of affairs be realized: (1) complete moral perfection of will must be attained and (2) happiness must be enjoyed insofar as it is deserved. If either of these states of affairs cannot be conceived possible, then the highest good as a whole cannot be conceived possible, and an antinomy of practical reason or *absurdum practicum* results. The respective arguments for immortality and for the existence of God as necessary postulates of practical reason are founded on the resolution of the dialectical threat to the conceivability, the practical possibility, of each of these two distinct states of affairs.

The argument for the first postulate, then, depends upon

the dialectical threat to the practical possibility of moral perfection in man. In the second critique itself, Kant's presentation of this dialectic is, to say the least, unsatisfying. For it consists simply of the assertion that holiness of will "is a perfection of which no rational being in the world of sense is at any time capable."[2] Kant evidently feels this contention to be an obvious one, of which our own moral struggles and failings would constitute sufficient proof. And though he has made this contention before, both in the second critique and in earlier writings, scarcely any more justification has been given for it on these occasions than is given here in the Dialectic.[3] But the relation of this contention to the critical moral philosophy is by no means so casual as these references would suggest, and it will be advisable for us to inquire further into Kant's reasons for making it.

The defining characteristic of the "holy will" for Kant is the *necessity* of its conformity to law, the fact that such a will requires no constraint of any kind in order to be in conformity with the law.[4] The holy will is thus opposed to the finite rational will as we see it in human persons, for finite rational volition requires self-constraint under the law as an *imperative*, in order that it become conformable to the objectively practical. Virtue (*Tugend*) for human beings consists in a "self-overcoming" (*Selbstüberwindung*), the successful discipline of oneself, and the conquest of obstacles (*Hindernisse*) which oppose the conformity of the will to the moral law.[5] Hence Kant sometimes says (somewhat paradoxically) that the holy will is *not* virtuous, because it lacks the obstacles to conformity of volition with law, which "virtue" as self-overcoming presupposes. But just for this reason, holiness of will is also the supreme moral good, and *perfect* virtue, since it is that state of moral perfection in which all obstacles to this conformity have ceased to exist. Kant's contention that holiness of will is impossible for a rational being in the world of sense amounts, then, to the claim that the obstacles hindering the conformity of the will with the law cannot *as a whole* be overcome by any rational being in the world of sense. And it is this claim which he must justify if he is to present successfully the dialectical argument for the first antinomy of practical reason.

The justification of this claim depends largely on the character of the "obstacles" which oppose the conformity of the finite rational will with law. According to one interpretation of Kant, these obstacles consist simply of man's natural inclinations, which it is his moral task constantly to suppress and frustrate in the interests of reason. The necessity of these obstacles would, on this view, be derived from man's finite and sensible nature itself, to which his reason is irreconcilably opposed. This seems to be the view of Greene's examined above, and it leads quite naturally to the charge that Kant's ethics involve an untenable "dualism" of two opposed natures in man.

It cannot be denied, of course, that the obstacles hindering the conformity of the finite rational will to law in some way involve inclination and sensibility. It is clear that for Kant a being (such as God) who is not burdened with needs and inclinations, and has only the objectively practical as a motive of volition, is necessarily a holy being.[6] But it does not necessarily follow that *only* beings unburdened by inclinations are capable of holiness. For it may still be the case that inclinations are not *sufficient* to produce obstacles to holiness of will, even though they are *necessary* for the existence of such obstacles.

Kant does not always seem to be of one mind concerning the role played by inclination in the constitution of obstacles to man's moral perfection. Because he recognizes that inclinations are necessary for the existence of such obstacles, he sometimes speaks as if inclinations themselves were the ene-

mies of morality. He says for example that "holy beings are
not virtuous, for the reason that they have no evil inclinations
to overcome." [7] He also says on occasion that rational beings
should wish to be completely free from all inclinations
whatever.[8] But accompanying this rather Schopenhauerian
tendency throughout Kant's works is a milder view of inclination. Kant criticizes all "morose" ethics, which "assume that
all amenities of life and all pleasures of the senses are opposed
to morality," and terms their "hostility to pleasure" a
"mistake." [9] In the *Lectures on Philosophical Theology*, Kant
expresses the view that evil does arise from the natural "limitations" (*Einschränkungen*) imposed on man by "sense" and
"animal instinct." But he denies unequivocally in the *Religion*
that evil could come about "from mere limitations in our
nature.[10] As Kant develops and clarifies his ethical views, it appears that the milder view, which does not hold inclinations
alone responsible for evil, comes to predominate. Too much
emphasis has been given to the "moroseness" of Kant's ethics,
and to his supposed hostility to inclination and sensibility.
This attitude is neither typical of Kant, nor characteristic of
his best and most mature thought. Nowhere can we find a better opportunity to observe Kant's *rejection* of this morose attitude than in his treatment of the character of those obstacles
which oppose conformity of the finite rational will to law.

From what we have already observed about the relation between reason and sensibility in the critical moral philosophy,
there are already good grounds prima facie for doubting that
inclinations alone constitute the obstacles hindering conformity of the finite rational will with law. The natural ends derived from inclination are not as such opposed to morality,
and in fact constitute a part of the good for morality, when
limited and conditioned by the worthiness to be happy.
Hence it is quite wrong to picture Kant as advocating simply

a suppression and frustration of inclinations. Although reason is pictured by him both in its prudential and moral function as disciplining and limiting the pursuit of natural ends, it does not have an exclusively repressive function. Kant strongly condemns that "monastic asceticism" which opposes all inclinations as such, and favors a more moderate form of self-discipline which "consists only in combatting the impulses of nature to the extent that we are able to master them when a situation comes up in which they threaten morality." [11] It is doubtful that Kant would have said this if he had felt that all inclinations as such constituted a threat and an obstacle to morality. Further, Kant even goes so far as to say that in cases of "wide duty" there are "limits to the extent of the sacrifice" of my own natural ends which I can be morally obliged to make. "These limits will depend, in large part, on what a person's true needs consist of in view of his temperament, and it must be left to each to decide this for himself." [12] Since, then, it is part of the task of moral reasoning to provide for the limited and conditioned satisfaction of natural needs, and not to oppose inclinations as such, it is difficult to see how inclinations by themselves could constitute a permanent obstacle to conformity of the will with law.

In the *Religion*, Kant denies unequivocally that inclinations by themselves can be a threat to the conformity of the will with law. For he lists both animal inclinations and prudential self-love as among the predispositions to *good* in human nature which "enjoin observance of the law." These predispositions can be "used contrary to their natural ends," but "it is not only futile to want to extirpate them but to do so would also be harmful and blameworthy." [13] Further he says explicitly that the "enemy" of morality "is not to be sought in the merely undisciplined natural inclinations" common to all sensuous beings.[14] Moreover, the ideal of humanity well-pleasing to God, the holy will, is there described as "being encumbered . . . with the very same inclinations . . . as ourselves" but possessed of an "unchanging purity of will" which "makes all transgression on his part utterly impossible." [15] If inclinations by themselves constituted the reason why holiness was unattainable for man, Kant could not have described a holy being as affected by them.

To understand the true character of the obstacles which oppose the conformity of the finite rational will with law, we must leave behind the oversimplified and uncharitable reading of Kant which opposes reason and inclination as two irreconcilable "natures" in man, and attend to the subtlety with which Kant develops his theory of the nature of a being who is both finite and rational, capable of autonomous action but also burdened in his very being with inescapable moral limitations. The maxims of any finite rational being, Kant tells us, contain the incentives both of moral reason and of sensible inclination.

Hence the distinction between a good man and one who is evil cannot lie in the difference between the incentives which they adopt into their maxims (not in the content of the maxim), but rather must depend on *subordination* (the form of the maxim), i.e. *which of the two incentives he makes the condition of the other*. Consequently man (even the best) is evil only in that he reverses the moral order of the incentives when he adopts them into his maxim. He adopts, indeed, the moral law along with the law of self-love; yet when he becomes aware that they cannot remain on a par with each other but that one must be subordinated to the other as its supreme condition, he [the evil man] makes the incentive of self-love and its inclinations the condition of obedience to the moral law.[16]

I do no evil simply by having natural desires for food, sex, human companionship, and so forth. And so long as these de-

sires of mine remain disciplined, conditioned by my reason
and limited to those ends which reason determines as being of
moral worth, they do not in the least constitute a threat or obstacle to the conformity of my will with the law. The natural
and quite deserved satisfaction and pleasure that we take in
the company of our friends, or in work well done, are, for example, no threat or obstacle to morality at all, except insofar
as we are disposed to deceive ourselves into thinking that acts
motivated by these pleasures are actually motivated by reason
itself. Here it is not the inclination which threatens us, but
our own impurity of will. Kant's occasional statements that
we should wish to be free of even such allowable inclinations
cannot be made compatible with his assertion in the *Religion*
that the desire to extirpate inclinations is "harmful and blameworthy." Such statements must be regarded as expressions of a
view which Kant correctly repudiated as his theory of man's
moral nature was clarifed and developed in the *Religion*. In
his expression of a desire to be free of inclination, Kant (like
the Stoics) had "mistaken his enemy." [17] For he confused the
fact that inclinations are necessary for the existence of moral
evil, with the mistaken view that *in man* inclinations are the
source of the threats to moral perfection.

It is not by having inclinations that we become evil, then,
but rather by a *free act of choice* in which we subordinate the
incentives of duty to those provided by these inclinations.
The moral obstacles in human nature are not constituted by
inclinations, by human finitude or sensibility as such, but by a
special characteristic of man's free power of choice
(*Willkür*). The permanent source of obstacles to conformity
of the human will with law is therefore not derived simply
from the concept of a finite rational being as such. Neither is
this permanent characteristic of human nature a part of "na-

ture" in the strict sense which is opposed to "freedom," for
then Kant would be attributing it just to sensibility and
inclination.[18] But just as little is this characteristic a "corruption of the morally legislative reason," since this would render
man utterly incapable of any goodness.[19] Rather it is conceived by Kant as an innate and natural propensity (*Hang*)
of the human power of choice, a propensity to invert the
moral order of incentives in the maxim of action. This propensity is not itself a natural inclination, nor is it a characteristic of these inclinations themselves. For if it were either, it
would again be traceable simply to human sensibility and finitude. Inclinations become the occasions for a moral danger to
us, then, only because of an innate propensity of *our free volition* to give them preference to the incentives of moral reason.
As such, this propensity "corrupts the ground of all maxims"
and constitutes what Kant calls the "radical evil in human nature." [20] In my discussion of Kant's theory of radical evil in
Chapter 6, I will be devoting special attention to this theory
and investigating Kant's reasons for holding it. Much of what
I say about it here will be subjected to critical examination
later. My present task is not, therefore, to see *why* Kant
holds that man has an innate propensity to evil; rather, it is
only to ascertain *what* his position is, and to see briefly how it
supports the dialectic of practical reason now under consideration.

In saying that the propensity to radical evil in man "corrupts the ground of all maxims," Kant does not mean that on
account of it all our maxims are evil, but rather only that
there exists, *antecedently* to our every adoption of a good or
evil maxim, a tendency to prefer the incentives of inclination
to those of duty. For this reason Kant says that radical evil is
"*inextirpable* [*nicht zu vertilgen*] by human powers, since ex-

tirpation could occur only through good maxims, and cannot take place when the ultimate subjective ground of all maxims is postulated as corrupt." [21]

Along with this propensity to evil, man has certain *predispositions* (*Anlagen*) to good, the highest of which is his moral personality as an accountable and free being. Kant describes this predisposition as a "capacity [*Empfänglichkeit*] for respect for the moral law as *in itself a sufficient incentive of the will* [*Willkür*]." [22] This predisposition is not a propensity (*Hang*) of the human *Wilkür* as it actually exists, but rather is "bound up with the possibility of human nature" and is part of the concept of finite rational volition as such. [23] It is in virtue of this predisposition that man has a susceptibility to goodness, but unlike the propensity to radical evil, it does not by its very existence make him good or evil.

When it is said, Man is created good, this can mean nothing more than: He is created *for good*, and the original *predisposition* [*Anlage*] in man is good; not that, thereby, he is already actually good, but rather that he brings it about that he becomes good or evil, according to whether he adopts or does not adopt into his maxim the incentives which this predisposition carries with it (which must be left wholly to his free choice). [24]

Radical evil, therefore, though it is "inextirpable," is at the same time possible to overcome, "since it is found in man whose actions are free." [25] The propensity to radical evil in human nature therefore does not mean that men necessarily adopt evil maxims, or that they are incapable of moral goodness in general. Rather it only means that in our moral strivings we do not begin from a "natural innocence," but must presuppose a "wickedness of the will" in the form of a propensity to evil, and must therefore "begin with the incessant counteraction against it." [26]

In the world of sense, this counteraction takes the form of

moral *progress* in time, an overcoming of the obstacles which this propensity places in our way. But since the propensity itself is "inextirpable by human powers," we can never remove the source of these obstacles at one stroke. For no good maxim of ours can remove a propensity antecedent to the adoption of all maxims, a propensity which "corrupts the ground of all maxims." Our counteraction against radical evil in time thus "always remains only a progress from *one* perfection to others," a progress which is always accompanied by "that failure which is inseparable from the existence of a temporal being as such, the failure, namely, ever wholly to be what we have a mind to become." [27]

Because the source of moral obstacles, the propensity to radical evil, is not capable of extirpation in time, man is forced to combat it by means of an overcoming of *each* of the obstacles which it puts in his way. Since these obstacles are constituted by the propensity to prefer the incentives of inclination to those of duty, man's moral progress in time always consists of a "gradual reform of his sensuous nature," the arduous "labor of moral reconstruction" which counteracts the propensity to evil by disciplining and limiting the particular inclinations which are the occasions for its manifestation.[28]

We can now see why Kant's doctrine of radical evil is the true exposition and ground for the dialectic of practical reason which leads to the first antinomy. The attainment of holiness of will is impossible for finite rational beings as we know them in the world of sense because this attainment by man would require not simply an overcoming of particular moral obstacles, but the overcoming of the source of these obstacles in his own moral nature itself. It would thus require not a progress in *degree* of virtue, but the attainment of a different *kind* of moral volition. But because the radical evil of man's own nature is both imputable to him (as a propensity of his

free *Willkür*) and inextirpable by him in time, the transition
from virtue to holiness is unattainable by him.

The dialectic leading to the first antinomy of practical reason, therefore, may be put thus: Complete moral perfection,
holiness of will, must be attained if the highest good is to be
attained. But I, who know myself as a finite rational being in
the world of sense, recognize that my own moral nature
makes it impossible for me ever to attain holiness of will. But
if holiness of will is unattainable, then the highest good as a
whole is unattainable, and I am committed not to make it my
end. But if I do not make the highest good my end, I cannot
rationally adopt any end in accordance with the command of
the moral law, since the highest good constitutes the unconditioned object of pure practical reason from which all other
objects are derived. But since I cannot will at all without the
representation of an end, this denial that the highest good is
possible commits me not to obey the moral law. But I recognize nonetheless that I am unconditionally obligated to obey
the moral law. The conflict of this rational commitment with
this moral obligation constitutes an *antinomy of practical reason*.

The Postulate of Immortality

Kant answers the first antinomy of practical reason with
the postulate of immortality. This postulate is necessary, he
claims, if we are to render the possibility of the highest good
conceivable to us and avoid the moral error with which this
antinomy threatens us. We must now proceed to see how
Kant proposes to justify this claim.

The first antinomy of practical reason, as we have just seen,
threatens the possibility of the highest good by reasoning
from our knowledge of the moral nature of men as we find
them in the world of sense, to the conclusion that for men as a

whole the moral perfection of holiness of will is unattainable. Because the attainment of holiness of will is a necessary condition for the attainment of the highest good for any single rational being, this conclusion also forces us to admit that the highest good as a whole is impossible, and hence to an *absurdum practicum*. In his treatment of the first postulate in the second critique, Kant does not tell us specifically why this argument involves a dialectical fallacy. But from what he has already told us about the dialectic of practical reason we may presume that the argument is dialectical because it infers from a fact about men as they exist in the world of appearances to the unattainability of holiness of will for them as they exist in themselves. All that can be said with justification is that men cannot attain holiness *in the world of sense;* the first antinomy arises when the further (unjustifiable) claim is made that holiness of will is *in general* unattainable by them. Now if this is Kant's way of resolving the first antinomy, we might expect the postulate of immortality to consist of the assertion that in some supersensible existence (a "future life") radical evil is somehow extirpable, and holiness of will is attainable. And we might also expect that any clarification of this postulate by Kant would consist in an analysis of the character which this supersensible existence must be presumed to have in order to fulfill its practical function.

But Kant rejects this relatively simple and straightforward way of formulating the first postulate; his reasons for this rejection seem to be largely moral ones. Kant is rather wary of any view which posits a miraculous kind of transformation in man's moral nature, and he gives no quarter to "fantastic theosophical dreams which completely contradict our knowledge of ourselves." [29]* The postulate of a future life in which

* Kant did not, it is true, always see that the "wish to be free of" all inclinations is a "fantastic dream" and even a morally blameworthy

holiness is suddenly and inexplicably made possible for man seems to Kant a morally dangerous postulate, much akin to the beliefs of the superstitious believer who praises and placates the Deity in the hope "that God can make him a better man without his having to do any more than *ask* for it." [30] A postulate of this kind would seem to make it rational for a man simply to wait until this future life to discover how holiness of will might be possible for him, and not to waste his time with the difficult and always incompleted labors of moral progress toward holiness in this life. In Kant's view, then, this postulate would lead to an *absurdum practicum* every bit as much as the dialectical argument it is supposed to answer. A properly formulated postulate must uphold the rationality of moral progress in this life as the proper road to the attainment of the final end of this progress.

Kant seems to be faced at this point with a truly insoluble problem. He wishes to postulate progress toward moral perfection as the necessary means of pursuing this perfection; and yet the very circumstances which make this progress necessary also guarantee that it alone can never bring about the fulfillment of its final end. Kant's attempt to avoid this dilemma in the second critique is extremely complex, subtle, and obscure in its brevity. Holiness, says Kant, is not attaina-

wish. It is only in his later writings (particularly in the *Religion*) that this radically stoical element in Kant's ethics is recognized as incompatible with his moral philosophy and discarded. Kant seems always to have maintained a great personal respect for stoical "apathy," a respect which is not always proportionate to its foundations in his moral theory itself. Here as elsewhere, Kant tended to assume that his philosophical insights would justify his own personal moral opinions when this was in fact not the case at all (*TL* 409g 70fe; cf. Matson, "Kant as Casuist," 335ff). The repudiation of certain elements in stoicism is plain throughout his works, and in the *Religion*, it becomes quite explicit (*Rel* 57ffg 50ffe; but cf, also *KpV* 126ffg 131ffe).

ble by man in the course of his moral progress from bad to better,

but since it is required as practically necessary, it can be found only in an endless progress to that complete fitness; on principles of pure practical reason, it is necessary to assume such a practical progress as the real object of the will.[31]

The first postulate, then, is not fomulated in order to insure the possibility of holiness itself, but rather to insure the possibility of an endless progress toward it, which is "the real object of the will." But why does Kant say that endless progress is the "real object of the will"? It would appear that, having *accepted* the dialectical argument showing the practical impossibility of holiness, Kant is now attempting to avoid the *absurdum practicum* by substituting a more attainable goal as "the real object of the will." If this were his procedure, it should certainly be accounted an extremely arbitrary and highhanded one. But it is not quite accurate to say that Kant has *substituted* "endless progress" for "holiness" as a component of the highest good. For he does say that holiness itself is to be "found" or "met with" (*angetroffen*) in an endless progress.[32] Now by this Kant cannot mean that holiness is actually a term or member of this series, for this would be simply to affirm that holiness is attainable within this progress, which is what Kant has denied. And it could hardly be said that holiness was attained at the *end* of an *endless* progress. In the second critique, Kant explains himself in this way:

Only endless progress from lower to higher stages of moral perfection is possible to a rational but finite being. The Infinite Being, to whom the temporal condition is nothing, sees in this series, which is for us without end, a whole conformable to the moral law; holiness . . . is to be found in a single intellectual intuition of the existence of rational beings.[33]

In some of his later writings, Kant goes into more detail on this point, referring to man's moral constitution (*Beschaffenheit*) as fulfilling the requirement of holiness by means of a constant disposition (*Gesinnung*) to progress from bad to better. For the purposes of the first postulate, he tells us, we are to

visualize a variation that progresses into the infinite (in time) within the perpetual progression toward the ultimate purpose in connection with which its *disposition* endures and is itself constant, a disposition which is not mutable like that progression, but is rather something supersensible and is, consequently, not fluctuating in time.[34]

It is therefore this disposition, regarded by Kant as the supersensible (and nontemporal) counterpart of an endless progression, which is to satisfy the moral requirement of holiness of will.

But it can hardly be said that Kant has solved his problem by referring to this disposition. For if the endless progress itself does not include holiness as any part of it, then neither is the disposition to progress (supersensible though it may be) in any way identical with holiness of will. In either case, then, Kant cannot claim that holiness of will is actually attained as part of an infinite progression; rather he seems to be claiming that this progression, and the supersensible "disposition" to progress, are regarded by God as in some sense morally equivalent to holiness and as constituting an adequate fulfillment of the supreme condition of the highest good. The disposition (*Gesinnung*) to progress toward holiness, Kant admits, is not the same as the deed (*That*) of actually attaining holiness, and for man the deed must always remain "defective" (*mangelhaft*). But Kant holds that this disposition somehow "counts for" (*gilt für*) the deed.[35] It is plain, however, that in order to formulate a postulate which adequately avoids the error of the first antinomy, it will *not* be sufficient for Kant merely to postulate that an eternal progression is possible. He must also indicate how this progression, or the supersensible disposition which corresponds to it, can *count for* the attainment of holiness. It is apparent from several of Kant's statements that in addition to an endless progress from bad to better, some form of divine cooperation is required if man is to fulfill his moral destination and attain holiness (or its moral equivalent).[36] In the *Religion,* where Kant discusses "Difficulties which Oppose the Reality of [the idea of holiness] and their Solution," he places most emphasis not on the postulate of immortality (though this postulate definitely does seem to have its place) but on the role of God's intellectual intuition and grace (*Gnade*) in making possible the attainment of a moral constitution which fulfills the moral requirement of holiness as the supreme condition of man's final moral end.[37]

Thus the second critique, by postulating the possibility of an endless moral progression, solves only *part* of the dialectical problem raised by the first antinomy of practical reason. It does not solve the *entire* problem, because it does not tell us how this endless progress (or the disposition corresponding to it) fulfills the supreme condition of the highest good. Until we know this, the first antinomy of practical reason cannot be regarded as fully resolved. And because Kant does not treat this matter in the second critique, his discussion of the first antinomy at this point must be regarded as incomplete. For the present, however, our task is only to examine his argument for the postulate of immortality, and we must postpone dealing with the larger question of the resolution of the first antinomy until Chapter 6.

Kant's justification for the first postulate is in its essentials simple and straightforward. Our belief in immortality is justified by our need to conceive the possibility of an endless moral progress toward holiness of will: "This infinite progress is possible . . . only under the presupposition of an infinitely enduring existence and personality of the same rational being; this is called immortality of the soul." [38] However straightforward this postulate may seem to be, it has not seemed wholly satisfactory to many of Kant's readers. Greene remarks that "Kant tells us very little about this future life." [39] Edward Caird objects on the contrary that Kant allows us to infer entirely too much about it, and faces formidable difficulties resulting from such inferences. By imagining immortality as a state in which men may progress morally, Caird maintains, Kant implies that this life involves a continuation of the temporal sequence. But, says Caird, since this future life is not part of the sensible world, "this would involve both that time is, and that it is not a mere form of our perception." If Kant attempts to flee this objection by referring not to a temporal sequence but to a nontemporal disposition, Caird replies that

if we put it in this way, immortality ceases to be a postulate of reason except as the way in which we are obliged to represent something which we cannot properly think, viz., the eternal realization of goodness of will of the rational being who determines himself according to the law of reason.[40]

Kant of course does agree that all practical postulates involve our assuming the possibility of something by postulating the conditions which alone allow *us* to conceive its possibility; [41] so this is not in question. What Caird seems to be urging, however, is that Kant is not postulating *immortality* in any proper sense unless he postulates an existence under the conditions of a *temporal* sequence. Kant addresses himself to the question of the nature of "eternity" or "infinite duration" in a 1794 essay, *The End of All Things*, and his remarks here are worthy of our attention:

We . . . say that we conceive a duration as infinite (as eternity) not because we have any ascertainable concept of its enormity, for that is impossible since eternity lacks time altogether as a measure of itself; but rather, that concept is a purely negative one of the eternal duration, because where there is no time also *no end* is possible.[42]

The "endless progress" is not, then, regarded as an endless temporal series, but as something quite outside time. The temporal progression of man within this life is to be thought of as "within" this eternal progression and a future life is thought of as a continuation of our temporal progress—" although . . . under other conditions." [43] Of course, if eternity is not to be thought of as an endless series of changes within time, it is just as little to be regarded as an endless period of stasis and rest. The latter idea, says Kant, "revolts our imagination." Since both these ideas are derived from our representation of phenomena *in* the sensible world, neither is adequate to represent a futue life *beyond* the sensible world. By means of the postulate of immortality

we do not proceed a single step further in our knowledge, but will have only declared that reason, in a practical sense, can never reach its ultimate purpose on the path of perpetual changes. And, too, if reason attempts by employing the principle of rest and immutability, it would not only be just as unsatisfactory with regard to its theoretical use, but, rather would end in total thoughtlessness.[44]

We should recall that the entire theoretical basis for the concept of immortality in the critical philosophy is to be found in the transcendental idea of a simple and indestructible substance, the abstract metaphysical conception which is treated in the first paralogism and in the second antinomy of the first critique. This idea is given an immanent use as an object of moral belief, but this adds no speculative content to it beyond what little metaphysical inquiry can tell us about it.[45]

It is our practical interest alone which could allow us further
to determine this idea, and give us a more detailed description of
a future life. No speculation about this life can have any consequence for us. "We know nothing of the future, and we
ought not to seek to know more than what is rationally bound
up with the incentives of morality and their end." [46] Thus
Kant tells us very little about our future life because he finds
it possible to know only very little about it. Such a life is
quite beyond our powers to conceive or describe in any concrete way. In attempting to describe it,

the speculative man becomes entangled in mysticism where his
reason does not understand itself and what it wants, and rather
prefers to dote on the beyond than to confine itself within the
bounds of the world, as is fitting for an intellectual inhabitant of
a sensible world.[47]

What is important about the postulate of immortality is not
any graphic or appealing description of a future life, but the
role played by this concept in allowing us to conceive the possibility of the fulfillment of our immanent moral strivings in a
transcendent existence. Moral belief in immortality is not a
"doting on the beyond" but a faith required by our rational
pursuit of the final end of our immanent moral strivings. It is
only insofar as the idea of immortality plays a role in the resolution of the first antinomy of practical reason that Kant's *absurdum practicum* argument justifies our postulating its object. Our speculative cravings for knowledge of the beyond
must always give way in Kant's view to our theoretically
more modest moral interests.

The Second Antinomy of Practical Reason

The highest good requires for its attainment that two distinct states of affairs be realized: (1) finite rational nature

must attain to complete moral perfection (holiness of will, or, as Kant has now told us, some moral equivalent to it); and (2) the enjoyment of happiness by finite rational beings insofar as they have made themselves worthy of it. The first antinomy of practical reason arose from the dialectical threat that the first of these states of affairs might be impossible of realization. The second antinomy, which prepares the way for the postulate of God's existence, concerns the threat that the second state of affairs might be impossible.

It might seem at first glance as though no dialectic could arise with respect to the proper apportionment of happiness and worthiness. "Since we know only a very small part of this world," we can never claim with any certitude that it is impossible that happiness and worthiness might not happen to be brought into exact proportion.[48] In view of our ignorance, no claims about the concurrence of worthiness and happiness can ever be more than conjectures, and it would therefore seem that no dialectic could ever succeed in grounding a *denial* that worthiness and happiness might not happen to be brought into conjunction.

This short way with the dialectic of practical reason fails to grasp the full character of the relation between worthiness and happiness which is required for the attainment of the highest good. Moral virtue, considered as the worthiness to be happy, is taken by Kant to be the condition for the moral worth of happiness. Happiness has moral worth, then, not simply when it accompanies virtue, but when it is combined with it in the concept of a single highest good; it is the unity of the highest good, as we have seen, which gives the conditional relation between the moral and natural good its meaning and function. Virtue (as the worthiness to be happy) and happiness are not components of the highest good when regarded simply as different goods which may happen to accompany one another in a given case. Rather, these two goods must be "necessarily combined in one concept," and therefore "must be related as ground and consequence." [49] The concept of the highest good is not brought to realization merely when the virtuous are also happy, but is only fulfilled when the virtuous can be said to be happy *because* they are virtuous. The highest good, to be realized as a single good, a *systematic unity* of two goods, requires a *systematic* connection between virtue and happiness, a connection which "is predicated upon virtue's producing happiness as something different from the consciousness of virtue, as a cause produces an effect." [50]

The question of the practical possibility of the highest good which we face in the second antinomy is not, then, whether happiness might happen in particular cases to accompany virtue; rather, the question is whether there might be a systematic relation between virtue and happiness, where the former is in some way the ground or cause of the latter. This systematic causal connection appears prominent, says Kant, when we consider the highest good as "a practical good, i.e., one that is possible through action." [51] When we seek justice in the world, we seek to establish a causal relation between desert and reward. We do not seek simply to make the good man happy and the evil man unhappy, but to reward the one for his goodness, and to punish the other for his wickedness. In pursuing the conditional relation between the natural and moral goods, we attempt to realize the highest good as a unity of two goods, a unity established by a systematic connection of cause and effect.

The possibility of the highest good rests, then, on whether a systematic causal connection between virtue and happiness can be conceived to exist, or to be possible of attainment. Kant does say that a highest good or Kingdom of Ends "would actually come into existence through maxims which the categorical imperative prescribes as a rule for all rational beings, *if these maxims were universally followed.*" [52] But Kant does not mean to assert that the highest good is therefore attainable by human means alone, for he gives two reasons why this cannot be. First, we have already observed that no man, strive as he may, is capable of action in perfect conformity with the moral law. Though he may strive to the full extent of his powers to bring about the highest good in the world, and though it may be possible for such striving to constitute a moral equivalent to the perfection of a holy will, men cannot, either individually or collectively, attain to the moral perfection in *deed* which would be required actually to bring about a Kingdom of Ends. Hence even the best-intentioned man, Kant emphasizes, cannot count on others doing their part to bring about the highest good [53] nor (though Kant gives this point less emphasis) can such a man even count on his own efforts to be equal to his own share in the accomplishment of the highest good. But second, even if it were possible for all men to will in perfect conformity to the law, both in disposition and in deed, it does not follow that their efforts would necessarily bear fruit in the world itself, and produce an exact causal relation between worthiness and happiness. A finite being is always limited in respect of his powers to control the consequences of his actions in the world of nature. The efforts of men in this respect are always "bounded" (*begränzt*).[54]

An exact causal relation between virtue and happiness in the world therefore requires more than human purposiveness, human volition, and effort. It can only come about, says Kant, if "the kingdom of nature and its purposive order works in harmony" with the moral efforts of men,[55] in order that each may enjoy happiness insofar as he is worthy of it. Hence the practical possibility of the highest good depends on whether there is in nature anything sufficient to compensate for the imperfection of human volition and the limitation on human powers, to bring about an exact causal connection between virtue and happiness.

But Kant claims next that nothing of this kind is apparent in nature at all. We may of course expect to find "here and there a contingent accordance" of worthiness and happiness, but we "can never expect a regular harmony agreeing according to constant rules." [56] At times we may see good men happy, and evil men fall prey to misfortune, but often we see the evil triumph, and good men "subjected by nature to all the evils of want, disease and untimely death." [57] Human justice may sometimes succeed in punishing wickedness and (more rarely) in rewarding goodness, but at the same time human society suffers from "the injustice of government, which favors certain men and so introduces an inequality of well-being [*Wohlstand*]." [58] Nothing in the laws of nature, then, or in their operations in the world of appearances, affords us even the slightest ground for belief in the practical possibility of a *systematic* causal connection between virtue and happiness:

Every practical connection of causes and effects in the world . . . is dependent not on the moral intentions of the will but on knowledge of natural laws and the physical capacity of using them to its purposes; consequently, no necessary connection, sufficient to the highest good, between happiness and virtue in the world can be expected from the most meticulous observance of the moral law.[59]

The morality of intention (*Absicht*), then, has a purposive relation to the natural good, and to its realization in the world of nature. The morally good man strives to bring about justice in the world, to develop his natural gifts, to promote the happiness of those who deserve it, and to remove from the undeserving those privileges which give them an unjust advantage over others. The man of good will also has his own needs and inclinations, the proper satisfaction and enjoyment of which he prizes as his own personal good. But his own efforts, and the efforts of those like him, are limited and subject to natural forces beyond human control. A finite creature, delivered over to the sensible world and bounded both morally and naturally in his capacities to transform this world in accordance with the idea of the final end of his moral volition, must look to nature itself to harmonize with his efforts, to embody a moral purposiveness which makes possible the justice he seeks and the deserved happiness he hopes for. But in nature he observes no such harmony, nothing corresponding to his moral intention and effort. A man who views his final moral end in terms of the world of sense, then, must view all his efforts and his moral volition itself as vain and gratuitous, and he must give up the highest good as impossible of attainment.[60]

Thus once again we are threatened with a dialectic of practical reason, an argument which apparently demonstrates the practical impossibility of the highest good. And as before, this dialectic threatens us with an *absurdum practicum*, a commitment not to make the highest good our end, and therefore not to obey the moral law. It is this dialectic which constitutes the second antinomy of practical reason, and leads us to the second practical postulate.

The Postulate of God's Existence

Kant resolves the second antinomy of practical reason by pointing out a dialectical illusion, an illusion engendered by our confusing the world of appearances with the intelligible world. The second antinomy successfully shows that a systematic causal connection between virtue and happiness cannot be found in sensible nature.

That a virtuous disposition necessarily produces happiness is not, however, *absolutely* false but false only in so far as this disposition is regarded as the form of causality in the world of sense. Consequently, it is false only if I assume existence in this world to be the only mode of existence of a rational being, and therefore it is only *conditionally* false.[61]

In order to conceive the practical possibility of the highest good, we must somehow postulate a systematic connection in nature between virtue and happiness, and purposive harmony with our moral volition which guarantees this volition an actuality and efficacy in the world. Such a connection does not exist in sensible nature, but it might exist in the world of moral action as a whole, if we expand our conception of this world to include the intelligible as well as the sensible. In the first critique, Kant seems to have conceived this world as the intelligible world itself, regarded as a "kingdom of grace" opposed to a "kingdom of nature." "This world is indeed an intelligible world only, since the sensible world holds out no promise that any such systematic unity of ends can arise from the nature of things." [62] The highest good, then, is regarded as attainable in a "moral world," which we must assume "to be a consequence of our conduct in the world of sense (in which no such connection between worthiness and happiness is exhibited), and therefore to be for us a future world." [63]

In the first critique, then, Kant justifies the first postulate along with the second, by arguing that only in a future life can we expect a systematic connection between worthiness and happiness to be brought about. Kant continues throughout his works to relate the two postulates in this way, by speaking of a future life as containing "rewards" and "punishments" for good and bad conduct; [64] but Kant does not continue to maintain that it is *only* in such a future life that a systematic connection between worthiness and happiness can be hoped for. Though in sensible nature *alone* no moral purposiveness can be discerned, it may nonetheless be the case that such a purposiveness does exist mediated by a causality in the intelligible world:

It is not impossible that the morality of intention should have a necessary relation as cause to happiness as an effect in the sensuous world; but this relation is indirect, mediated by an intelligible Author of nature. This combination, however, can occur only contingently in a system of nature which is merely the object of the senses and as such is not sufficient to the highest good. [65]

Kant does not seem to have related these two conceptions of the second postulate to one another in an explicit way, though they evidently exist side by side in many of his mature works. [66] But it is clear that the two conceptions are not incompatible with one another. The "rewards" and "punishments" of a future life can only constitute an over-all moral purposiveness in the world if they *complete* a systematic connection between worthiness and happiness which must be postulated as existing—in part, at least—in the sensible world. Moreover, assuming that we have already postulated a future life for rational beings, we must postulate a systematic relation between worthiness and happiness in this life as well as in the present one. The two conceptions seem in this way even to require one another, in order to be adequate to the demands of the second postulate.

The conception of "rewards" and "punishments" in a future life, however, has seemed problematic to some of Kant's critics. Greene takes Kant to task for speaking of happiness or unhappiness in any future life. Since, according to Greene, happiness is enjoyed only by "man's sentient nature," it fol-

lows that happiness is only "a minor matter which pertains to
the phenomenal world," and Kant cannot "consistently maintain now that this phenomenal self will continue after death
or that in the next life man will continue to desire the happiness which he craves in this." [67] Kant does maintain, of
course, that man's desire for happiness is due to man's finitude
and is related to sensibility in this life. But if he (or Greene)
were to claim that happiness is *not* part of a future life, he
would be making a claim to theoretical knowledge of transcendent existence, a claim which can never be made good.
Kant clearly does not deny that man will continue to have
needs in his future life, and even seems in places to claim positively that he will have them.[68] Again, whether we hold that
happiness is a part of man's future existence, and even
whether we consider this question worth asking, depends
solely on our *practical* interest in it, and on whether an answer to it will be relevant to the definition of any practical
postulate. No speculation about our future existence can ever
have any theoretical claim to validity.

What is of course most crucial about Kant's postulate of an
intelligible ground for a systematic connection between virtue
and happiness is that Kant claims that this ground must be
conceived by us as an "Author" of nature "through understanding and will, i.e. God." [69] Kant is most emphatic that a
personal being is required for the second postulate, a "*living
God.*" [70] To see why Kant requires this, we must recall that
we are attempting to conceive the practical possibility of a
systematic causal connection between worthiness and happiness, where this connection itself is regarded as an object of
purposive volition and action. The second antinomy shows us
that a merely human purposiveness is not sufficient for the attainment of this systematic connection. Human volition is imperfect, and has only a limited capacity to make use of the

laws of sensible nature in order to achieve its final purpose. We must postulate in nature, then, a cooperating agency with the ability to give efficacy to our moral efforts in a systematic way, a way not subject to human limitations. Such an agency is conceivable by us, says Kant, "only on the supposition of a supreme cause of nature which has a causality corresponding to the moral intention." Hence we must postulate a being "which is capable of actions by the idea of laws." Such a being, Kant says, "is an intelligence (a rational being), and the causality of such a being according to this idea of laws is a will." [71]

Beck claims that Kant's argument for the second postulate is in fact not a moral argument at all, but a "revision of the teleological argument, which is purely theoretical." [72] Beck admits that Kant's argument is not a physicotheological argument, an argument from an observed purposiveness in nature to a purposive designer. But he does claim that it is a "teleological" argument, an "analogy" to the physicotheological argument. Kant's argument for the second postulate, Beck says, is "based not on the moral command in question but on the moral pheonomenon as requiring a designer for the adjustment of two disparate things to each other." [73]

Beck's argument, however, is far from lucid. It is not at all clear what he means by "the moral phenomenon," nor is it clear how in Beck's view Kant has argued (theoretically) that there is such a "phenomenon" requiring a designer. Kant's argument does, however, have an important similarity to teleological arguments from the design of nature, a similarity which may have led Beck to advance his claim that Kant's argument is really a theoretical one. Kant clearly does infer from the assumption that there is a purposive systematic connection in nature between happiness and worthiness, to the conclusion that there exists an intelligent volitional agent capable of intending and carrying out such purposiveness. But this inference is hardly a crucial one, even in the physicotheological argument. In examining the physicotheological argument, we might question whether the design of nature warrants our assigning it to a purposive intelligence, or we might be unsure what purpose or purposes (if any) we are justified in finding in the operations of nature; but once we have decided that nature *is* something which exhibits a purposive design, and its operations do have a definite final end, it is hardly possible then to deny the existence of an intelligence capable of producing the purposive order we have assumed to exist. The inference from something designed to a designer, is an inference common both to Kant's moral argument and to physicotheological argument. But even here, Kant says only that we cannot conceive a purposive harmony of nature fulfilling our moral aspirations unless we assume an intelligent author of nature; he does not argue that we have theoretical knowledge that such a being must exist in order that this harmony may come about.[74]

Even in the theoretical physicotheological argument, the crucial point is not whether an admittedly purposive design requires a purposive designer, but whether nature can be said to embody a purposive design, to be a product of intelligence and volition. And Kant's argument on *this* point is in no sense theoretical. He argues, rather, that if we are to conceive the possibility of our final moral end, we must postulate the purposive cooperation of nature in aiding and giving efficacy to our moral intentions. Without such a final purpose in nature, we cannot conceive the systematic connection of worthiness and happiness as a possible result of purposive volition. Hence the final purpose in nature is not proved on theoretical grounds, nor does Kant give us one shred of theoretical evidence for it. It is clear for Kant that the discovery of a final purpose in nature is "far more than theory can accomplish." [75] That nature is the product of purposive design is not proved theoretically, but postulated, assumed in order that the final end of morality may be conceived possible, and our efforts toward reaching it may be conceived to be efficacious. Kant's moral argument is a "teleological" argument, an "argument from design"; but it is not a theoretical argument, for it does not argue on *theoretical* grounds that the world embodies a design or a final purpose. Rather, it postulates on practical grounds that nature must possess a final moral purpose if we are to be able to make the highest good the object of our own finite rational volition.

Beck's desire to show that the moral argument is really "theoretical" seems to have been prompted by a feeling that the second postulate in some way "displaces" the command to pursue the highest good. By postulating the existence of a morally perfect author of nature, Kant seems to have postulated the actual *existence* of the systematic connection between worthiness and happiness, and not merely its *possibility*, which is what morality required. Beck's real objection, then, is that once we postulate the existence of a God "the alleged command to seek to establish the *summum bonum* now contributes nothing to the conception of the distribution of happiness in accord with worthiness." [76] Now this observation does give rise to a formidable objection to the second postulate, but not the objection stated explicitly by Beck. The most forceful and perceptive development of this objection against the second postulate is rather to be found in Hegel's *Phänomenologie des Geistes.* Hegel considers the Kantian postulate of the harmony of morality with nature on two occasions in the *Phänomenologie:* in his discussion in Chapter V of *Die Tugend un der Weltlauf,* and in more detail in Chapter VI where he attempts to show the *Verstellung* into which the "moral *Weltanschauung*" necessarily must fall.

Moral action is for Hegel (as it is for Kant) something purposive, it is done "for the sake of the actual [*wirkliche*] harmony of purpose and reality." [77] But the moral consciousness, Hegel says, is aware of its limitations, of its inability through its own effort to bring about its final moral end. This end is therefore "posited as *not actual* [*nicht wirklich*], as beyond [*jenseits*]."

The end of reason, however, as the universal, all-encompassing end, is nothing less than the entire world; [it is] a final end [*Endzweck*] which reaches beyond the content of the individual action, and hence in general is to be placed beyond all real [*wirkliche*] action.

But at the same time, the moral consciousness cannot accept the inactuality of its end. "Pure duty is essentially [*wesentlich*] *active* consciousness; thus it ought to be put into action, absolute duty ought to be expressed in the whole of nature and the moral law become the law of nature."

Because absolute duty *ought* to be actualized in the world, says Hegel, the moral consciousness is led to postulate it. Thus arises for the moral consciousness "the postulate of the harmony between morality and actuality [*Wirklichkeit*]—a harmony postulated by the very concept of moral action." At this point, Hegel notes the "shift" (*Verstellung*) which the moral consciousness has undergone, a shift which in Hegel's view necessarily defeats the purpose of the moral consciousness:

Thus if we let the highest good count as being [*das Wesen*], then consciousness is not in general in earnest with morality. For in the highest good, nature has no other law than that of morality.

But then moral action itself falls away, for action *is* only under the presupposition of something negative [*eines Negativen*] which action is to cancel [*aufheben*]. . . . On this assumption, then, a situation has been admitted as essential [*wesentlich*], in which moral action is superfluous and does not take place at all.[78]

In Chapter V, Hegel expresses the resulting situation for the moral consciousness as follows:

In fact for the knight of virtue his own *action* [*Tun*] and struggle is really a sham-fight, which he *cannot* take in earnest, because he has already placed his true strength in the good being *in and for itself*, i.e. bringing about its own fulfillment—a sham-fight which he *must* not allow to become in earnest.[79]

The moral consciousness, then, is seen by Hegel as requiring both that its own action be *necessary* for the fulfillment of the highest good, and also that the highest good be postulated as already existing, so that moral action is *superfluous*. And Hegel hints darkly that in this shift there is something not quite honest going on, that morality itself is behaving rather shabbily. What Hegel has in fact presented is more like a dilemma: Either the highest good exists, or it does not. If it does not, the moral agent cannot hope through his own limited efforts to bring it about, and consequently he must regard his moral action as gratuitous and ineffectual, and his final end as a practical impossibility. But if, on the other hand, the highest good does exist, his moral action is also gratuitous, for it is no longer required for the attainment of the highest good. The moral agent must either take his own action to be superfluous, to be a "sham-fight," or he must fall into moral despair and, what is even more dangerous, into an *absurdum practicum*.

Hegel finds the "shift" in the moral consciousness to be a suspicious *Verstellung* only because it seems evident to him that moral consciousness is somehow contradicting itself, deceiving itself (and trying to deceive us) by shifting between two *incompatible* views of moral action. Likewise, the dilemma arises because it appears that we cannot maintain both that the systematic connection between worthiness and happiness requires our moral action for its realization, and that this connection is part of the order of the world, created by God. But if we could maintain these two views without contradiction, then both Hegel's accusation of *Verstellung* and the threat of the moral dilemma would be groundless. For we could not maintain that our moral action toward the systematic connection between worthiness and happiness is *useless* if we also maintain that this connection is fulfilled in God's plan. But neither could we hold that our moral action is *superfluous*, if we can also hold that our action is required for the attainment of the systematic connection between worthiness and happiness. And we will attempt to rescue Kant from Hegel's objection by maintaining that these two standpoints on moral action need not be incompatible with each other.

Let us see again precisely what these two standpoints are. The postulate of God's existence is the postulate of a systematic moral purposiveness in the world. All events are—from one standpoint—the effects of God's causality. God is the *ens originarium*, the *Urwesen*, the ground or root of the very possibility of all other things.[80] At the same time, some events are also regarded as the effects of human action, of free finite rational volition. These events are the result of human purposiveness, and men can be held responsible for them. The postulate of freedom of the will is the postulate that some events in the world are the results of human causality and can be imputed to men. Some events in the world, therefore, must be viewed *both* as the result of divine causality, as fulfilling God's final moral purpose in the world, and as the result of human causality, furthering human ends.

Let us examine the differences between these two stand-points a bit more closely. Kant conceives God as creating the world as a whole by his intuitive understanding. This under-standing, and hence the creation of the world-order as a whole, is not a temporal event. For God, says Kant, "nothing is past or future; for he is not in time at all. He knows *every-thing* intuitively, at one [*auf einmal*], whether or not they are present to our representation." [81] God's purpose is therefore not something actualized *in* time, but is postulated as obtain-ing throughout time, and even in an intelligible world. Time, says Kant, was created by God along with the world.[82] Hegel is therefore misdescribing the second postulate when he calls it "the postulate of the harmony of morality and actual-ity [*Wirklichkeit*]." Neither is God's world-order a kind of "status quo," as Hegel would seem at times to suggest.[83] This world-order does not exist at one time and not at another. Hence it is neither "actual" (*wirklich*) nor "not actual"; for both of these alternatives imply that it is something which is to be brought about *in time*, and which therefore has either been brought about in time, or has not (yet) been brought about. Kant describes God as the highest *original* good, order-ing the world in such a way as to make possible the highest *derived* good, the unconditioned totality of the object of pure practical reason.[84] The systematic connection between happi-ness and worthiness, therefore, is *not* something which is pos-tulated as "already existing" in time, but as a morally purpo-sive world-order obtaining irrespective of time.

Viewed from the standpoint of human action, however, this systematic connection is a *human* purpose, an object of finite rational volition. Although human freedom is postulated by Kant as pertaining to the intelligible world, it nonetheless re-mains true that the objects of *finite* rational volition, its ends, are represented as something future, something to be realized in time.[85] Therefore, Hegel is correct in saying that the highest good is regarded by the moral agent as "not actual." But since the second postulate does not say that this object *is* actual, that it "already exists" or has been brought about in time, there is no contradiction between maintaining that the world-order *contains* this connection as its final purpose, and maintaining that human volition *seeks to realize* the connection by finite purposive action.

In order for Kant to hold that the systematic connection between worthiness and happiness is the effect of a *cooperation* between human volition (which can pursue this end only imperfectly and weakly) and God's creation of a good world, he must be able to maintain that the two standpoints are not incompatible with each other. He must hold, that is, that a systematic connection between worthiness and happiness in the world involves both the purposiveness of free human action, and the purposiveness of an Author of nature, and that the "concurrence" between divine and human action is not an impossibility.[86] Kant realizes the relevance of this question when he says,

For to be a creature and as a natural being to follow the will of one's author, and nevertheless to be a free-acting being . . . to be responsible and yet to regard one's own action at the same time as an effect of a higher being: the compatibility of these concepts is one which we must think together in the idea of the highest good.[87]

But both the freedom of human action and the purposive order of the world are postulated in the intelligible world. Whether they are compatible with one another, and, if so, what relation they bear to each other, is therefore quite beyond our power to know. We cannot regard as impossible that God's world-order includes free human volition and its effects, and that some effects are due both to divine and to human agency.[88] But neither can we see how free action may be a part of the purposive order of the world. The compatibility of the two standpoints, then, "can only be seen into by one who breaks through to an acquaintance with the supersensible (intelligible) world: . . . —An insight to which no mortal can attain." [89] It is a "mystery" of rational religion, in Kant's view, that "beings may be *created* to a free use of their powers." Thus, although the two standpoints "cannot be reconciled through the insight of our reason," neither can they be shown to be incompatible with one another, and it is still possible for us to hold both of them.[90]

With this in mind, let us return to Hegel's claim that for Kant moral action must be "superfluous" and must "not take place at all." As moral agents, of course, we are aware of the command of morality upon us, and we are aware also that moral action (the determination of the will by the legislative form of its maxim) could take place even if it were "superfluous." Even if man could no nothing, or needed to do nothing, to bring about the ends of moral action, volition motivated by duty would still be commanded of him, and would still have its unconditioned worth. But Hegel might still argue that if moral action were recognized as "superfluous," as unnecessary for the attainment of its final end, then it would be pointless to engage in moral action, because it would be pointless to adopt an end which will be realized *whether or not* one does anything to further it. Hegel's argument, then, seems itself to be a kind of *absurdum practicum*. His argument is not that moral action would not take place if the second postulate is assumed, but that under this assumption moral action is pointless and (rationally) should not take place. Thus Hegel remarks ironically that "the absolute end is that moral action should not take place at all." [91] This also seems to be what Beck is stating (though far less clearly than Hegel) when he speaks of the second postulate as "displacing" the moral command.[92]

Now if it were impossible for us to maintain that some effects are due *both* to free human volition and to the operation of God's final purposiveness in the world, then the postulate that the systematic connection between worthiness and happiness is brought about by an omnipotent world-governor would entail the admission that this connection is *not* due to human volition, that human action *is* "superfluous." And thus the second postulate would lead us to an *absurdum practicum*. But since it is possible (and even morally necessary) to maintain that this connection is *both* the result of God's creation of the world and of human volition in the world, the *absurdum practicum* does not follow.

But we might try to introduce the *absurdum practicum* argument from a different quarter. Even granting the compatibility between divine and human causality of events in the world, the second postulate still might be said to render our moral effort "superfluous" by the assumption that the systematic connection between worthiness and happiness will obtain *however men may act in the world*. Whether or not I promote the highest good, this postulate guarantees that a systematic connection between worthiness and happiness will be found in the world. All my action, good or evil, thus contributes equally to this connection. My *moral* strivings, at least, are superfluous, in that I could equally well contribute to the realization of the highest good by pursuing justice and by pursuing injustice. For the second postulate says only that the systematic connection *will* obtain, and does not say that *my* good will is required for it. But here we ignore, in the first place, the radically *ad hominem* character of Kant's moral arguments themselves. Kant's arguments are not objective proofs, but subjective arguments "sufficient only for moral beings." [93] I can be required to accept the postulates only so long as I view myself as seeking to obey the moral law. For if I do not, then clearly I do not need to make the highest good my end, and do not need to conceive the practical possibility of this end. An amoral man, then, would not need to view his own action as part of a world-order in which a systematic connection between virtue and happiness obtains. Indeed, to do this would be for him *irrational*, since it would be to *postulate* that his evil deeds would somehow be punished. It is only to the morally good man himself, then, that the moral arguments are directed. And it is presupposed that anyone who can be made to accept the argument for the second postulate already views his own action as action toward the highest good; for if he did not, the argument for the second postulate would not apply to him.

Nevertheless, it may be urged that the moral man *himself* might wonder how much his own efforts toward the highest good contribute to the attainment of the systematic connection between worthiness and happiness. And if he had already postulated that this systematic connection exists in the world-order in which his actions are a part, would he not discover that his efforts are then superfluous in view of the practical postulate he has assumed? In Kant's view, he positively would not. Indeed, since he postulates this world-order only on the assumption that *his* action contributes to the highest good, he may well say that his contribution is necessary for this world-order to exist. But more importantly, the discovery that his action is "superfluous" would require that he know *how* his efforts contributed to the systematic connection in the world-order he has postulated, *how* these efforts relate to all the other events in the world to bring about the systematic connection between worthiness and happiness which he has assumed. Presumably, God would have such knowledge, but the finite moral agent positively does not have it. He does not and cannot *know* whether or how his efforts are required for the existence of a good world; he knows his duty, and his end, and he works toward this end as best he knows how, using the knowledge of nature which he gains through experience. Such a man

finds himself impelled to believe in the cooperation and manage-ment of a moral Ruler of the world, by means of which [the highest good] can be reached. And now there opens up before him an abyss of mystery regarding what God may do [toward the realization of this end] whether indeed there is *anything* in general and if so, *what* in particular must be ascribed to God. Meanwhile, man knows concerning each duty what he himself must do to be worthy of that supplement, unknown, or at least incomprehensible to him.[94]

To know whether Hegel's objections to Kant were valid at this point, we would have to be capable of adopting the stand-point of God [95] in order to see whether human freedom is compatible with divine omnipotence, and to see whether and how a purposive world-order arises from the acts and events that we can experience. But from the human standpoint, which is (as Kierkegaard had to point out to Hegel's followers) after all *our* standpoint, there is no incompatibility, and no hypo-critical *Verstellung*, between a man's moral action toward his highest moral end, and his belief that the effects of this action are part of a world-order in which this end is purposively em-bodied; and none between his moral desire to bring about a systematic connection between worthiness and happiness in the world, and his hope and trust that his efforts, imperfect and feeble as they are, do constitute a part of an over-all pur-posive order in which this connection does obtain in the long run. Rather, as the *absurdum practicum* argument shows, such belief, hope, and trust are required if we are to be consistent purposive moral agents.

The Postulates and Their Practical Function

Kant argues, as we have seen, that we must postulate the existence of a God and a future life if we are to conceive the possibility of the highest good as an end of action, and thus escape an *absurdum practicum*. His arguments for the postulates are valid, then, only if we can conceive the possibility of the highest good by means of the ideas of God and immortality, and cannot conceive this possibility without them. But we may still doubt whether Kant has convincingly argued either of these points. How, in the first place, can Kant deny that *other* ideas might do equally well in conceiving the possibility of the highest good? Perhaps Kant has justified *some* form of moral belief, but we may seriously question whether he has justified faith in the traditional Christian conceptions of God and immortality, which he certainly pretends to do.

In his 1899 inaugural dissertation, Albert Schweitzer correctly argues that the selection of the ideas of God and immortality (and that of freedom as well) depends on *metaphysical* considerations.[96] In his resolution of the antinomies of practical reason, Kant has made it clear that the practical postulates must be postulates of supersensible existence. Moral belief, then, requires belief in the objects of transcendental ideas. Now in the first critique, Kant sought to "determine the sources, extent and limits" of metaphysics not only concerning what may be *known* a priori, but also what may be *thought*. Because the supersensible is totally inaccessible to the human faculty of knowledge, we are radically limited even in our ability to think or conceive of supersensible objects. In the Dialectic of the first critique, Kant investigates systemati-

cally the number of definite concepts of supersensible existence which we may form, and describes the totality of such
concepts as the "system of transcendental ideas." Though this
system may be viewed in a number of ways, Kant states that
"Metaphysics has as the proper object of its enquiries three
ideas only: *God, freedom* and *immortality*." [97] Since the
practical postulates must be drawn from concepts of supersensible existence, these postulates are restricted by the nature of
finite rational thought to these three ideas only. Kant does not
pretend that "reason can *objectively* decide" whether God
and immortality are required for the possibility of the highest
good; but he does hold that these ideas are "the only way in
which it is theoretically possible for us to conceive" the possibility of the highest good.[98]

Kant, then, does argue consistently that we must postulate a
God and a future life if we are to escape an *absurdum practicum*. But his argument may still leave us somewhat unsatisfied.
For we may still ask whether Kant's own account of the
practical postulates suffices to give us a satisfying conception
of the world of our moral action as a world in which the
highest good is a practical possibility. Kant claims that moral
perfection can be conceived possible by us only if we postulate a future life. But he gives us no definite account of how
such a perfection is made possible by a future life. As we have
seen, he even denies that any definite account of a future life
can be given. Similarly, he claims that a systematic connection
between worthiness and happiness can be conceived possible
by us only if we postulate a God. But again he does not tell us
how God makes this connection possible, and again even denies that we can ever know precisely *what* is contributed by
God. In what sense, then, do the ideas of God and immortality allow us to "conceive" the possibility of the highest good?

This question, of course, does not challenge the validity of the moral arguments. For it cannot be denied that God and immortality must be postulated if we are to escape an *absurdum practicum;* and this is all the moral arguments needed to show. But these arguments cannot satisfy us completely until we know how the practical postulates actually do perform the function which Kant has shown they must perform. In order to see how our question may be answered, we must be clear on the relation between the rational origin of the transcendental ideas of God and immortality, and their function as practical postulates. The ideas of God and immortality do not and cannot constitute theoretical *explanations* of the possibility of the highest good. The sense in which the postulates allow us to "conceive" the possibility of the highest good cannot be that these postulates constitute *objective conditions* for its possibility. It is true that in postulating the existence of a God and a future life, we make a theoretical commitment, a belief in the reality of *some* supersensible existence adequate to the possibility of the highest good, which takes the definite form only by means of the transcendental ideas of God and immortality. It is for this reason that Kant says that the question of moral faith is at once "theoretical and practical," and that it is *theoretical* reason which assumes the existence of a God and a future life.[99] But for the practical postulates to function as theoretical explanations of the possibility of the highest good, we would require more knowledge of these objects than can be given in the mere transcendental concepts of them, which is all theoretical reason can give us. The postulates of God and immortality, then, must allow us to "conceive" the possibility of the highest good in some distinctively practical way, which does not involve us in theoretical claims which we would have to justify by appealing to something beyond the transcendental ideas as they are given to us. The postulates, Kant says, "have not to do with theoretical knowledge of the ob-

jects of these ideas, but only with whether they have objects
or not." [100]

A transcendental idea gives us no theoretical knowledge of
its object (even if that object is presumed to exist). The transcendental ideas are, for theoretical reason, "only ideas"; an
idea is "a mere idea, a *focus imaginarius*." [101] But this does
not mean, as Hans Vaihinger claims, in his *The Philosophy of
As-If*, that a transcendental idea is a "fiction," an idea to
which *no* object corresponds, "i.e., only a representation
without an object." [102] Kant cannot possibly have meant to
assert this. For the claim that the transcendental ideas do *not*
have objects, like the claim that they *do*, is a theoretical claim
about the supersensible, a claim which no theoretical grounds
can ever justify. And Kant is most explicit in saying that it is
beyond the power of theoretical reason to prove that there
are no objects corresponding to these ideas.[103] Vaihinger is
mistaken when he takes phrases like "only an idea" to be remarks about the relation of ideas to their objects. Instead, such
remarks should be taken as pertaining to the rational origin of
the ideas themselves, as objects of thought.

An *empirical* concept is one whose object is an (actual or
possible) appearance, and which can therefore be given in
some possible experience. Such concepts typically originate
from experiences of their objects, and every empirical concept
can be shown to have a real or possible object corresponding
to it.[104] In contrast, pure concepts or transcendental ideas
can never arise from the experience of their objects (since
these objects cannot be given in experience, even if they
exist) nor can it even be shown that the objects of these concepts are possible (just as it cannot be shown that they are impossible). The origin in reason of transcendental ideas, therefore, does not stand in any direct relation to the *objects* of

these ideas (even if these objects exist). It is in no sense the case that we *think* these concepts because of their objects. Rather, reason itself is the origin of these concepts, by means of inference.[105] Reason infers for any series of conditions to an idea of an unconditioned with respect to that series, in order to think the series in its totality.[106] But since only a finite part of any series can be given in experience, every idea is essentially "a problem to which there is no solution." [107] Reason sets this problem for itself, and thus originates ideas whose objects cannot be given in experience. Such an idea, because its *origin* bears no direct relation to its object, is called "only an idea"—that is, an idea whose existence in *thought* is independent of whether any object corresponds to it. Kant's view at this point is, especially as regards the idea of God, a sophisticated alternative to the view expressed by Descartes in the Third Meditation. But it does not involve in any way the claim that transcendental ideas are "fictions," that objects corresponding to them do *not* exist.

Because transcendental ideas arise not from experience of their objects, but as "mere ideas," we are never capable of making claims to theoretical knowledge about the objects of these ideas, even if (on other grounds) we concede that these objects exist. Thus Kant asserts that "no synthetic proposition is made possible" by the postulates.[108] In one obvious way, of course, this is false: for the proposition "God exists" is synthetic. But Kant means only that *beyond* this proposition, no further synthetic claims *about* God or his relation to the world, are justified. We may assert that God is an *ens reallissimum*, that He is simple, infinite, a substance, and so forth; but all these predicates are contained in the *idea* of God itself, and to predicate any of them of God is to make a claim which is analytic. Even those "natural" predicates applicable to God but derived from experience (his understanding, will, and so on) follow in Kant's view from the concept of an *ens realissimum* itself. We may predicate understanding, will, and other natural qualities of God only by *analogy*, and only insofar as these qualities are "pure realities," compatible with and indeed consequences of the nature of an *ens realissimum*.[109]

It is evident that Kant feels himself to be strongly committed to an *idea* of God much like the God of Leibnizian rationalism. But we must not let this fact about the transcendental idea of God obscure the *practical function* of this idea as a *postulate*. "Religion," says Kant, "has no need of a speculative study of God." [110] Even the idea of God is relevant to the practical postulate only insofar as it fulfills a moral function:

It concerns us not so much to know what God is in Himself (his Nature) as what He is for us as moral beings; although in order to know the latter we must conceive and comprehend all the attributes of the divine nature . . . which, in their totality, are requisite to the carrying out of the divine will in this regard. Apart from this context we can know nothing of Him.[111]

What we seek, then, is the *practical function* of the ideas of God and immortality in allowing us to conceive the possibility of the highest good. We seek to know what the postulates are "from a practical point of view" or "for practical use." [112] Kant contrasts this "practical use" of the transcendental ideas with their *regulative* use in theory. He argues that while for theory the objects of the ideas need not be presupposed, and remain transcendent, in their practical use the ideas become "immanent and constitutive." [113] Faced with an account of this sort, we may reasonably wonder *what* the ideas of God and immortality, ideas whose objects transcend all experience, can be said to be "immanent" in, and how they can be "constitutive" of anything. But before we dismiss these remarks as hopeless jargon and obscurantism, or attempt to see in them an espousal of a radical new doctrine (such as an *"Immanenz Gottes im Menschengeist"*), we ought to consider the possibility that what Kant is saying here (albeit in his own jargon) is something quite simple and straightforward.

We have seen earlier that purposive action commits a rational agent, as part of this action, to believe in and conceive his end as possible of attainment. "The subjective effect" of the moral law, says Kant, "i.e., the intention which is suitable to this law and which is necessary because of it, the intention to promote the practically possible highest good at least presupposes that the latter is possible." [114] This *presupposition* can be said to be "constitutive" of and "immanent" in moral volition in the sense than an attitude or outlook involving belief in the practical possibility of the highest good is, or rationally ought to be, ingredient or implicit in the intention and frame of mind of the moral agent himself (as a part of the "subjective effect" of the moral law upon him). Now insofar as the *belief* in the transcendent objects of the ideas of God and immortality are subjectively necessary for this attitude, and constitute part of it, these ideas too, as defining objects of this belief, can be said to be "immanent" in and "constitutive" of moral volition as well. It is, then, simply because an *outlook* involving moral belief is for Kant part of the "subjective effect" of the moral law that he says that the *ideas* of God and immortality are "immanent and constitutive" in their "practical use."

If we are to discover Kant's true conceptions of God and immortality as objects of moral faith, then, we must go beyond the transcendental ideas of God and immortality, and beyond the *absurdum practicum* argument itself, to a consideration of the function that moral belief, moral faith, fulfills immanently in the frame of mind of the moral agent. For these ideas are only introduced in practice, and their objects postulated, as *objects of moral faith,* and we have faith in them only as they are "for us as moral beings." It is to Kant's account of moral faith, then, that we shall now turn.

5. Moral Faith and Rational Religion

Our inquiry thus far has dealt with the subtle and complex reasoning of Kant's *absurdum practicum* arguments, and with their foundation in the critical moral philosophy. I have tried to show that these arguments can be stated in a fairly precise and plausible way, and that they follow consistently from Kant's critical doctrines. In following out these arguments as I have done, I have traced the natural dialectic of practical reason through the idea of the unconditioned final end of finite rational action into the moral perplexity of the antinomies occasioned by our pursuit of this end, and we have seen that belief in a God and a future life are required as part of a rational response to the problematic situation in which finite reason finds itself. But we saw at the conclusion of the last chapter that Kant's justification of this belief is still in a sense incomplete. For in order to see precisely how belief in God and immortality are required by the *absurdum practicum* argument, we need more than can be given us in a merely speculative account of the ideas of a "Highest Being" and a "simple and indestructible substance." We must also understand the uniquely practical function fulfilled by the belief in the objects of these ideas, and the way in which this belief is "immanent" in moral volition itself.

Kant is not attempting in his justification of moral faith to re-erect the claims of speculative metaphysics which were exposed as "dialectical illusions" in the first critique. Instead, he is trying to formulate the ultimate problems which confront human existence in its dialectic of finite rationality, and to provide a rational response to these necessary problems. It can be seen from an inspection of the *absurdum practicum* argument itself that the faith justified by this argument is *not* primarily an assent to certain speculative propositions. In order to obey the moral law, I must make the highest good my end. If I am to make the highest good my end, I must conceive the highest good as possible of attainment. I must, that is to say, hold beliefs about the *situation* of my moral action as a whole, and view this situation in such a way that the highest good is conceivable to me as a practical possibility. Moral faith, then, is justified primarily as a response to the dialectical perplexities of the human situation, an *outlook* on or *attitude* toward man's problematic condition in terms of which he may continue rationally to pursue the destination marked out for him by his reason. Moral faith is, as Hegel saw, a *moralische Weltanschauung*, a *"praktische Weltauffassung."* [1]

The moral arguments, properly understood, are thus not merely arguments for the acceptance of certain speculative propositions; they are arguments for a "moral outlook," a "moral faith," in which speculative belief play (in Kant's view) a prominent role. In order to understand this role, we must examine further Kant's conception of the problematic and dialectical situation in which the finite rational agent finds himself, and make more explicit the character of the outlook on his situation which Kant suggests as a rational response to it. Such an examination should help us to give a further answer to the questions we raised at the end of the last chapter, and it will complement Kant's *absurdum practicum* arguments by providing us with a more detailed description of the outlook, the faith, which these arguments justify.

Our task at this point is made much more difficult because Kant himself gave concrete expression to the "outlook" of moral faith only in scattered remarks throughout his writings, and usually expressed himself best in his more popular writings, where the moral arguments themselves are stated least rigorously. Kant seems to have considered the attitudes and emotional content of faith too "personal" a matter to deal with in a context of abstract philosophizing, and this accounts in part for his reluctance to discuss the precise manner in which the ideas of God and immortality are "immanent" in moral volition. But I think we must demand of Kant's moral faith a more explicit account of itself, and cannot conclude that we have truly appreciated the strength of the *absurdum practicum* arguments until we understand better the outlook of moral faith on the problematic condition of the finite rational moral agent.

A sympathetic examination of the moral arguments as I have presented them, along with careful attention to Kant's remarks about this faith, will, I think, afford us with a reasonably clear and explicit account of the moral outlook Kant is recommending. When we have gained a better understanding of this outlook, we can proceed to a brief consideration of Kant's "philosophy of religion" proper, his conception of a religion based on this rational outlook, and the relation of this "pure religious faith" to the plurality of "ecclesiastical faiths" found in human society.

Moral Despair

Kant states plainly in a number of places that moral faith is *not* an outlook to which only the philosophical mind has access. This outlook may be justified philosophically by the moral arguments, but it does not require these arguments in order to be intelligible to the ordinary man. Thus in the third critique, Kant remarks that "this moral proof is not one newly discovered, although perhaps its basis is newly set forth, since it has lain in man's rational faculty from its earliest germ."[2] Moral faith is taken by Kant to be part of the ordinary man's moral attitudes, as part of the "moral way of thinking" (*moralische Denkungsart*).[3] Morally good men, in Kant's view, habitually *do* and rationally *should* maintain faith in God and in immortality as part of the frame of mind appropriate to moral volition. Moral faith, he says, "is so interwoven with my moral disposition that as there is little danger of my losing the latter, there is equally little cause for fear that the former can ever be taken from me."[4]

If we are to bring to light the character of moral faith as an outlook, a "way of thinking," we must attempt to see what ordinary situations, problems and facts of the moral life correspond to the philosophical line of reasoning which Kant presents in his *absurdum practicum* argument. Such parallels will be accessible to us, I think, if we reflect for a moment on the moral arguments as we have seen them in our previous chapters. We have seen that in Kant's view the good man is not concerned merely with the goodness of his own intentions, but that the good will itself involves a positive concern with the establishment of goodness in the world. Further, we have seen that the moral man's concern with moral purposes is not limited to the pursuit of the particular ends which he may set for himself from time to time; beyond these, the moral man acts purposively to establish a *good world*, to realize a final end which is the sum total and the ground of all particular moral ends.

Of the possible ways in which goodness may be established in the world, some are in the power of the moral agent, while others are not. It is part of his moral wisdom to address himself to tasks which suit his situation and talents, and in which he has the most chance of success. Some of his efforts will appear to bear fruit, while others will not. When he succeeds, he experiences an "intellectual satisfaction in his object" [5] and is able to view himself as having contributed materially to the betterment of the world. When he fails, he may still be conscious of an inner self-contentment in having a good will,[6] and he may proceed to his next task in the hope that he may yet do something toward the betterment of the world as a whole, even if in this one instance his best efforts do not appear to have proved successful in making the world a better one.

Thus we can say that the concern of the moral man with the attainment of the particular ends he pursues in obedience to the moral law is not a morally indispensable concern. If I attempt to institute a legislative reform of some kind in order to make my society better, but fail in my attempt, this does not indicate that my hope for a better world, and my concern with bringing such a world about, are vain. Particular moral projects may be abandoned without the abandonment of moral action as a whole. In response to particular failures, the moral man can turn to his next task sustained by a continuing concern for his final moral end, the sum and the ground of all particular ends, and hopeful that a better world may be attained in the long run. Each particular project is only a skirmish in the struggle for a better world, and to meet one setback is not necessarily to be defeated in the struggle as a whole.

And yet in the face of failure and frustration in his pursuit of particular moral ends, the moral man may also begin to wonder whether his ultimate purpose itself may not also be doomed to failure. He is constantly aware, in his concern for the attainment of this final end, of his own finitude, of his limitations in bringing about the betterment of the world. He re-

solves to do what he can; but he often fails in his attempt to
bring about even the merest part of his final moral end, and
unforeseen events might easily nullify completely the small
contribution he might make to this end. If he is to continue to
pursue and concern himself with the realization of his ultimate
purpose, therefore, the moral man must depend upon and concern himself with matters beyond his own powers of accomplishment. He must turn to sensible nature with his moral concern in mind, and ask whether there is any hope for the realization of his final end to be found in the nature of things as he
knows them.

Now when the moral man thus questions the possibility of
his final end, he is questioning a concern which *is* morally indispensable. He may take comfort in each of his failures by
the hope that his ultimate end, the goodness of the world itself, may not be impossible. But if he were to discover that
this final end itself must be abandoned as an impossibility, he
could not so abandon it without at the same time ceasing to
act purposively in obedience to the moral law. Pursuit of his
final end, indeed, could not be abandoned without the abandonment of moral volition itself. The question whether the
final end of morality is a practical possibility is therefore a
question which threatens the rationality of moral volition as a
whole, and in asking it the moral agent enters upon what
Kant calls "the natural dialectic of reason in its practical employment."

When the moral man turns to sensible nature with this
question in mind, he experiences the perplexity and dismay
characteristic of any Kantian "dialectic," and is at once threatened with what we have called the "second antinomy of
practical reason." For it is discovered at once that sensible nature exhibits *no* regular moral purposiveness, and the world
seems not to reflect in any way the good man's striving to

bring about goodness in it. In the course of his life, every man meets with moral and social evils and with natural catastrophes which cannot but provide a foundation for serious doubt that any force for good exists in the world beyond the feeble and wavering intentions and efforts of the moral individual himself and others like him. Neither in nature nor in the actions of men does he perceive any kind of purposive cooperation sufficient to maintain his hope that his ultimate moral purpose may be attainable in the long run. Doubt and uncertainty about the attainability of this final purpose must assail him, and he is strongly tempted to abandon his moral concerns as empty illusions. In the face of failure and suffering, unable to find a shred of positive evidence that his moral purpose is a practical possibility, the moral man is in grave danger of falling into *moral despair*. Kant characterizes the dialectical perplexity of such a man in a remarkable passage in the third critique:

Deceit, violence, and envy will always surround him, although he himself be honest, peaceable and kindly; and the righteous men with whom he meets will, notwithstanding all their worthiness of happiness, be yet subjected by nature, which regards not this, to all the evils of want, disease, and untimely death, just like the beasts of the earth. So it will be until one wide grave engulfs them together (honest or not, it makes no difference) and throws them back—who were able to believe themselves the final purpose of creation—into the abyss of purposeless chaos of matter from which they were drawn. The purpose, then, which this well-intentioned person had and ought to have before him in his pursuit of moral laws, he must certainly give up as impossible.[7]

Once the moral man has fallen into despair, and has abandoned his final moral end as an impossibility, he must view himself as either a "visionary" or a "scoundrel."[8] If he continues to pursue the ideal of a morally good world, he must see himself as a "visionary," and his efforts as directed toward an empty and impossible goal. But if he abandons his pursuit of the final end of morality, he must cease to act purposively in obedience to the moral law and must be, in his own eyes, a "scoundrel." In either case, Kant says, if I deny the practical possibility of the final end of morality, "I would have to deny my own real nature and its eternal moral principles; I would have to cease to be a rational human being." [9]

The second antinomy of practical reason thus corresponds concretely to the attitude of moral despair, where the moral agent is driven by his experiences of suffering, failure, and frustration in his pursuit of moral ends to abandon as hopeless the project of establishing a morally good world. Such a despair must always be premature, in the sense that it is always beyond the power of a finite being to know absolutely that the world is destitute of moral goodness, that it provides *no* ground for the realization of his final end. His despair is always therefore a presumptuous judgment about the world. His hope for a good world is not positively *refuted* by suffering and failure, but only rendered *groundless*. His despair is not positively justified, but neither is there any reason in the world itself why he should *not* despair. His situation is not so easy, then, as it would be if experience afforded him positive knowledge that there is no place for moral hope. The uncertainty of the world and the finitude of his knowledge rather leave man suspended between hope and despair. Failure, suffering, and the evils of the world do not so much refute hope as *exhaust* it.

Moral Faith in God

Moral faith is the outlook of the rational man who has chosen not to succumb to moral despair, who has chosen hope rather than despair. Concretely, then, moral faith consists in a view of the situation of moral action which gives a rational and conceptual expression to confidence and hope that the processes of the world are ordered purposively and cooperate with our moral volition. This outlook must also guide the attitude of the moral man in situations of suffering and apparent moral failure, and function as a response to moral despair. In Kant's view, the source and the condition of the possibility of such an outlook for any finite rational being is a belief in God. The moral man for Kant views the world as the product of a morally perfect creator and ruler, a

self-subsistent reason, equipped with all the sufficiency of a supreme cause, which establishes, maintains, and completes the universal order of things, according to the most perfect design [*Zweckmässigkeit*]—an order which in the world of sense is in large part concealed from us.[10]

Belief in a God, then, gives concrete expression to the moral man's faith that the world of his action is a moral world, a world which cooperates with his moral volition, and into which the effects of his moral striving do not fall stillborn and empty.

Kant has often been described by his interpreters as a "deist," a believer only in an abstract and metaphysical conception of God, as one for whom any personal relationship between man and God is entirely lacking. And this view does gain some support from the abstract and metaphysical way in which Kant usually speaks of God in his writings. But it would be a great mistake to see in the God of Kant's moral faith no more than an abstract, metaphysical idea. For Kant moral faith in God is, in it most profound and personal signification, the moral man's *trust in God*. In the third critique, Kant introduces the term "trust" (*Zutrauen*) into his definition of "faith" in general: "Faith (absolutely so called) is

trust in the attainment of a design, the promotion of which is
a duty, but the possibility of the fulfillment of which is not to
be *comprehended* [*einzusehen*] by us." ¹¹ The term "trust"
appears in a number of Kant's characterizations of faith.
What is most significant about Kant's use of this term, however, is that "trust" denotes, in at least some of these uses, a
personal relationship between man and God, or a personal attitude of the moral man toward the God in whom he has
faith. Kant refers most explicitly to this in the *Lectures on
Ethics*, in a section entitled "Trust in God under the Concept
of Faith": "Faith, then, denotes trust in God that he will sup-
ply our deficiency in things beyond our power, provided we
have done all within our power." ¹²

If we view moral faith in God as a kind of trust in God,
several things become clearer to us about the moral outlook
and attitudes Kant is presenting. First, we may see that the
God in whom we believe is not presented to us first as an object of speculative knowledge, and only afterward as a being
to whom we stand in a personal relationship. For Kant, our
belief that there is a God is precisely the belief that there is a
being in whom we can place our trust, a being who governs
the world justly and beneficently, with the power and wisdom to order the world as is best. The *belief* in God is fundamentally a *trust* in Him, and the God in whom we believe is
essentially that being in whom we can place our absolute
trust.

This observation allows us to see, secondly, how the "attributes" of the Deity are introduced into Kant's moral theology. We saw in the previous chapter that the possibility of
the highest good, postulated in an intelligible world, could not
be an object of speculative knowledge, and hence that no
speculative inferences as to the conditions of this possibility
could be warranted. These conditions, as objects of moral

faith, were rather to be defined by the "subjective" conditions under which a finite rational being can *think* (rather than know) the character of the practical possibility of the highest good. Kant thus directs us to the "task" of the idea of a moral world-ruler, a task not of discovering "what God is in Himself" but rather "what He is for us as moral beings." [13] To fulfill this task, we turn not to metaphysical speculation, but rather we examine our own moral faith in God, and discover in the character of this faith what its object must be for us. "The only argument which leads to a definite concept of the object of theology is itself moral." This fact is significant for Kant as regards the specifically religious character of our belief in God:

Even if a religion could be established by the theoretical path, it would actually, as regards sentiment [*Gesinnung*] (wherein its essence lies), be different from that in which the concept of God and the (practical) conviction of His existence originate from the fundamental ideas of morality.[14]

Thus when Kant speaks of "omnipotence," "omniscience," "holiness," "blessedness" and other divine attributes as "required" for the possibility of the highest good, he does not (and cannot) mean that we have *speculative* knowledge that a being with these attributes must exist if the highest good is to be possible. Rather, these attributes define God as an object of our faith, our moral trust. If our moral faith is to be faith in a being in whom "we must place our trust . . . absolutely and unconditionally," then our concept of the object of this faith must be the concept of a being who is adequate to such a trust.[15] It is this "immeasurable trust" in God which motivates us to attribute to him "omnipotence," "omniscience," and other infinite attributes.[16] These attributes are not ascribed to God for the purpose of advancing speculative knowledge, but in order to show reverence (*Ehrfurcht*) for a being in whom we place an absolute trust.[17] In these attributes we honor God "as the Lord of life and the whole world . . . who cares for men." [18]

It is quite clear, then, that Kant's position is not to be described as "deistic." Kant himself certainly denied in a forceful way that he was a deist. The "deist" says Kant, "understands by the concept of God merely a blindly working eternal nature, as the root of all things, a primordial being or a highest cause of the world." [19] But, he asks, "do I in this way come to be in the least acquainted with God? The concept of the deist is thus completely vain and useless, and makes no impression upon me, if I assume it alone." [20] In contrast to the emptiness and abstractness of deism, Kant describes his own position as that of "Moral Theism": "Theism consists in believing not merely in a God, but also in a *living* God, who has produced the world through knowledge and free volition." [21]

A concept of God which is to be adequate for moral faith must include not only "ontological" perfections, but the perfections of a living and personal being, and, most important, *moral* perfections. It is God's moral attributes, all of which are of necessity specifically personal, which Kant sees as fundamental to the concept of God.[22] Kant sometimes describes such a concept of God as "anthropomorphic," but he does this only qualifiedly.[23] It is more common for him to criticize "anthropomorphism" as endangering the moral purity of our idea of God by representing God as all to similar to man.[24] Kant expresses himself most clearly on this point when he distinguishes "dogmatic" anthropomorphism from "symbolic" anthropomorphism.[25] The former asserts that God actually possesses characteristics found in finite things, while the latter limits itself to an "analogical predication of unlimited perfections of God, and "in fact concerns language only and not the object itself."²⁶ Kant seems to have been greatly impressed by the dilemma between deism and anthropomorphism presented by Hume in his *Dialogues* and devoted considerable effort to avoiding this dilemma.²⁷ A full exposition of his theory of "symbolism" and "analogy" would take us far off our course, but we should note the use made of these theories by Kant in order to preserve a concept of God which is both that of a "living God," a personal being, and at the same time that of a perfect and infinite being. Kant expresses himself most clearly on this point, perhaps, in the third critique:

If we are to give the name "cognition" [*Erkenntnis*] to a mere mode of representation (which is quite permissible if the latter is not a principle of the theoretical determination of what an object is in itself, but of the practical determination of what the idea of it should be for us and for its purposive use), then all our [cognition] of God is merely symbolical; and he who regards it as schematical, along with the properties of understanding, will, etc., which only establish their objective reality in the beings of this world, falls into anthropomorphism, just as he who gives up every intuitive element falls into deism, by which nothing at all is cognized, not even from a practical point of view.²⁸

The outlook of moral faith itself has often been misunderstood by Kant's readers, and it is such misunderstandings which have been involved in most of the claims that Kant's moral arguments "corrupt" his ethics. Hegel's criticism, discussed in the previous chapter, takes the moral outlook (or one of its two mutually incompatible "moments") to be a sort of moral complacency, where the moral agent "puts all his true strength in the good bringing itself about." As a matter of fact, however, any such attitude is quite foreign to Kant's thinking. Our "absolute trust" in God, as we have already seen, presupposes that we have already "done all within our power" to bring about our moral final end. Kant emphasizes this point countless times in his writings. The use of "trust in God" as an excuse for moral complacency may be found in some forms of *"moralische Weltanschauung,"* but it is not found in Kant:

> Of course, we have reason to leave ourselves entirely in God's hands, to let His will hold sway; but this does not imply that we ought to do nothing, leaving Him to do all. We must do what is in our power; we must do what we ought; the rest we should leave to God. That is true submission to the divine will.[29]

Another—and even more common—misunderstanding of the outlook of moral faith consists in seeing Kant as advocating faith as a "means" to our own happiness. This blatant misreading of Kant is expressed baldly by Greene when he says:

> However we conceive of the reward which He is postulated to guarantee in the next life, God still remains in Kant's argument, a *deus ex machina* introduced to resolve our moral perplexities, the great Paymaster who is to reward us for our moral efforts. But surely if, on Kant's own principles, it is wrong to use men merely as means to our ends, we are not entitled to bring God into our scheme of things primarily as a means to our ultimate happiness.[30]

There can be no doubt, of course, that for Kant faith in God is introduced as a response to the dialectical perplexities which threaten practical reason. Moral faith is the attitude of a finite rational being before the uncertainties of the world in which he must act purposively toward his final moral end. It can be said, then, that we do "bring God into our scheme of things" in order to "resolve our moral perplexities," or at least in order to *face* these perplexities rationally. But Greene, like many of Kant's readers, does not think this is all that is going on. For he depicts the attitude of moral faith as a kind of anticipation of our future rewards, as an attitude which looks

upon God as a "great Paymaster" who will dole out to us
what we really—but not morally—desire.* It should seem
clear that nobody—including Kant—would have *recom-
mended* so shabby and hypocritical an attitude as this, and it
ought to have occurred to Greene and others that this description of moral faith was bound to be a caricature. So gross a
distortion of Kant's meaning, indeed, would not even be
worth our consideration here, were it not for the appalling
fact that it is such a common interpretation of the moral outlook Kant is advocating.

The view that in moral faith we are using God as a "means
to our own happiness" derives, without doubt, largely from
the hard-dying conviction that Kant's ethics is "corrupted"
by the inclusion of human happiness in the ends of morality.
We have already shown in detail that this conviction is quite
without foundation, and that it presupposes confusion of motives and ends which is completely opposed to the most fundamental doctrines of the critical moral philosophy. If our pursuit of and hope for happiness is motivated not by our private
desire to be happy but by the fact that it is objectively *good*
that we be happy, then there is no impurity in our volition.
And in this case we do not look upon God as a "great Paymaster"—as though our only interest in a moral world-order
were "what I can get out of it"—but rather as a moral ruler
of the world, in whose goodness and justice we can trust as
moral beings.[31] It is true, of course, that some men *do* hypo-
critically pursue their private happiness while only *pretending*

* Noah Porter gives us a characterization of the God of moral
faith which is in some ways even more amusing. Kant's God is in his
view not a "paymaster" but a "sheriff," whose task it is to "enforce"
the moral law (Porter, *Kant's Ethics*, 226). Kant of course would
shun the reduction of moral to legal obligation implicit in this image,
as well as its ludicrous inappropriateness as a description of the moral
man's trust in God.

to be motivated by their obedience to the law. But Kant condemns such "impurity" as one of the fundamental forms of human wrongdoing, and he certainly is not *advocating* it.[32]

Greene's caricature of moral faith, apart from this common and fundamental misunderstanding, has other difficulties of its own. In the first place, it would be absurd in itself for anyone to think that he could actually increase his chances of receiving the "big payoff" merely by believing in the existence of a "great Paymaster"; thus moral faith would in any case be a rather feeble "means" to our "ultimate happiness." Perhaps some people *do* think that their believing in a "great Paymaster" does increase their chances for a future reward of some kind. But Kant is not such a person, and in fact he sharply condemns this way of thinking as a form of "religious illusion." [33] Second, as we noted earlier, Kant is not particularly fond of the notion that we can expect justice only in a "future life." He does, it is true, express this view in some of his earlier critical works, and he continues to speak of "future rewards" in his later writings. But as we have already seen, he regards God's justice as applying as much to the sensible world as to the intelligible, and regards it as a moral ordering of *this* world by an intelligible author whose purposes are not, as such, knowable to us.

But it might be said by Greene that Kant at least does advocate that the moral man should believe that God will "reward" him, even if he does not regard his belief as a "means" to obtaining such a reward. It is true that Kant recommends an attitude of trust, a belief that we will in the long run enjoy as much happiness as we deserve. But it is rather odd for Greene to infer automatically that we thereby believe that we will obtain some special "reward" either in this life or in another. In Kant's view is it presumptuous for even a good man to suppose that life has thus far dealt with him unfairly, and that if the world is to be just, he must look forward to a future "reward" for his troubles. In Kant's view, a man would have a duty to pursue and desire the realization of justice in the world "even though, in accordance with this idea, he saw himself in danger of paying in his own person a heavy price in happiness—it being possible that he might not be adequate to the demands of the idea." [34] Kant does not look upon moral faith as an outlook in which man is to anticipate a great "future reward." Rather, trust in God's goodness is described as a reverent *submission* to God's will. "Practical faith," says Kant,

does not consist in saying: "If only I trust implicitly in God He will do what I want"; but rather in saying: "I will myself do all I can, and if I leave myself in God's hands, He will strengthen my weaknesses and make up my shortcomings as He knows best." [35]

Moral faith does not consist so much of an expectation of future happiness as an acceptance of present sufferings. Moral faith does not promise me a world better than the actual one, but consists in the courage to trust that this world, as it is, a world in which there is suffering and apparent moral failure, is itself a morally good world. In moral faith, I do not flee this world to a better one; rather, I *choose* this world, I refuse to despair of it, I make it by my choice the world in which I will rationally act in pursuit of my final moral end. Trust in God is thus not characterized by the gleeful anticipation of my "future rewards," but rather by "humility and modesty, combined with resignation." [36] The man of moral faith, far from looking upon God as the "great Paymaster," looks upon every event which befalls him as coming from God's wisdom, and regards God with "thankfulness and resignation." [37] The attitude of moral faith is well expressed by the words of the beautiful Cantata Number 56 by Bach:

> Ich will mein Kreuzstab gerne tragen,
> Er kommt von Gottes lieber Hand.*

The outlook of moral faith is for Kant "immanent" in moral volition itself, and functions as part of the moral sentiment or disposition of a finite rational being as he wills and acts. This outlook thus guides his attitudes toward the particular events that befall him, and his responses to his successes and failures in his attempt to bring about a good world. Trust in God, as we have seen, enables the moral man rationally to face moral setbacks and suffering without falling into moral despair. Moral faith does not "explain away" or erase our sufferings, but gives us the hope and courage to be content and rationally to pursue a good world in spite of them. Kant discusses the attitude of moral faith toward suffering with great sensitivity when he says,

Contentment with the divine will consists in ready and joyful acquiescence in God's rule. It must be absolute and universal—whatever the circumstances in which we might find ourselves, be these good or bad. But is such contentment possible? We must guard against making man a hypocrite, for it is contrary to his nature to live in want and wretchedness and yet to thank God for it. If I thank God for my state, it follows that I must be content, and I cannot, therefore, be wretched. But how can I thank God for that which I wish had not happened? And yet is it not possible to have peace and contentment, great though our wretchedness and trouble may be? . . . In the course of the world taken as a whole everything is grounded in His good providence, and we may hope that everything, in general, happens in accordance with the foresight of God. . . . Not our senses but our reason might

---

* I will bear my cross gladly,
  It comes from God's loving hand.

recognize—and this, too, gives us a basis for belief,—that the ruler of the world does nothing without purpose. Thereby we find consolation in, though not for, the evils of life, a solid contentment with the course of life as a whole.[38]

In moral faith, then, we trust in the wise purposiveness of the creator and ruler of the world, we maintain the conviction that the world is not without moral purpose, and that its purpose harmonizes with our best moral intentions to bring about a good world. Moral faith is therefore also a *moral teleology of nature*, not one derived from empirical observation, but one which we as moral agents apply to empirical events. "We believe," says Kant, "that we perceive in the case of the wicked the traces of a wise purposive reference, if we only see that the wanton criminal does not die before he has undergone the deserved punishment of his misdeeds." [39] We do not pretend, of course, to justify claims about a final moral purpose in the world by appealing to the course of events themselves, but such purposes are part of the faith of "the judgment of human reason reflecting morally on the world." [40]

This observation allows us to make clear the status of "the teleological argument" in Kant's moral theology. In the previous chapter, we examined Beck's claim that the moral arguments are really "teleological" arguments, or something "analogous" to them, and saw that there was no reason to think that the moral arguments, as we have understood them, are "analogous" to the physicoteleological argument in any way which is inimical to them or to Kant's claim that they are not theoretical in character. But it is Beck's further contention that as Kant grew older (and, presumably, wiser) he repudiated the moral arguments in favor of a "purer" form of the physicoteleological argument. (This, of course, is quite at odds with Adickes' view that as Kant grew older and wiser he repudiated the moral arguments in favor of a more "subjec-

tive" moral faith, and repudiated these arguments precisely because—according to Adickes—he recognized them as theoretical. Perhaps Kant's haste to rid himself of the moral arguments is like the haste of the proverbial rider who "leapt to
his horse and rode off hurriedly in all directions"). The
"fact" that the moral argument is really theoretical, says Beck,

is not made clear in the *Critique of Practical Reason*, . . . But it
dominates the final theological sections of the *Critique of Judgment*, and the moral argument of the second critique has already
been assigned to the obscurity of a difficult footnote by the time
Kant wrote the treatise on religion.[41]

Now it is certainly inaccurate for Beck to say that the
physicoteleological argument "dominates" the theological discussion in the third critique, in view of the amount of space
Kant devotes to showing the *inadequacy* of this argument
(sections 85 and 90 and the Concluding Note all have this
aim), and in view of Kant's summary statement of his findings
on the teleological argument in section 90:

The result then is this. For the existence of an original being as a
Godhead or of the soul as an immortal spirit, absolutely no proof
in a theoretical point of view is possible for the human reason
which can bring about even the least degree of belief.[42]

It is also plainly false to say that the moral argument is discussed in the *Religion* only in "the obscurity of a difficult
footnote." Kant rather *begins* the preface to the first edition
of the *Religion* with this argument, and evidently regards it as
the starting-point for any rational discussion of religion from
a critical point of view. The moral argument is plainly presupposed throughout the *Religion*, and is even stated *again* in ab-
breviated form on two other occasions.[43] The "difficult footnote" to which Beck presumably refers follows upon an ex-

tended discussion in the text of the preface, and is intended to clarify *part* of that discussion.[44] Any implication that Kant was beginning to be "ashamed" of the moral arguments in the *Religion* is clearly without any textual foundation, and in fact the text of the *Religion* strongly supports the very opposite conclusion.

Beck's claim, however, does seem to receive support from Kant's "Moral catechism" in the *Metaphysic of Morals* (which was written later than either the third critique or the *Religion*):

Teacher: But even if we are conscious of a good and active will in us, by virtue of which we consider ourselves worthy (or at least not unworthy) of happiness, can we base on this the sure hope of participating in happiness?

Pupil: No, not merely on this. . . . Our happiness always remains a mere wish which cannot become a hope unless some other power is added.

Teacher: Has reason, in fact, grounds for admitting the reality of such a power, which apportions happiness according to man's merit or guilt—a power ordering the whole of nature and ruling the world with supreme wisdom?

Pupil: Yes. For we see in the works of nature, which we can judge, a wisdom so widespread and profound that we can explain it to ourselves only by the ineffably great art of the creator of the world. And from this we have cause, when we turn to the moral order, which is the highest adornment of the world, to expect there a rule no less wise.[45]

"This passage," says Beck, "is especially noteworthy. There is no discussion of the *summum bonum* in the *Metaphysik der Sitten*. The proof of God's existence is an argument from design, pure and simple." [46] But before we decide that Kant has in the *Metaphysic of Morals* reverted to an argument of which he himself is often credited with having given the definitive refutation, a few points must be considered. Statements like the one in the catechism are, in the first place, not restricted to the *Metaphysic of Morals*. In the first critique, Kant says, "The belief in a wise and great *Author of the world* is generated solely by the glorious order, beauty, and providential care everywhere displayed in nature." [47] The "privileged status" of the physicoteleological argument is, then, nothing new in the *Metaphysic of Morals*. But in view of the refutation of this argument which occurs in the first critique itself, we might reasonably question whether this status is (as Beck assumes) the status of a valid theoretical argument.

In both the first critique and the *Metaphysic of Morals*, the context of these "physicoteleological" remarks is *not* a philosophical discussion of the theoretical question of God's existence, but rather an examination of the justified religious faith of the *ordinary man*. The remark in the first critique is intended to deprecate scholastic philosophy, to point out to philosophers that "they can lay no claim to higher and fuller insight in a matter of universal human concern that that which is equally within the reach of the great mass of men." [48] Similarly, the moral catechism is *not* intended as a piece of academic philosophy. Kant rather regards it as a "methodological" device for "developing ordinary human reason" and "cultivating" it.[49]

What impresses Kant about the physicoteleological argument is that it, unlike the other speculative arguments, "produces a similar effect in the way of conviction upon the common understanding as upon the subtlest thinker." [50] To understand the "privileged status" of the physicoteleological argument, then, we must see why, in Kant's view, it is capable of commanding the respect of the ordinary man. "Physical teleology," says Kant, impels us, it is true, to seek a theology, but it cannot proclude one. . . . By the constitution and principles of our cognitive faculty, we can think of nature, in its purposive arrangements which have become known to us, in no other way than as the product of an understanding to which it is subject.[51]

Thus far, Kant agrees with his "pupil," when the latter says that "we see in the works of nature, which we can judge, a wisdom so widespread and profound that we can explain it to ourselves only by the ineffably great art of a creator of the world." [52] But here we have only "sought" a theology, utilized purposiveness in nature as a *regulative* principle of reflective judgment. We still have no natural theology because "the theoretical investigation of nature can never reveal to us whether or not this understanding may also, with the whole of nature and its production, have had a final design (which would not lie in the nature of the sensible world)." [53]

Kant's pupil seems, then, to have drawn this unwarranted conclusion when he infers that there actually exists a world-author with a final moral purpose for the world. If Kant's pupil has any reply to Kant's objection to the physicoteleological argument in its theoretical form, he does not tell us what this reply is. Kant, however, does tell us in the third critique why it is natural for the ordinary man to draw this inference:

That the physicoteleological proof convinces, just as if it were a theoretical proof, does not arise from our availing ourselves of the ideas of purposes of nature as so many empirical grounds of proof of a *highest* understanding. But it mingles itself unnoticed with that moral ground of proof, which dwells in every man and influences him secretly, . . . and by which therefore we arbitrarily fill up the lacunas in the design argument.[54]

The moral faith which, in Kant's view, is the true faith of the ordinary man, causes him to look upon nature as the product of divine authorship, and disposes him to have faith that nature is endowed by its creator with a final moral purpose. Hence the ordinary man "sees" nature as the work of God, and discerns in it—what no amount of empirical evidence could have demonstrated—the signs of a divine and morally purposive creation. "The emotions aroused by the manifold purposes of nature," says Kant,

have something in themselves like *religious* feeling. They seem in the first place, by a method of judging analogous to moral to produce an effect upon the moral feeling (gratitude to and veneration for an unknown cause) and thus, by exciting moral ideas, to produce an effect upon the mind, when they inspire that admiration which is bound up with far more interest than theoretical observation could bring about.[55]

Moral faith in God is an outlook on the world, a way of viewing, interpreting, evaluating, and judging the events of the world, which is not—and could not be—justified by empirical evidence or speculative demonstration, but forms part of the *Weltanschauung* which the moral man must have in order rationally to pursue his final destination. As such, it might be termed a moral "blik," to use the terminology of R. M. Hare.[56] But moral faith in God is at the same time for Kant a personal trust in God's goodness and wisdom, a reverent submission to the divine will, and a hope that his final moral purpose will, in the long run, obtain in the world as a whole.

Moral Faith in Immortality

If concrete descriptions of the outlook of moral faith in God are rare in Kant's works, such descriptions of moral faith in immortality are practically nonexistent. But again, we may try to determine what this outlook is by examining Kant's *absurdum practicum* argument as sympathetically as we can, with this interest in mind. We have seen that for Kant the moral agent has a final end not only as regards the establishment of goodness in the world, but also a supreme and unconditioned end as regards the moral goodness of his person. But we also saw that every man, however he may strive toward this end, finds that the character of his free volition itself forever excludes the absolute perfection of holiness from the series of his moral acts in time. Kant thus pictures the moral man as concerned with the attainment of the ideal of moral perfection while at the same time realizing that he is always "on the way" toward this ideal, that his deed (*That*) always falls short of the ideal of holiness. Hence the moral man must, if he is to continue a rational pursuit of the moral perfection of his person, sustain a hope that somehow through his constant progress he may satisfy the ideal of perfection. A full account of his attitude of hope must, as we saw earlier, be postponed. What interests us now is the response of moral faith to a particular threat to the possibility of the ideal of perfection, the response of moral faith in immortality.

As the moral man contemplates his own action and character with his ideal of moral perfection in mind, he sees that he must stake his hope for the attainment of this ideal on some moral reality which is attained in or through his particular acts and the moral character he manifests in them. But at the same time he is forced to admit that these acts themselves, and his moral character as he is able to discern it, are at all times far from perfect, and exhibit only a progress "from one virtue to others," a progress sustained only by a constant effort on his part. He must stake his hope on the permanence, the constancy, the absolute moral reality of this progress itself, since this alone—unlike his acts and his states of moral character in time—is capable of exhibiting some unqualified moral good. But this progress itself, so far as he can discern it, depends on his own effort in and through his particular acts. This progress *is* in fact—so far as "virtue's empirical character" is concerned—only the series of his acts themselves.

The moral man must hope, however, that somehow in this series is manifested something more permanent, something which can stand as a moral reality and attest to an unqualified kind of moral perfection. But there is in the world as he finds it a serious threat to this hope: the threat of his own *death*. Death will terminate, so far as his senses are able to discern, the very existence of his moral personality, leaving him at the end of his life still far distant from his moral ideal, and ending violently and arbitrarily the entire series of his moral action and progress. His very existence will be "thrown back into the purposeless chaos of matter from which it was drawn," [57] leaving even his best efforts at moral perfection behind as a mere collection of events, embodying in them no trace of moral perfection, no constant and permanent moral reality, but only a painful and feeble striving toward an empty and meaningless goal. The profound threat of death for Kant is not to be found in our fear of the physical pain of dying, or even in the melancholy thought that in death we will cease to be able to do and experience all those things which give life meaning and enjoyment. All this might well be borne without difficulty by any courageous person. What truly threatens us is that the goal which gives our life its moral meaning—the goal of moral perfection—is apparently rendered impossible of attainment by the prospect of death. The permanence and moral reality of the progress on which we must stake our hope for the attainment of this ideal is threatened with dissolution into a mere series of feeble and imperfect acts and empirical events. It is not the pain of death or the disturbing thought of the "cessation of consciousness" which threatens the moral man; the threat which death poses to him is rather the threat of *moral despair*.

This despair cannot be answered merely by a Heideggerian "anticipatory resoluteness," by a resolve in the face of death to give life a "wholeness" by finding meaning in what remains to us to do in life.[58] For Kant our moral goal is defined by reason prior to any "resolve" on our part, and the "wholeness" constituted by the attainment of moral perfection is precisely what *cannot* be fully attained in the series of empirical events of life. It is a characteristic of our rational nature, says Kant, "never to be satisfied with what is temporal (as insufficient for the capacities of its whole destination)." Thus, although we might find some kind of "meaning" in life through a resolute attitude toward our "being unto death," such a resolve cannot preserve a *moral* meaning to life, and is thus from the point of view of the critical philosophy a form of moral despair.

The response of moral faith to the threat posed by death must be, like all faith, "a trust in the attainment of a design, the promotion of which is a duty." As moral agents, it is rational for us to look upon the prospect of death with courage and trust, and not to dwell on it in morbid anticipation or to hide the thought of it from ourselves in fear and despair. But how is such an attitude of courage and trust to be related to moral faith, to a *belief* in immortality? Does this attitude even require such a belief? It does, in Kant's view, if we are rationally to avoid the threat that death may constitute the utter destruction of our entire moral personality, and with it our hope for a moral reality capable of manifesting our attainment of moral perfection. Something of our moral personality must persist beyond the particular acts and states of character manifested in the empirical world, if we are rationally to hold out any hope for the attainment of our moral final end as regards the goodness of our moral person.

This permanent existence of our moral personality is described by Kant in his later writings as a man's supersensible "disposition" (*Gesinnung*), which manifests itself empirically in the progress of his moral character in time. It is this disposition which (in a manner to be considered in the next chapter) "counts for the deed," and constitutes the moral equivalent of holiness of will.[59] It might be thought that by identifying immortality with a supersensible moral disposition, Kant has in effect identified the postulate of immortality with that of freedom. But this suggestion must be sharply qualified. The postulate of freedom is never more than the postulate of a capacity or predisposition (*Anlage*) of human nature, its inherent capability of autonomous action. The possession of this capacity constitutes a *condition* for moral personality, but it cannot be identified with the "moral person himself as a good or evil man." No man is good merely by the possession of a predisposition to good; rather, the moral person himself is constituted by the exercise of his own freedom, by the use he makes of his predisposition to autonomous action.[60] His true moral self, then, is not to be identified with the mere capacity of this self to act autonomously. But it may be identified with his freely adopted moral *disposition* in the use of this capacity. Hence to postulate the supersensible endurance of this disposition beyond the empirical acts and states of character manifested in life is to postulate more than that man is free; it is to postulate that the essence of the moral person himself is somehow deathless, and endures eternally as a morally significant reality. To maintain a moral faith in immortality is thus to trust and believe that my "self in its eternal validity"—to use Kierkegaard's phrase—will *not* be "thrown back into a purposeless chaos of matter" but will continue to have moral significance and manifest moral perfection in spite of my physical death and dissolution. And it is this faith which Kant's *absurdum practicum* argument is aimed at justifying.

We may well question whether Kant has justified belief in a "future life" in any proper sense by his *absurdum practicum* argument. It seems somewhat confused to apply the temporal designation "future" to a supersensible existence, which is presumably not temporal at all—at least in the way that sensible things are temporal. It is also unclear whether such a supersensible disposition would be in any proper sense a "life"—since we cannot pretend to say whether such an existence would be in any sense "conscious" or what sort of "consciousness" it might have. Kant's moral faith in a supersensible disposition can therefore hardly be of any comfort to those who hope for a "future life" to console themselves in their fear and melancholy at the prospect of the termination of their conscious life in the world. The only comfort moral faith can rightly hold out to such persons is to be found in the attitude of courage and trust which it commends to them. Still, we may be able to find some minimal force of the terms "future" and "life" preserved in Kant's conception of immortality. The moral disposition grounds the sum of a man's acts and states of character in time, and thus embodies his acts in life in something like the way that a man's future character (in time) contains within it his past actions and states of being. A man's moral disposition is also the essence of his moral personality, and manifests his "life" in this sense. Yet it must be admitted that this conception of immortality lacks the definiteness which might be demanded by many as part of the usual consolation in the thought of eternal life. Considered as part of the outlook of moral faith, however, it seems to me that the very indefiniteness of Kant's conception of such a "future life" has a great deal to recommend it. The man who faces death with true courage and trust will not concern himself greatly with the precise character of his "future state," just as the good man who truly trusts in God will not spend his time ruminating on his "future rewards." Both of these tendencies constitute a "doting on the beyond" which is most strongly condemned by Kant.[61] Moral faith always consists in trusting of the goodness of the life which God has given, and not in seeking a fantastic remedy for this life in an imaginary world.*

Moral Faith and Illusion

In a footnote in the second critique, Kant raises a possible objection to his doctrine of moral faith by referring to the work of a contemporary whom he evidently admired greatly:

* There is considerable evidence that Kant seriously questioned the doctrine of a "future life" during the period in which the *Religion* was written. The concept of man's "supersensible disposition" clearly constitutes a radical revision of the doctrine of "endless progress" found in the second critique, and a reduction of the notion of "future life" to a "purely negative function" (*EaD* 334g 77e). On account of this good disposition, Kant says, "man may, notwithstanding his permanent deficiency, yet expect to be *essentially* (*überhaupt*) well-pleasing to God *at whatever instant his existence be terminated*." (*Rel* 67g 61e). And in a manuscript probably dated August, 1794, we find Kant questioning the doctrine of a "future life" and an "eternal existence" quite seriously. Kant states that we must believe in God out of a moral need, in order to direct our efforts to the attainment of the highest good. He then continues: "In the same way, we believe in a future life. But the latter is only a belief of the second rank [*Glaube vom zweyten Range*]. For it is not necessary that we exist, or exist eternally, but only that so long as we live we conduct ourselves so as to be worthy of life" (*RR* 644). Since this passage itself is equivocal, and since it is not drawn from Kant's published writings, it would be absurd to conclude that in it Kant had "repudiated" his belief in a future life. But this passage, along with Kant's continual attention to the problems of immortality and the first antinomy of practical reason, does show that these were questions to which Kant returned time and again in his own philosophical thinking about religion.

In the *Deutsches Museum* for February, 1787, there is a dissertation by a very subtle and clear-headed man, the late Wizenmann, whose early death is to be lamented. In this he disputes the right to argue from a need to the objective reality of the object of the need, and he illustrates his point by the example of a man in love, who has fooled himself with an idea of beauty which is merely a chimaera of his own brain and who now tries to argue that such an object really exists somewhere.[62]

Wizenmann's objection is one which must be faced by any defense of a religious "leap" of faith, and it is one which has been frequently brought against religious belief in general. Probably the most cogent and powerful statement of this objection is to be found in Sigmund Freud's reflections on the character of religious belief. Freud's claim is that religious beliefs, one and all, have the psychological character of "illusions." "We call a belief an illusion (*Illusion*)," says Freud, "when a wish-fulfillment is a prominent factor in its motivation, and in so doing we disregard its relations to reality just as the illusion itself sets no store by verification." [63] Viewing religious beliefs in this light we see that such beliefs usually represent the world not as we have learned of it through the labors of empirical science, bur rather as we would like it to be:

It would be very nice if there were a God who created the world and who was a benevolent Providence, and if there were a moral world-order in the universe and an after-life; but it is a very striking fact that all this is exactly as we are bound to wish it to be.[64]

Freud, like Wizenmann, attacks the logic of arguing from a "need," from some desire or wish that we have, to the reality of the object of that need. It is irrational and unjustifiable to believe that something is so because one desires or wishes it were so. But Freud does not only criticize the "inference" involved here; he condemns this entire way of thinking as harmful and pathological in character. An "illusion" (*Illusion*) is closely akin to a psychiatric "delusion" (*Wahnidee*). (In *Civilization and Its Discontents*, Freud refers to religion as a "mass-delusion" (*Massenwahn*), though the distinction between *Illusion* and *Wahn* seems to be drawn somewhat differently in this later work.)[65] Any belief motivated by wish-fulfillment is in Freud's view an "intimidation to the intelligence," [66] which fetters human rationality and prevents it from dealing honestly with itself and the world. Only the man who is able to "renounce his infantile wishes" and to "accept with resignation" that the world is not entirely as he wishes it to be, is free to confront reality in a rational, constructive and unprejudiced way. Only such a man is truly in a position to bring about the progress of humanity as a whole, and to give his own "intellect" ascendency over his "instinctual life." [67]

Freud's penetrating study of religious belief is a powerful moral attack on all forms of "faith" and is doubtless a correct diagnosis and assessment of the actual religious convictions of many persons. And it appears, at least at first glance, to apply to Kant's moral faith as well. I shall try to argue, however, that Kant has a formidable defense against any charge that moral faith is a form of pernicious "illusion."

We may first point out that Kant and Freud are in essential agreement on a number of issues of relevance here. For both the proper goal of human life is the rule of "intellect" over "instinct," and neither the critical philosophy nor the outlook of Freudian psychoanalysis condones any uncritical acceptance of traditional religious beliefs and practices. Both men felt a deep sense of moral revulsion at the unquestioning religious dogmatism of many religious authorities and believers.[68] But the similarities go deeper than this. Both Kant and Freud recommend a sober, even stoical outlook on the world, and for both the term "resignation" (*Ergebung*) occupies a key place in the character of this outlook. Both Kant and Freud were men of scientific temperament, who were nonetheless capable of great sensitivity and deep thought about the universal problems and concerns of mankind.

But the differences which made Kant a believer and Freud an unbeliever are not, for all this, "illusory" differences. The most fundamental of these differences concerns the role of reason in human desire. For Freud, who was always in this respect deeply akin to Schopenhauer, all desire is fundamentally irrational. All desires are, for him, "wishes" arising from the blind irrationality of the "instinctual life" of the human organism. The function of reason for Freud is not to *originate* desire, but rather to *adjust* instinctual wishes to "reality" as much as possible. The essential tasks of reason, then, are to seek the satisfaction of desire (the alleviation of human suffering), and to recognize and reconcile oneself to the necessary disharmony between instinctual wishes and reality. We must adjust ourselves to reality as it is, and avoid harmful fantasies which only perpetuate our frustrating desires. Reason must teach us to *abandon* (as far as we can) the desire for objects which are unattainable to us, and content ourselves with the happiness reality allows. It is always harmful, therefore, to attempt to sustain any desire or wish for an object whose possibility of attainment is threatened by reality. Such desires must be controlled by our sober perception of reality, and insofar as our suffering from them is inevitable, our reason must counsel resignation rather than the illusion of hope. Hence we must especially avoid letting our desires influence in any way our beliefs about reality. Our very rationality, rather, depends on submitting each desire to the test provided by reality, and accepting absolutely the results of that test.

Kant, too, of course, regards the "limitation" of sensible desire as an important function of reason, and he too warns against "hollow and fantastic desires." [69] But in Kant's view the relation of reason to desire is nonetheless very different. In Kant's view it is not true that all desires have their origin in instinct. And for him reason's function is not limited to the control of irrational wishes. Reason itself, rather, is practical, capable of originating desire and defining purposes for human action independently of the contingencies of "sensible nature." Reason is not simply a means for *reconciling* oneself to reality, but provides man with the destination of *transforming* reality itself, desiring and striving for the attainment of a rational ideal in his own person and in the world as a whole. Reason itself thus defines an object of desire whose pursuit is itself motivated by reason. To abandon this ideal end, to limit or "control" one's desire to establish it, because its possibility appeared to be threatened by reality, would in Kant's view be precisely to abandon rationality itself, it would be positively *irrational* and morally condemnable.

Kant stresses the unique character of man's final moral end and our rational "need" or desire of it in his reply to Wizenmann's objection:

I concede that [Wizenmann] is right in all cases where the need is based on inclination, . . . which is . . . merely subjective ground of wishes. Here we have to do, however, with a need of reason arising from . . . the moral law, which is necessarily binding on every rational being: this, therefore, justifies a priori the presupposition of suitable conditions in nature and makes them inseparable from the complete practical use of reason.[70]

Moral faith is therefore "the only case where my interest inevitably determines my judgment," [71] because only in this case do I deal with the *unconditioned* object of a desire which derives from reason itself, whose pursuit reason cannot and will not abandon, limit, or qualify. The final end of all rational action cannot be "tested" by reality, both because it is beyond the powers of human reason ever to perform this "test" in a theoretically conclusive way, and because reality itself must be "tested" and transformed by our action in pursuit of this final end.

Moral faith, however, is in no sense a form of "wishful thinking," or a Jamesian "will to believe." It is true that our rational commitment to believe does arise from a personal choice on our part: the choice to obey the moral law which rationally obligates us and to pursue the object which our reason sets before us as our final moral end. But we do not believe the highest good to be possible because we *want* it to be possible; we believe it to be possible because we *must* do so if we are rationally to continue our pursuit of it. There is no question here of our justifying our belief in something by our "will to believe" it, because it would make us happier to believe it, or because we *wish* it to be so. Presumably, of course, if we desire to *attain* the highest good, our belief that it is possible will be a hopeful and comforting belief. But this hope and comfort do not justify, and should not by themselves motivate our belief. Rather, they proceed, along with moral faith, from a rational pursuit of the highest good.

Religion and the Church

Kant often uses the term "religion" in a loose and everyday sense to refer to particular social institutions and beliefs that we commonly distinguish as "religious." And on some occasions he seems to regard "religion" as identical with "moral faith." But Kant also uses the term "religion" in a very strict and technical sense, which he expresses in several places: "Religion is the recognition [*Erkenntnis*] of all duties as divine commands." [72] What, we may ask, is the significance of this

strict sense of the term "religion" in Kant's thought? It is
clear for Kant that morality has no need of a divine will or
command to insure the *validity* of the moral imperative.[73] So
why must we, in Kant's view, "recognize all duties as divine
commands"?

In the second critique, Kant seems to be answering this
question when he says that our duties "must be regarded as
commands of the Supreme Being because we can hope for
the highest good . . . only from a morally perfect . . . will;
and therefore we can hope to attain it only through harmony
with this will." [74] But this argument is hardly a convincing
one. It is true, of course, that *our* only conception of a divine
will (a morally perfect will) must be derived from our rational standard of goodness—from the moral law. We must
believe, then, that the performance of our duties is in *harmony* with the divine will. But this does not show that we
must recognize our duties as commanded by God.

In order to understand the function and justification of "religion" in human life, we must turn to Kant's argument in the
first part of Book III of the *Religion*. Kant is concerned at
this point with the practical means by which men may best
undertake their pursuit of their highest moral end. We noted
earlier that for Kant the highest good is sought not in the virtue and happiness of a single individual, but in an entire *world*
of persons, each with an absolute value and dignity as an end
in himself. The highest good consists in a "systematic union
of rational beings under common objective laws," *moral* laws,
and is in this way a "social end" and a "social good." The
highest good, says Kant,

cannot be achieved merely by the exertions of the single individual toward his own moral perfection, but requires rather a union
of such individuals into a whole towards the same goal—a system

of well-disposed men, in which and through whose unity alone the highest moral good can come to pass.[75]

Moral faith, of course, provides us with a hope for such a unity of wills by means of "the presupposition of . . . a higher moral being through whose universal dispensation the forces of separate individuals, insufficient in themselves, are united for a common effect." [76] But this, in Kant's view, is not sufficient for *our* purposive action toward the highest good. Trust in God, as we have seen, does not mean complacently waiting for God to accomplish our moral ends. "Man is not entitled," says Kant, "to be idle in this business and to let Providence rule, as though each could apply himself exclusively to his own private moral affairs and relinquish to a higher wisdom all the affairs of the human race (as regards its moral destiny)." [77]

Beyond moral faith, then, there is a further need for men themselves to work toward a systematic unity of rational beings in a *community* under a common moral law. Such a union of men, says Kant,

is attainable, so far as men can work towards it, only through the establishment and spread of a society in accordance with, and for the sake of, the laws of virtue, a society whose task and duty it is rationally to impress these laws in all their scope upon the entire human race.[78]

What sort of community is this to be? A *moral* community of men, says Kant, must differ essentially from every *political* community. Its laws cannot be *statutes*, derived from an arbitrary human authority, but must instead be purely *moral* laws which recommend themselves to each man through his own *reason*. But in addition to this, the very *principle* of a moral community of men will differ from that of a political one. The legislation of every political or "juridical" state "proceeds from the principle of *limiting the freedom of each to those conditions under which it can be consistent with the freedom of everyone else.*" [79] The laws of a political state, then, concern only "external rights," concern only the manner in which the freedom of each man must *limit* the freedom of others. But the human race has the duty also to work toward a moral community of its members, to take responsibility for all men as persons, and for the moral relations *between* men. No political community, however, can work toward this goal. The laws of such a community are always "coercive laws" (*Zwangsgesetze*), which compel men to an outward "legality" in their actions, but can never bring about *morality*, the inward improvement of the disposition of a free person.[80]

Each man naturally prescribes the moral law to himself, and recognizes it as binding on him. To found a moral community (*ethisches gemeine Wesen*) of men is to transform the moral law into a *public* law, uniting all members of this community under common, noncoercive, and moral laws, laws valid universally for all men as rational beings: "All single individuals must be subject to a public legislation and all the laws which bind them must be capable of being regarded as the commands of a common law-giver." [81] Now if the community in question here were a *political* one, the law-giver could be taken as the people itself. "But," says Kant, "if the community is to be *moral*, the people, as a people, cannot itself be regarded as the law-giver." [82] The member of a community, simply as men, cannot presume to be capable of legislating universally, and for *all* men.[83] Nor can men presume to legislate concerning the *inner* morality of their fellows.

There must therefore be someone other than the populace capable of being specified as the public law-giver for a moral community. . . . Only he can be thought of as highest law-giver of a moral community with respect to whom all *true duties*, hence also the moral, must be represented as *at the same time* his commands; he must therefore also be "one who knows the heart," in order to see into the innermost parts of the disposition of each individual. . . . But this is the concept of God as moral ruler of the world. Hence a moral community can be thought of only as a people under divine commands, i.e. a *people of God,* and indeed *under laws of virtue.*[84]

"Religion," then, "the heart's disposition to fulfill all human duties as divine commands," is derived from the *social* character of man's highest end. In my pursuit of the highest good as a social good, I must recognize the moral law not only as pertaining to me as a rational being, but also as a law binding morally on all rational beings, a law which obliges me to see myself as part of a moral unity with such persons, a *member* of a Kingdom of Ends, under a divine *head.*[85] Kant's "philosophy of religion," then, in the strictest sense, is part of his social philosophy, and it is in his philosophy of religion that Kant gives decisive expression to the role of human community in his ethics. To give a fully adequate account of this complex aspect of the critical ethics is beyond the scope of the present inquiry. We should, however, examine briefly Kant's conception of pure religious faith and its relation to the religious practices found in human society.

Each man, says Kant, has the duty to join a moral community of men, and to regard all rational beings as members of such a community. In this minimal sense, men are *already* a "people of God" prior to the actual founding of any such community as a human institution. But in a fuller sense, men are to *become* a "people of God" by their own realization, in practice, of their social end.* Human reason, says Kant, al-

* Max Adler, in his book *Das Soziologische in Kants Erkenntniskritik,* attributes a predominantly social meaning not only to the ideal of the highest good and the kingdom of ends, but to Kant's doctrine

lows us to form an *idea* of a moral community of men as a goal of our actual social endeavor. A moral community must be under laws of reason alone; God is thus thought of as the "highest law-giver" for this community, but it is reason, and not His arbitrary will, which is the "author" (*Urheber*) of these laws.[86] God commands morally because he is holy and not because he has the power to coerce. A moral community of men must also be *universal;* its laws, deriving from reason, are equally binding on all men. No political state—not even a "theocratic" one—can begin to realize the idea of such a community.[87] A political state concerns only the external relations of men with one another, and such a state is essentially restricted to the persons who happen to found it, and cannot include all mankind under its laws.[88] A moral community of men is not to be sought in the form of a political state, but in the form of a church (*Kirche*), a community devoted to the strengthening in its members of *religion*, the inner disposition to fulfill all duties as divine commands.

[Such a moral community,] then, in the form of a church, . . . really has, as regards its basic principles, nothing re-

of moral faith itself. In Adler's view, the "intelligible world" in which we postulate the providence of God is the *social* world, the *human* world as opposed to the world of *nature* (Adler, 342ff). Adler's interpretation overlooks, of course, the obvious fact that for Kant the "intelligible world" is a supersensible and an unknowable world, a world to which we have access—if it can even be called that—only through the outlook of moral faith. And yet Adler does bring strikingly to our attention the even more important fact that Kant's moral idea is a *social* ideal, an ideal world of *persons,* and that the moral man's trust in God is closely associated with his hopes for progress in the human world of history (*IAG* 17fg 11fe, 30g 25e; *EF* 377ffg 124ffe; *VE* 317ffg 252fe; *SF* 82 ff). And his discussion does much to cast doubt on Greene's hasty conclusion that Kant, along with his entire century, was distinguished by an "uncritical individualism," and a "lack of historical imagination" (Greene, "The Historical Context and Religious Significance of Kant's Religion," lxxiv).

sembling a political constitution. . . . It could best of all be lik-
ened to that of a household (family) under a common, though
invisible, moral Father . . . , a voluntary, universal and enduring
union of hearts.[89]

How is such a Church to be founded by men? Kant is not
recommending, as Auguste Comte was later to do, that men
should found a *new* religion, with no other basis than an abstract philosophical one. To attempt such a thing would not
only be quixotic, but it would be to ignore the fact that men
already have, albeit in an imperfect way, attempted to form
moral communities of this kind. In the plurality of world-reli-
gions or "ecclesiastical faiths" (*Kirchenglauben*) Kant sees
the single aim of establishing a pure religious faith (*reine Reli-
gionsglaube*). These attempts are, to be sure, imperfect and
conditioned by historical circumstances, but they are nonetheless recognizable approximations to the idea of a "people of
God." Any attempt to found a *new* religion on reason alone
would inevitably meet with the same obstacles in men themselves which have caused the imperfections in these ecclesiastical faiths, and would become only one of them. Thus pure religious faith alone is never sufficient to found a church as a
human institution:

Pure religious faith is concerned only with what constitutes the
material of reverence for God, namely, obedience, ensuing from a
moral disposition, to all duties as His commands; a church, on the
other hand, as the union of many men with such dispositions into
a moral community, requires a public commitment, a certain ecclesiastical form dependent upon the conditions of experience.[90]

Pure religious faith is therefore not the *alternative*, the "opposite" of ecclesiastical faith.[91] Rather, it is the true and rational *essence* of ecclesiastical faith. Ecclesiastical faith is the
"vehicle," the "conducting substance," of pure rational faith;

it is the "shell" (*Hülle*) which contains the rational kernel of
pure religious faith.[92] Thus religion, like human knowledge
and practice, has both a *pure* and an *empirical* part. Ecclesiastical faith, conditioned by historical circumstances and basing
itself on claims to divine revelation, is an *empirical* religion.
But it also contains principles which do not depend on the acceptance of a historical tradition or scriptural accounts of a divine revelation, but recommmend themselves to men universally, and base their claim solely on moral reason. "Religion
within the limits of reason" is thus to be found *within* ecclesiastical faith, which contains also "religion *outside* the
limits of reason," a *revealed* religion. Thus Kant explains the
title of *Die Religion innerhalb der Grenzen der blossen Vernunft:*

Regarding the title of this work . . . I note: that since, after all,
revelation can certainly embrace the pure religion of reason,
while, conversely, the second cannot include what is historical in
the first, I shall be able to regard the first as a wider sphere of
faith, which includes within itself the second, as a *narrower* one
(not like two circles external to one another, but like concentric
circles).[93]

Ecclesiastical faith, however, is at its best only an imperfect
vehicle of pure religious faith. Ecclesiastical faiths are numerous, divided into competing sects. Further, they base their
claims not on reason, but on empirical revelation, as transmit-
ted through a historically conditioned tradition. For both
these reasons, no ecclesiastical faith can lay claim to true *universality*. "An historical faith," says Kant, "grounded solely
on facts, can extend its influence no further than tidings of it
can reach, subject to circumstances of time and place and dependent on the capacity of men to judge the credibility of
such tidings." [94] The imperfection of ecclesiastical faith, however, often shows itself in even more positive and objectiona-

ble ways. Such faith often replaces *moral* duties recognized as divine commands with special duties *to* God, promulgated as "statutes" by a quasi-political hierarchy.[95] Thereby ecclesiastical faith restricts the *freedom* which is essential to all genuine religion. Ecclesiastical faiths are moreover often not content with the service of God through obedience to His will, but hope to placate God, or to win divine favor by means other than morally good conduct. Ecclesiastical faith is thus subject to the danger of "religious illusion" (*Wahn*), the belief that man can become well-pleasing to God by means other than a morally good disposition.[96] Falling prey to such illusions, ecclesiastical faith indulges in a "pseudo-service" (*Afterdienst*) of God, in the form of cultic worship and outward obedience to (morally indifferent) ecclesiastical statutes.[97] Kant does not condemn practices of this kind as such, but condemns the belief that they constitute a genuine duty to God, or an essential part of religion. This belief transforms faith (*Glaube*) into *superstition* (*Aberglaube*).[98]

We cannot rest content, therefore, with ecclesiastical faith as the vehicle for pure religious faith, but must attempt to further the ideal of a moral community of men through the use of our reason. Ecclesiastical faith is thus not only the vehicle for pure religious faith, but it is also the historical prerequisite for a moral community of men founded on pure religious faith. Men must "set free" pure religious faith from its "shell." [99]

But how is this to be done? It cannot be done through the *abolition* of ecclesiastical faith by "external revolution," says Kant, but must, like all human progress, be carried out "through a gradual reform according to fixed principles." [100] The principle of progress toward a moral community is *enlightenment*. The service of God must become "first and foremost a free and hence a moral service." [101] Through enlightenment, man is "released from his self-incurred tutelage," freed by his own use of reason from his subjection to arbitrary statutes and the particular historical tradition through which ecclesiastical faith has presented itself to him. Man must "grasp with mature reflection" the rational kernel in ecclesiastical faith, and so expand the horizons of his religion to include all men universally as rational beings in the only true *ecclesia catholica*, the *ecclesia* of a *catholicismus rationalis*.[102] Toward this end, ecclesiastical faith must guard itself against religious illusion and

must contain within itself, along with the statutory articles with which it cannot as yet wholly dispense, still another principle, of setting up the religion of good life-conduct as the real end, in order, at some future time, to be able to dispense with the statutory articles.[103]

Kant does not, however, intend that ecclesiastical faith, its practices and its historical tradition shall be *abolished* by progress. Rather, it is to come to an understanding of itself as a vehicle for pure religious faith, so better to serve the pure faith which is its essence. Kant thus looks forward to an epoch when ecclesiastical faith will be no longer any more than a mere vehicle for pure religious faith, and he expresses the hope that

in the end religion will gradually be freed from all empirical determining grounds and from all statutes which rest on history and which through the agency of ecclesiastical faith provisionally unite men for the requirements of the good; and thus at last the pure religion of reason will rule over all, "so that God may be all in all."[104]

It has been not infrequently noted that Kant's conception of pure rational faith contains many distinctly Christian elements.* Kant, indeed, does say that "of all the public religions which have ever existed the Christian alone is moral," and this has led some to think that Kant's "pure religious faith" is a "compromise" between Christianity and a faith based on

---

* Kant, indeed, has not only been characterized (by Nietzsche) as "an underhanded Christian" (Nietzsche, *Twilight of the Idols*, 74g 484e), but has been frequently lauded as "the philosopher of protestantism." This latter characterization seems to me particularly harmful and misleading. Even those who do accord Kant this title, of course, recognize that it is not one which Kant himself would have accepted willingly (Paulsen, "Kant der Philosoph des Protestanismus," 2). There was certainly little love lost between Kant and the Orthodox Lutheranism of his own time. But even more important, Kant's thought clearly has little in common with the narrowly biblical religion of Luther, Calvin and Zwingli, and has even less in common with their Augustinianism and their deprecation of human reason. Kant's doctrine of evil and grace, indeed, has even been said by Karl Barth to be predominantly Roman Catholic in its conception (Barth, *Protestant Thought from Rousseau to Ritschl*, 187). As Delekat observes, in his account of religious progress "Kant declined . . . any repetition of the Reformation—for him it was a revolution—and chose instead the path of gradual reform" (Delekat, *Immanuel Kant*, 369). Truly Kant's was more the spirit of Erasmus and Nicholas of Cusa than of Luther and Calvin.

In fact, nothing more than the most tenuous "spiritual" connection between Kant and protestantism is ever claimed. Even if, as Bauch concludes, "In Kant Luther's moral-religious feeling has attained the standpoint of reason" (Bauch, "Luther und Kant," 492). It is still highly doubtful that Luther himself would have regarded this "attainment" as being of much worth in comparison with God's revelation of Himself in Jesus Christ, which is certainly in Luther's view the source of all his "moral-religious feeling." Paulsen sees the greatest "protestant" elements in Kant to consist in his championing of "freedom of thought" and his opposition to "external, human authority" in matters of conscience and religion (Paulsen, "Kant der Philosoph des Protestantismus," 14). This characterization of Kant as the "protestant" philosopher is put most precisely by Staeps: "If one understands by protestantism the entire collection of ecclesiastical practices proceeding from the reformation, then Kant would never have aligned himself with protestantism. But if, instead, this expres-

moral reason or a "coalition" between them.[105] But Kant
makes claims of this sort because, in his view, Christianity is
"represented as coming *from the mouth of the first Teacher*
not as a statutory but as a moral religion." [106] On Christianity as a historical faith, however, he pronounces a different
judgment: "At any rate, the history of Christendom . . . has

---

sion means religious independence, the self-certainty of the spirit freed
from every external authority and grounded only on a conviction of
faith personally recognized, discovered, won and experienced, then
Kant is throughout a protestant philosopher, and one who placed
protestantism on a philosophical foundation in the autonomy of the
moral personality" (Staeps, "Das Christusbild bei Kant," 112f).

Unfortunately, however, it was just Kant's assertion of the autonomy of the rational and moral personality in relation to other persons, his affirmation of freedom of thought and his opposition to
"external authority" which set him against the social and ecclesiastical
reality of protestantism as he found it. Surely he was not speaking
only of distant Catholic countries when he warned the enlightened
sovereign not to support "the ecclesiastical despotism of some tyrants
in his state over his other subjects" (*WA* 40g 8e). Kant's assessment
of protestantism in his own time was expressed with ironic precision
in the *Religion*, where he remarked: "If a church which claims that
its ecclesiastical faith is universally binding is called a *catholic* church,
and if that which protests against such claims on the part of others
. . . is called a *protestant* church, an alert observer will come upon
many laudable examples of protestant Catholics and, on the other
hand, still more examples, and offensive ones, of arch-catholic Protes-
tants: the first, men of a cast of mind (even though it is not that of
their church) leading to *self-expansion;* to which the second, with
their *circumscribed* cast of mind, stand in the sharpest contrast—not
at all to their own advantage" (*Rel* 109g 100e).

In truth, Kant was as far from the radicalism, irrationalism, and
antihumanism of the reformation as he was from the dogmatism and
reactionary traditionalism against which the reformers protested. To
characterize Kant as a "protestant" philosopher is to imprison his
thought in the sectarian squabbles which he detested above all else
in matters of religion. It is to do a disservice to the ecumenicism, the
rationality, and universal communicability which lies at the very

served in no way to recommend it on the score of the beneficent effect which can justly be expected of a moral religion." [107] Kant thus regards Christianity both as a "natural
religion" a religion of reason, and as a "learned religion," an
ecclesiastical faith based on revelation. And it seems fair to
say that any ecclesiastical faith, containing a rational kernel
within an historical shell, must be regarded in this way by the
critical philosopher of religion.

A more cautious assessment of the relation of Christianity
to Kant's moral faith is expressed by the great theologian Karl
Barth. Struck by the similarity of Kant's conception of the
Church to the traditional Christian conception, Barth asks,

is this still the Church of the religion of mere reason? If it is, it is
certainly at the same time a picture of the Christian conception
of the Church showing no lack of careful study. And if the philosopher should answer that it is precisely in this that the occasional happy coincidence of the Christian with the reasonable element comes to light, we could then ask in return whether it was
in fact the reasonable element which served as the archetype in
this construction, . . . or whether perhaps things turned out differently from what Kant had planned and intended, whether he
might have used the text of a religion other than that of his religion within.[108]

It would of course be absurd to deny that Kant's conception
of the Church, or indeed that his religion and ethics generally,
were profoundly influenced by the Christian tradition in
which he lived. But unless we dismiss all attempts at "rationality" as mere "rationalizations," or claim that history itself is a
product of a metaphysical "reason," we cannot assume that
Kant's pure religious faith is *based* on the historical tradition

foundation of his conception of religion and of the church as a
"moral community" of all mankind.

from which his conception itself was drawn. Whether this is so must depend on the strength of Kant's purportedly rational arguments, and not on the historical tradition in which his view stands.

But, further, there is every reason to think that for Kant at any rate, it would be certain elements in Christianity which would come to the fore in his presentation of religion. Kant does discuss Judaism, Islam, and Hinduism in the *Religion* as well as Christianity, and he is concerned to show that many historical religions exhibit a morally based conception of God; [109] but in his own view it is the Christian faith which "has enriched philosophy with far more definite and purer concepts of morality than it had been able to furnish before," and it is Christianity whose development provides the topical issues which guide the discussion throughout the *Religion*.[110] Kant's foremost task in the *Religion*, indeed, was not to advance a thesis concerning "comparative religions," but to ask how far the faiths we see in human society (and, most particularly, the Christian faith) can be justified "within the limits of reason alone." The great, and much-neglected nineteenth-century theologian Albrecht Ritschl thus expresses the relation of Kant's pure religious faith to the faith of Christianity in a way which is both truer and more sympathetic, when he says:

In Christianity, the Kingdom of God is represented as the common end of God and the elect community, in such a way that it rises above the natural limits of nationality and becomes the moral society of nations. In this respect, Christianity shows itself to be the perfect moral religion. . . . Kant was the first to perceive the supreme importance *for ethics* of the "Kingdom of God" as an association of men bound together by laws of virtue.[111]

Religious Experience and Revelation

To found a "religion within the limits of reason," a pure religious faith, is not to establish a *new* human institution, but it is rather to perform a rational *critique* of existing ecclesiastical faiths, and to attempt to guide these faiths in slow progress toward the ideal of a universal moral community of men. In religion, too, for Kant, the *critical* function of reason, reason as *self-knowledge* is man's primary instrument of enlightenment and self-improvement.

It has seemed to many, however, that Kant is mistaken in thinking that a critique of religious belief and practice properly falls within the scope of human reason. It is only a "shallow rationalism," according to such persons, that could not recognize in the phenomena of religion something quite *outside* reason, a form of awareness not properly amenable to the judgment and criteria of mere human reason. Kant is thus frequently criticized for his "inability to recognize a distinctive religious experience," giving "knowledge of God" and affording us "communion" with him.[112] Kant neglects, it is said, the role of *feeling* in religion, and is led in this way to underestimate the role of cult and worship in religious practice.[113] Rudolf Otto, who indeed acknowledges a great debt to Kant in the formation of his own philosophy of religion, nonetheless provides a sustained indictment of Kant, charging that Kant neglected the "irrational" in the concept of the "holy," impoverishing this concept by reducing it to its purely rational and moral elements.[114]

It is most misleading to say, as some of Kant's critics have, that he simply "overlooked" or "neglected" the "irrational" aspects of religion. Kant never undertook a systematic psychological investigation of mystical or other religious feelings, but he certainly was aware—indeed, at times all too aware—

of the role played by "the irrational" and by "inner feeling" in ecclesiastical faith and its practices.[115] Kant's "inability to recognize" such phenomena does not consist in an ignorance of their existence, but rather in his attempt to make a *rational* assessment of them.

For Kant, the rational validity of any judgment rests on its *universal communicability*.[116] The validity of rational religion also rests on its universality, its basis in a faith and duty which can be required of all men. Now Kant would not undertake to dispute with anyone about the completely private content of his "inner feelings," but he would deny that the presence of such feelings—of whatever sort—could ever give to any belief or action the justification and validity which can come only with universal communicability. Kant is therefore not interested in the "inner" content of religious feelings, but focuses his attention on the *justifiability* of the claims made by those who argue from their own private feelings. No belief or action could ever be justified by the presence of a private feeling of any kind. This is just as true of moral feelings as it is of any other sort. It is true that both moral faith and moral volition have an emotional aspect, that they involve the incentive of "moral feeling" and a "felt need of reason" to trust in God.[117] But it is the *rationality* of moral faith and volition which justifies them, and not the mere presence of these feelings. Still less could "inner feelings" give us any "experience" or "knowledge" of God. For no finite being could be capable of such supersensible experiences: "The feeling of the immediate presence of the Supreme Being and the distinguishing of this from every other . . . feeling would constitute a receptivity for an intuition for which there is no sensory provision in man's nature.[118]

It is common for critics of Kant's position on this point to claim that Kant has drawn a "false distinction" between theoretical and practical reason. "Religious experience," it is said, is neither theoretical knowledge nor moral volition but is either a kind of combination of them or else some third sort of thing which is "yet higher or deeper than they." [119] Those who criticize Kant in this way appear to be suggesting a possible way of "expanding" Kant's critical project, supplementing it with an examination of a fundamental human faculty which Kant "overlooked" or "neglected." But this appearance is usually highly misleading. Were Kant's critics suggesting an expansion or revision of his conception of human rationality to include transcendental factors in human experience which were unnoticed by Kant, their suggestions would not at least be in spirit opposed to the critical project. Kant's own examination of the transcendental factors in human feeling, to which he devoted the third critique, certainly constitute an "expansion" of this kind. But for Kant, criticism is always rational self-knowledge, the awareness by man of his capabilities and limitations, comprehended systematically in terms of concepts with an universal and necessary validity.

Of course, insofar as "the holy" is for Otto a transcendental category of "pure reason," his treatment of this concept might fall within a genuinely critical approach to religion.[120] And in this respect his project would differ essentially from that of Schleiermacher, and of all those who would "supplement" a critique of reason with a doctrine of feeling which is altogether outside and above reason. But even for Otto, the "numinous" in religious experience is "irrational," incapable of being communicated or even conceived. The human "faculty of divination" stands altogether apart from human reason, and its judgments are quite incapable of being given universal validity except by an appeal to a "completely unique" kind of *feeling*.[121] Otto's project, too, then, is not a completion of criticism but an inversion of it, placing a

"category" of blind and irrational feeling completely beyond
the critical scope of reason.[122] Such an inversion is for Kant
"the death of reason," and necessarily puts an end to any
attempt systematically to criticize and determine the bound-
aries of human insight.[123] The sobriety and caution which
Otto himself exhibits in his brilliant examination of the
"numinous" factors in religious experience does not alter the
fact that he has attempted to introduce a category of pure
feeling which is in no way amenable to systematic criticism,
since it lies altogether outside the limits of man's rational
nature.[124] Kant perceives that critical self-knowledge must
of necessity be *rational*, and agrees with Freud that "there
is no court above reason." [125] Kant recognizes that only the
universal communicability of reason can provide us with a
genuine mark of truth and validity, and that religion, as well
as ethics and science, must be made to rest on *reason* if it is to
command the belief and reverence of free and rational men.

In so doing, however, Kant is careful to maintain the *critical* function of reason in dealing with religion. Kant does not
dogmatically *deny* the possibility of a divine revelation to
man. Reason, he says, "will never contest either the inner
possibility of revelation in general or the necessity of a revelation as a divine means for the introduction of religion; for
these matters no man can determine through reason." [126] Kant
even suggests cautiously that we may regard the continued
existence of the Jewish people throughout the ages as evidence of a special divine purpose.[127] But though divine revelation itself is not possible, it *is* impossible for any man to *know*
through experience that God has in any instance actually revealed Himself:

For if God actually spoke to a man, he still could not *know* that
it was God who spoke to him. It is absolutely impossible that a

man should grasp the Infinite through his senses, distinguish Him from other sensible things and thus be *acquainted* with Him.[128]

In the *Lectures on Philosophical Theology*, Kant draws a distinction between "outer" revelation "in works and words" and "inner" revelation "through our own reason." [129] When we regard our moral duties as divine commands, when we believe in God through rational faith, we may see these commands and this faith as a kind of "revelation" to us by God himself, a revelation through universally communicable human reason, rather than through experience or feeling. Regarding our rational faith and moral duties in this way does not, of course, add anything materially to them, and it certainly does not provide us with any sort of "knowledge" of God. Thus there is nothing totally new or revolutionary about Kant's remarks concerning "divine revelation through reason" in the *Opus Postumum* and this way of speaking occurs throughout his critical works.[130]

Why does Kant introduce the concept of "inner" and rational revelation? Kant notes that an important aspect of ecclesiastical faith as a vehicle for pure religious faith is its guardianship of a sacred *scripture*, through which divine revelations are allegedly made available to men.[131] Ecclesiastical faith interprets this scripture as a set of *statutes*, through the discipline of "biblical theology." [132] In its critical approach to religion, human reason must also deal with this scripture, and distinguish within it between that which belongs to pure religious faith and that which falls within the larger circle of empirical or ecclesiastical faith only. Pure religious faith, then, requires its own principles of scriptural interpretation, its own "hermeneutics." [133]

The "inner" revelation of moral reason provides a *criterion*, a "norm" or "touchstone," for our judgment of the genuine-

ness of "outer" revelation in a scriptural document.[134] Only
the revelations of a *good* God can be binding on us, and only
our moral conception of God provides us with a means of determining the moral purity—and consequently the possible au-
thenticity—of the alleged revelation of such a God. Nothing
can possibly be a genuine revelation of a morally perfect
God unless it can be brought into harmony with "inner" and
rational revelation. It is the project of pure religious exegesis,
therefore, to find that in scripture which harmonizes with and
exhibits the truths of "inner" revelation. It is in this sense that
inner revelation "precedes" all other claims to revealed doctrine, and that all "outer" revelation in experience "presupposes" the "inner" revelation of moral reason.[135] When a
scriptural document is interpreted in this way, says Kant,

> God in us is himself the interpreter, for we can understand no
> one who does not speak with us through our own understanding
> and our own reason, and thus the divine origin of a doctrine is-
> sued to us can be recognized through nothing but the concepts of
> *our* reason, insofar as they are purely moral and in that sense
> infallible.[136]

I cannot pretend to have discussed Kant's treatment of ecclesiastical faith, religious experience, or revelation with anything like the thoroughness which the complexity of these
subjects and the subtlety of Kant's analysis properly demand.
But we have seen, I think, how Kant's conception of the
Church completes his conception of man's pursuit of his final
moral end as a specifically *social* goal; and I have filled out the
concept of rational faith by giving brief consideration to
Kant's attitude toward a religion founded on claims which
transcend reason. What is most significant here is that Kant
has attempted a *rational critique of religion*. He has tried to
distinguish between those questions in revealed (and particu-

larly in Christian) theology which are amenable to a rational solution, and those which are not so amenable. In the final chapter, I will consider Kant's endeavor to treat rationally one of the most fundamental problems in Christian theology: the problem of radical evil and divine grace.

6. Radical Evil and Divine Grace

In Chapter 4 we saw how Kant's moral argument for the postulate of immortality arises out of a dialectical threat to the practical possibility of moral perfection in man. We were forced to recognize, however, that Kant's treatment of the whole question of man's moral perfection and the dialectical threat to it, as provided in his works prior to the *Religion*, remains seriously incomplete in several ways. We saw in Chapter 4 that Kant's argument at this point requires his doctrine of radical evil, and that the dialectic leading to the first antinomy cannot be made to rest simply on the finite and sensible character of human volition. We also noted that Kant's postulate of immortality is not, by itself, sufficient to resolve the first antinomy, and to guard us against the threat that moral perfection may be impossible for man. It is not until the *Religion* that Kant undertakes to fill these lacunas in his argument by examining the problem of radical evil in detail, and by giving a broader consideration to the response of moral faith to this problem.

Although Kant neither dealt with these questions in any detailed way nor attempted to relate them systematically to his doctrine of moral faith until the *Religion*, it is not true that he altogether neglected them. Kant recognized man's moral need for "divine aid" in his striving for moral perfection long be-

fore the *Religion,* and indeed had given expression to views
very similar to the doctrine of grace found in the *Religion.*[1]
Kant had even addressed himself to the question of radical
evil, though his early discussion exhibits nothing of the sophis-
tication found in the *Religion's* treatment of this question.[2] In
the *Religion,* then, Kant is for the first time giving *detailed* attention to questions which had already been of concern to
him, and he is trying to relate this detailed treatment of these
questions systematically to the doctrine of moral faith developed in the three critiques.

In the *Religion,* Kant reopens the whole question of man's
moral perfectability, and attempts to give a more complete
answer to this question than he did in any of his earlier works.
Our discussion of radical evil and grace will therefore round
out our examination of Kant's critical system of thought concerning the practical dialectic and its resolution. Kant's treatment of the questions of radical evil and grace, however, also
has considerable interest in its own right. In the *Religion,*
Kant attempts to deal rationally with the problem of the alien-
ation and reconciliation of God and man, a problem central to
religious life and thought generally, and particularly to Christian faith and theology. Kant attempts in the *Religion* to determine the extent to which this problem is susceptible of rational treatment, and to produce within these limits a rational
account of the reconciliation of man to God. Kant's discussion of evil and grace in the *Religion* does, it is true, exhibit a
certain tentativeness and incompleteness. Kant has not defined
as clearly as we might wish the limits of reason in dealing
with the questions of evil and grace, nor has he produced an
altogether clear account of divine grace itself. And yet,
though we are bound to notice these difficulties, I think we
cannot help realizing that Kant's discussion of radical evil and
grace ranks as one of the great achievements of the human in-

tellect in attempting to give a rational account of the reconciliation of man to God.

The Concept of Radical Evil

In Chapter 4, I discussed in some detail the doctrine of radical evil which grounds the first antinomy of practical reason. Before giving further attention to this doctrine, therefore, it will be wise to review our earlier findings. Human nature, according to Kant, possesses three "predispositions" (*Anlagen*) to good: (1) the predisposition to *animality*, as a *living* being, from which man's natural needs and inclinations are derived; (2) the predisposition to *humanity*, as a *rational* being, from which is derived man's ability to exercise *prudence* with respect to his own needs and desires; and (3) the predisposition to *personality*, from which derives man's awareness of his obligations and his accountability before the moral law.[3] These predispositions all belong to "human nature" in the sense that they are "bound up with the possibility of human nature." They are predispositions *to good* in the sense that they are considered in themselves "not a matter of reproach" and that through them man is created "for good." [4] *

* Kant, therefore, along with Kierkegaard, "parries the rationalistic view that the sensual itself is sinful" (Kierkegaard, *The Concept of Dread*, 53). Sin is not for Kant, as it was for Ritschl, "the contradiction in which man finds himself, as both a part of the world of nature and a spiritual personality claiming to dominate nature" (Ritschl, *The Christian Doctrine of Justification and Reconciliation*, 199). Certainly the contrast between man's finitude and his rationality, his sensible needs and inclinations and his unconditional moral destination, is of great significance for Kant's view of man and his condition. But this contrast itself does not make man an evil, a sinful being. Here again, Kant repudiates the stoical rationalism with which he is usually charged. The valiant stoics, he said, were mistaken in seeing evil only in "undisciplined natural inclinations," when in fact evil is really "an invisible foe who screens himself behind reason and is therefore all the more dangerous" (*Rel* 57g 50e).

No man, says Kant, is *actually* good or evil on account of his possession of these predispositions.[5] Hence, if man is to be said to be "by nature" good or evil, this goodness or evil cannot consist in the predispositions bound up with the *possibility* of human nature. The very concept of moral good and evil involves, rather, the actual use man makes of his capacities, and prevents us from regarding these capacities themselves as morally good or evil. Good or evil must "lie only in a *rule* made by the human will (*Willkür*) for the use of its freedom, that is, in a *maxim*." [6] All moral good and evil, as we have already noted, has reference to maxims of human volition, and all objects of the human will derive their goodness from inclusion in the matter of a morally valid maxim. Further, as we have also noted, *all* maxims of finite rational volition (be they good or evil) contain *both* the incentives of moral reason and of sensible inclination; [7] every maxim must contain both these incentives if it is to be the principle from which a finite rational subject acts, since both incentives belong to the predispositions of such a subject. The goodness or evil of a maxim, therefore, does not consist in the incentives it contains, since if it did, then man would at all times be "at once good and evil." [8] The goodness or evil of a maxim rather consists in its "form," in the "order" or "subordination" of the incentives it contains, on "which of the two incentives [the agent] makes the condition of the other." [9] The maxim of the good man differs from that of the evil man only in that the former conditions the incentives of inclination by those of duty, whereas the latter reverses the moral order of incentives, and makes it a rule to do his duty only on the condition that it be consistent with the pursuit of inclination.

If man is by nature evil, then, this evil cannot consist in a lack of the incentive to be good, in a "corruption" of moral reason.[10] If man is to be conceived as a morally accountable being at all, it must be presupposed that he understands the moral imperative as binding on him, and consequently recognizes this imperative as an incentive to action. But if man is not a morally accountable being at all, then he cannot be an *evil* being. Man's predisposition to personality, his moral accountabiliy, is a condition for the possibility of being good or evil, and his possession of it cannot render him actually good or evil. In a similar way, evil in man cannot consist in any "natural impulse," in any incentive or inclination to do evil simply for evil's sake. Man's natural impulses and inclinations all arise from a predisposition to good, from the nature of man as a finite living being, and none of them are essentially evil.

Kant is sometimes criticized for rejecting the possibility of an impulse to evil in man, an inclination to rebel against the law or to disobey the law simply for the sake of disobedience.[11] In fact, however, it is not difficult to see that he had extremely sound reasons for rejecting it.* In the first

* Kant does not hold, of course, that *all* forms of rebellion are impossible. If morality has been presented to a man through the arbitrary and despotic will of a real or imagined sovereign, it might not at all be unlikely in Kant's view that this man, feeling his dignity as a person affronted and abused by such a despotism would develop a strong natural inclination to disobey the commands of this sovereign and to rebel against them. From a Kantian point of view, the representation of duties as positive commands of God rather than as the commands of our own autonomous reason may even have fostered such a rebellion. An irrational morality may indeed bring with it "a secret hatred for virtue's command" (*TL* 485g 159e; *Rel* 24ng 19ne). What Kant denies is that man, as a rational creature, can have a natural inclination simply to be *irrational*. He may rebel against his family, against society, and even against God (a God falsely conceived as an arbitrary despot), but he cannot rebel against *himself* as a rational being. Silber claims that "Kant's insistence to the contrary, man's free power to reject the law in defiance is an ineradicable fact of human experience" (Silber, "The Ethical Significance of Kant's *Religion*," cxxix). This, however, is a fallacy endemic to philosophical criticism: the supposition that by pointing to "facts" (which no one disputes)

place, an inclination of this kind could not in itself be regarded as morally evil at all, since it would be derived from
nature rather than from man's use of his freedom, and he
could not be held morally responsible for it. But, more important, to admit an inclination of this kind would be tantamount
to denying that man is capable of rational action at all, either
good or evil. As we have just seen, the incentives of moral reason and inclination can be contained in the same maxim. For
Kant, these incentives are in principle compatible with one another, and may be subordinated one to the other in a self-consistent maxim of action. The good man makes it a rule to do
his duty, and to pursue the satisfaction of inclination only
when this is compatible with the performance of duty. The
evil man, on the contrary, seeks first his own happiness, but in
Kant's view does do his duty when it is compatible with this
end (although, since he is not motivated unconditionally by
the legislative form of his maxim, his volition has only legal
and not moral worth). But the good man does not cease to
have natural needs and inclinations, nor does the evil man
cease to understand his moral obligation and to recognize it as
an incentive for action. Both the good and the evil man form
rational principles for their volition, for both are finite rational agents. If we assume, however, that men are affected by

---

that one can give a philosophical justification of the manner in which
one has expressed the facts. Also puzzling is Silber's contention that
in Kant's view an evil man must be a "weak personality," from which
he infers that because certain evil men in fact and fiction (Hitler,
Napoleon, Ahab) were not weak personalities, Kant's view must be
wrong. Surely a man who, disregarding his duty and denying his
natural feelings of sympathy and humanity, consistently follows the
maxim of pursuing his own happiness to the detriment of others—
surely such a person is not what we would call a "weak" personality.
And yet precisely this is described by Kant as the "wickedness" or
"corruption" which, along with the "weaker" vices of "frailty" and
"impurity," the nature of man exhibits (*Rel* 29fg 24fe).

an inclination to do evil simply for evil's sake, then no self-consistent rational principles of volition—good or evil—are possible for them. I can make it my maxim to pursue happiness on the condition that I do my duty or to do my duty on the condition that it is consistent with the pursuit of my happiness; but I cannot consistently make it my principle to "obey the law on the condition that I disobey it" or to "disobey the law on the condition that I obey it." I cannot consistently incorporate both the incentive of moral reason and the incentive to do evil for evil's sake into the *same* maxim. Hence, if man were to have an inclination to do evil for evil's sake, he could frame no self-consistent maxims of any kind, and could not be a finite rational agent at all. To suppose an inclination of this kind would indeed be to divide man into two "irreconcilable natures," to assume a manichaean view of human nature.

Man is not, then, a merely *animal* being, devoid of moral reason; nor is he a *devilish* being, who possesses incentives to violate rather than to obey the moral law.[12] He is a finite but rational and moral being, aware of his moral obligations, and capable rationally and consistently both of obeying and of disobeying the moral command. Radical evil is not to be sought in man's predispositions, in the moral capacities of man as a finite rational being, but must, if it exists at all, be found in man's use of his capacities through his power of free choice, his *Willkür*. It is only in a very special sense, then, that we may call man good or evil "by nature." It can never be possible to infer from the *concept* of human nature as such that man is either good or evil.[13] Nor can human "nature" in this case be taken in the sense opposed to "freedom," for it is precisely in man's use of his freedom that his goodness or evil must lie. By "human nature," says Kant, we here intend only the subjective ground of the exercise (under moral laws) of man's freedom in general; a ground—whatever its character—which is the necessary antecedent of every act apparent to the senses.[14]

"Human nature," then, will not in this sense be opposed to freedom, but rather designates a "property (*Beschaffenheit*) of the will (*Willkür*)" itself.[15] Kant also refers to "human nature" in this sense as "the ultimate subjective ground for the adoption of maxims." [16] We must be clear as to the meaning of this formula if we are to understand what Kant means when he says that man is evil "by nature."

By calling man's moral nature a "subjective" ground, Kant is emphasizing the fact that he is concerned with man's character as a free subject, with the human power of choice or will (*Willkür*) and its maxims, the "principles on which the subject acts." He is not concerned with the moral nature of man as derived merely from the *concept* of man (man could not in this sense be called either good or evil) but with the character exhibited by the human will in the actual and subjective use of its freedom. As a "subjective ground," man's moral nature is something "acquired" by man, something which man has "brought upon himself." [17] "Nature," says Kant, "is not to bear the blame (if it is evil) or take the credit (if it is good) but man himself is its author." [18]

Man's moral nature, furthermore, is thought of by Kant as a "ground for the adoption of maxims." Kant tries to clarify what he means here by calling this ground a "propensity [*Hang*] to evil," a "subjective ground of the possibility of an inclination. . . . so far as mankind in general is liable to it." [19] This explanation, however, may do more to confuse than to clarify. For if "inclination" is taken to mean an incentive arising from man's predisposition to animality, then it would be a contradiction to speak of a "subjective ground" of its possibility. Such a "subjective ground," as we have just seen, would consist in the free adoption of a maxim of finite rational volition; but this itself, in turn, would already presuppose a will affected by the incentives of inclination. Hence there can be no "subjective" ground for these incentives themselves. Further, a "propensity to evil" would seem, on this account, to mean the subjective ground for an inclination *to do evil;* and this, as we have seen, Kant has ruled out.

What, then, can Kant mean when he describes a "propensity to evil" as a "subjective ground for the possibility of an inclination?" The only plausible explanation seems to be the following: Kant usually uses the term "inclination" (*Neigung*) to refer to a natural incentive in all finite rational volition, an incentive derived from man's predisposition to animality. But he also uses it on occasion to refer to a kind of *volition,* namely, volition motivated by such an incentive.[20] If we take him to be using "inclination" in the second of these two senses, then the phrase "subjective ground of the possibility of an inclination" would mean: the property of the human will which makes it possible for this will to invert, in accordance with a rule or maxim, the rational and moral order of its incentives, to prefer the incentives of inclination to those of duty, and hence to do *evil.* Kant seems to confirm this interpretation when he says:

Here, however, we are speaking only of a propensity to genuine, that is, moral evil; for since such evil is possible only as a determination of the will, and since the will can be appraised as good or evil only by means of its maxims, this propensity to evil must consist in *the subjective ground of the possibility of deviation of maxims from the moral law.*[21]

And, finally, Kant calls this subjective ground "ultimate" or "primary" (*erste*). By this, he seems to mean two things.

First, this ground is "posited as the ground antecedent to every use of freedom in experience." [22] Since it is antecedent to all the subject's acts in time, Kant calls it "innate" (*angeboren*).[23] The subjective ground is the source, in the subject's moral character, of all his particular acts. Hence Kant describes it at times as the subject's "highest maxim" (*oberste Maxime*), the "underlying common ground, itself a maxim, of all particular . . . maxims." [24] Because this ultimate subjective ground of man's moral character is expressible as a good or evil maxim, an ultimate subjective *principle*, Kant speaks of the radical evil in human nature as an "evil principle." [25] A particular evil act, in Kant's view, is possible only through the adoption of an evil maxim. Thus the propensity to evil in man does not refer to the inversion of the moral incentives of particular acts; it refers to the human propensity to adopt *maxims* which invert these incentives. The propensity to evil is thus a propensity to follow an evil principle, to adopt a maxim or policy of evildoing, and hence to have an evil will.

This subjective ground or highest maxim is also "ultimate" for Kant in the sense that every man can be said to have it; it can be "predicated of man as a species" (though it is not derived from the concept of man as a species).[26] If this subjective ground is evil, the evil is "radical" in the sense that it lies at the "root" of man's character as a free being, and is "woven into human nature." [27] And since it lies at the ground of all man's free action in time, this subjective ground conditions man's volition in general. It is therefore "inextirpable by human powers" and belongs essentially to the freedom of every man.[28]

Kant distinguishes three "stages" (*Stufen*) in which a propensity to *evil* might exhibit itself.[29] The lowest of these is the "frailty" of the human will in its "observance of adopted maxims." A man may "resolve" or "intend" to do good, but succumb to temptation. Here Kant quotes the words of St. Paul: "The good that I would, I do not" (Rom 7:15). In this stage, however, the agent's evil *maxim*, his policy of inverting the moral order of incentives, does not show itself plainly. Still, the agent's "deviation" from his good maxim requires the positive adoption of an evil maxim for which he is responsible. The second stage of evil is the "impurity" of the human will, the confusion of incentives of duty with those of inclination, and the perpetration of a self-deception, a belief that volition is motivated by the law when in fact it is not. Here too, the adoption of evil maxims has been disguised, this time by the pretense that an evil maxim (a maxim whose adoption is motivated by inclination) is really a *good* maxim, motivated by moral reason. The third and highest degree of evil is "wickedness" or "corruption," the *conscious* neglect of the incentives of duty in favor of those of inclination, and the *deliberate* adoption of the inversion of the moral order of these incentives into the maxim of action. It is in this stage that evil shows its character most clearly, and it is evils of this stage ("acts done with consciousness of their evil" [30]) that Kant will employ in support of the thesis of radical evil in human nature.

The concept of radical evil shows a great similarity to Kant's conception of a "passion" (*Leidenschaft*). Passion for Kant is a form of desire which "presupposes a maxim of the subject, to act from an end given him by inclination." [31] A passion, then, is an "inclination" in the same sense that the propensity to evil is a "ground for the possibility of an inclination." [32] A passion, further, is a desire "which can be mastered by the subject's reason with difficulty or not at all." [33] Both passion and the propensity to evil are deliberate and even "rational" choices to oppose reason itself, and to subvert it in favor of the incentives of inclination. Both use the natural incentives of inclination "contrary to their ends" [34] by deliberately inverting the rational order of the will's incentives. It is this rational opposition to moral reason itself which Kant calls "perversity of heart," the third and highest stage in which man may exhibit a propensity to evil.

The Critique of Man's Moral Nature

We now have a fairly clear idea what "radical evil in human nature" must be, if there is to be such a thing at all. But we have not yet seen whether man is *by nature* good or evil, or indeed whether it is possible for us to say that he is either. Kant attempts to answer these questions through an investigation which is *critical* in character, in that it aims at human self-knowledge obtained systematically by means of an examination of the "sources, extent and limits" of human capacities. At the same time, however, this must be a critical investigation *sui generis;* for by inquiring after the limits of man's moral capacities in virtue of which man is said to be "by nature evil," we are no longer inquiring simply into the extent and limits of those capacities which make man's moral nature possible. We are asking instead about the extent and limits of man's own *use* of capacities which, as a finite rational being, he is already presumed to have. To say that man is evil is to say that, having the capacity to be good, he is *nonetheless* evil. And to say that he has a propensity to evil is to say that, having the incentives of moral reason in virtue of a natural predisposition, he nonetheless limits his capacity for good by his tendency to prefer the incentives of inclination to those of moral reason.

When we turn to the consideration of a critical inquiry

into man's moral nature, we are immediately confronted by a possible objection. We might question, in the first place, whether "the moral nature of man" is even a coherent concept. If the human will is truly free and completely spontaneous, as Kant maintains, how is it possible for it to be limited "by nature," to possess an "innate propensity" of any kind? Such a "propensity" or "nature" would seem to be contrary to Kant's libertarianism and to be ruled out in principle by his radical concept of the spontaneity of the human will. Kant himself does not consider an objection of this kind in the *Religion,* but I think it is quite clear what his answer to it would be. For Kant moral good or evil does not attach primarily to objects, or acts, but to maxims, and even more fundamentally to the persons whose maxims they are. In order to regard persons as responsible agents, we must presuppose that they are free, that they themselves are the spontaneous authors of the maxims of their acts. But it is equally necessary to suppose that an agent's discreet actions and his particular maxims must have in his spontaneity a common ground or source, in the form of the agent's own "highest maxim," the subjective ground of the adoption of all his maxims. Only through a definite and determinate *moral character* can an agent be the author of his own acts. Kant does not, therefore, make the mistake common to libertarians of equating freedom or spontaneity with indeterminacy. A free being is not something indeterminate, something possessing no fixed character, but is rather something which *determines itself* spontaneously in accordance with its own character. A free act *requires* a subjective principle or maxim in accordance with which an agent determines himself, just as the concept of freedom generally requires a moral law governing it in order to be a coherent concept at all.[35]

Kant, along with Hume, sees that the moral accountability

of a man depends on his possession of a fixed character or disposition. In Hume's words:

Actions are, by their very nature, temporary and perishing; and where they proceed not from some cause in the characters and dispositions of the person who performed them, they infix not themselves upon him, and can neither redound to his honour if good, nor infamy if evil.[36]

Kant and Hume differ here only concerning the account they give of the moral characters and dispositions of men, and not on their existence. Hume regarded the human moral character as a pattern of events and actions within the sensible order of causes and effects, and hence for him "liberty" could mean only indeterminacy. For Kant, however, the possession of a moral character by an agent is required by the structure of finite rational volition itself, and belongs to the agent's own spontaneity in the intelligible world, rather than to the sensible order of cause and effect. Hence a fixed moral character in human freedom, a "moral nature of man," is far from being ruled out by Kant's conception of the spontaneity of the human will.

To show that a good or evil character applies universally to all men, that it is "entwined with and, as it were, rooted in humanity itself," [37] however, is quite a different matter. And in asking for Kant's justification of this claim, we enter directly upon Kant's critical investigation of man's nature. Kant has made it abundantly clear that we cannot hope to demonstrate by abstract reasoning that man is by nature evil; if we are to be able to predicate evil of the human species, or indeed of any particular person, we must somehow base this predication on what we can observe of the actions of men through experience. But, indeed, though we may be able to judge with reasonable certainty the moral characters of many particular acts (especially of evil ones), we cannot pretend to judge the

222 KANT'S MORAL RELIGION

highest maxim of any man with any assurance.[38] "The depths of the human heart," says Kant, "are unfathomable." But according to Kant it *is*

> possible *a priori* to infer from several acts done with consciousness of their evil, or from one such act, an underlying evil maxim; and further, from this maxim to infer the presence in the agent of an underlying common ground, itself a maxim, of all particular morally-evil maxims.[39]

Now from this passage, and others like it,[40] we might be tempted to think that Kant means to infer that because a person sometimes knowingly commits evil actions, the *highest maxim* of such a person is necessarily evil, and therefore the person himself is essentially evil. But surely this cannot be what Kant means. For in this case it would also seem proper to infer that because a person had in some case performed a morally good action, his highest maxim must be morally good; but in this case, it would be proper to infer that because a person performs both good actions and evil actions (which all, or nearly all, men certainly do in the course of a lifetime) the highest maxim of such a person is both good and evil, which is a contradiction. Kant does seem at times to be holding the position that the radical evil in man's nature "unfits him for all good," [41] renders it impossible for him ever to do any good. Such a view, however, would not only involve insuperable difficulties of its own for his moral theory, but it would also contradict his assertions that man may "reverse the highest ground of his maxims" and adopt a new disposition to progress which counteracts and may even "overcome" or "get the upper hand" over the evil principle in his nature.[42]

These difficulties can be most easily solved, I think, if we return to Kant's argument itself, and examine it on its own merits. Suppose I observe that some person, that I myself for example, have knowingly committed an evil act or a number of evil acts. Now what might I be entitled to infer about my own moral character, the "ultimate subjective ground of my adoption of maxims," from such an observation? Clearly I cannot infer that because some of my maxims are evil, all of them must be evil. But since it is my character, my free use of my will, which is responsible for the evil that I observe, I may certainly trace this evil to its root in my character. Because I have in fact adopted evil maxims I may legitimately infer that my moral character is such that I am *liable* to the adoption of evil maxims. I may legitimately say that my character contains a "formal ground for all unlawful conduct" which I in fact exhibit, that my will contains a "propensity to evil" consisting in a "subjective ground of the possibility of deviation of maxims from the moral law," a "general subjective ground of the adoption of transgression into my maxim." [43]

Kant does not show, then, that men are *incapable* of good, or that the moral character of every man is necessarily evil. We do indeed know that the character of each man, his highest maxim, must be either good or evil; but no man can ever say with certainty—even in his own case—whether this maxim is one or the other.[44] From the evil actions of men we observe, we cannot say that man is incapable of good, but we can say that he is incapable of the perfection of holiness, of an "unchanging purity of will" which "makes all transgression utterly impossible." [45] We do not know whether our highest maxim itself is good or evil, but we do know from the evil we do that our moral nature contains a "propensity to evil." And since this propensity is one for which we ourselves are culpable, we could not have derived its existence merely from the finitude of human nature. The *moral* imperfections of our volition are limitations we impose upon ourselves, limitations for which we ourselves are responsible, and which must be inferred from our *use* of our freedom, and not merely from the concept of finite rational volition in general.

Everyone who reflects on his actions morally, in Kant's view, is bound to notice that he himself, through his own moral failures, exhibits a propensity to evil. But Kant now wants to make the further claim that "we may presuppose evil to be subjectively necessary to all men, even to the best," and that the evil we find in ourselves and others is "woven into" human nature, "entwined with and, as it were, rooted in humanity itself." [46] Kant's language at this point might lead us to think that he is seeking some sort of explanation for the evil of the individual's will by tracing it to a "propensity" characteristic of his species. But this is definitely not the case. Every evil action, says Kant, "must be regarded as though the individual had fallen into it directly from a state of innocence." [47] The individual himself has brought his propensity to evil upon himself by his own choice, and manifests this choice in each evil act. Kant thus anticipates Kierkegaard's statement that "with the first sin came sin into the world. Exactly in the same way this is true of every subsequent first sin of man, that with it sin comes into the world." [48]

Man's propensity to evil, because it is the propensity of a *free* will, has no explanation in anything other than the spontaneous exercise by this will of its freedom. We cannot "*explain* the contingent existence" of this propensity by referring it to anything but human freedom itself, and we cannot ever pretend to *prove* that a propensity to evil is necessary to all men.[49] Yet we should not take this fact to weaken in any way the assertion that all men are evil, and evil by nature. If it cannot be *proved* that I am evil by nature, this does not make me any less evil than I have shown myself to be. Instead, this fact should make me realize all the more clearly that this evil "must be set down in our account," that the only "explanation" for the evil I do should be sought by recalling that I myself am *responsible* for it.[50] Kant's position is again in essential agreement with that of Kierkegaard, who says:

If men have so often wasted the time of dogmatics and ethics, and their own time, by pondering about what would have happened in case Adam had not sinned, this merely shows that they have brought with them an incorrect mood and an incorrect concept. To the innocent man it can never occur to ask such a question, but the guilty man sins when he asks it; for with his aesthetic curiosity he would like to obscure the fact that he himself has brought guilt into the world, has himself lost innocence by his guilt.[51]

When Kant says that man is evil "by nature," he does not mean to *explain* evil, but only to point out the *universality* of evil in man. Kant thus looks for evidence supporting the claim that all men, without exception, exhibit a propensity to evil; and he finds such evidence in "the multitude of crying examples which experience of the actions of men puts before our eyes." [52] But Kant does not merely exhort us to recognize and condemn the many evils which we see men commit. His argument is rather designed to show the *universality* of evil, to show that all men, despite the many differences between them, exhibit alike a radical propensity to do evil. Kant is first mindful of Rousseau's claim that primitive man, man "in the state of nature," is good. So he first considers men in an uncivilized condition, and argues that the cruelty and brutality of the primitive peoples of America and the Pacific Islands give little grounds for thinking of such men as pure or noble. Kant then considers the alternative hypothesis, that men in a more advanced state of civilization "in which their predispositions can more completely develop" are truer examples of moral goodness in man.[53] He notes with sad irony the even more in-

sidious vices of hypocrisy, ingratitude, envy, and the lust for
power and for superiority over his fellow men that characterize man in the civilized state. And he turns his attention, as if
just for good measure, to the conduct of men in the relation
of civil states to one another. In war, "that scourge of human-
kind," men seem to exhibit both the worst hypocrisy of civilization and the unmitigated barbarism of the worst savages.[54]
Thus, in spite of the differing conditions in which we find
man, a propensity to evil, to lie, to kill his fellows, or to en-
slave and exploit them, to adopt any course of action which
leads to the satisfaction of personal wishes, is always characteristic of him. And hence Kant concludes that each of us has
grounds for saying, in the words of Romans 3:9: "They are all
under sin,—there is none righteous, no, not one." [55]

Moral Progress and Perfection

The unconditioned component of the highest good is the
moral perfection of finite rational beings. It is each man's duty
to strive for the attainment of this perfection in himself, and
to do what he can to promote it in others as well. We noted
in Chapter 4 that the thesis of radical evil in human nature
offers a serious challenge to the practical possibility of moral
perfection in man, and threatens us with moral despair over
this end. We are now prepared to see how Kant raises this dialectical threat in the *Religion*, and how he uses the thesis of
radical evil to give a more comprehensive statement of the
problems involved in it than he had in his earlier writings.

The thesis of radical evil, says Kant, does not affect moral
"dogmatics," does not soften or in any way alter the *precepts*
which determine what our duties are. The rational command
of morality is unchanged by it. And yet this thesis does have
something to say to moral "discipline" (*Ascetik*), and carries
with it definite implications regarding the manner in which

man can and should set about fulfilling what the law commands of him.[56] The radical evil in human nature therefore
does determine how man may pursue moral perfection, and
contributes significantly to our formulation of the dialectic of
practical reason which threatens the practical possibility of
this end.

The thesis of radical evil, according to Kant, tells us about
the pursuit of moral perfection

that in the moral development of the predisposition to good im-
planted in us, we cannot start from an innocence natural to us,
but must begin with the assumption of a wickedness of the will in
adopting maxims contrary to the original moral predisposition;
and, since this propensity to evil is inextirpable, we must begin
with the incessant counteraction against it.[57]

The radical evil we have brought upon ourselves thus imposes
on us definite conditions under which alone we may pursue
moral perfection. For man as he knows and observes himself
in the world of appearances, says Kant, the "incessant counteraction" against this propensity to evil takes the form of "a
continual progress from bad to better," a "gradual reform of
his senses." [58] In a progression of this kind, a man wins virtue "little by little" through the discipline and limitation of
each of his inclinations.[59] This discipline, however, is not itself *necessarily* a counteraction against the propensity to evil,
but may equally be brought about by reason as prudence:

The immoderate person, for instance, turns to temperance for the
sake of health, the liar to honesty for the sake of reputation, the
unjust man to civic righteousness for the sake of peace or profit,
and so on—all in conformity with the precious principle of
happiness.[60]

The distinction between progress in disciplining inclinations
for the sake of prudence and a genuine moral progress coun-

teracting the propensity to evil does not lie in "virtue's empirical character (*virtus phaenomenon*)." [61] It must rather be
sought, along with the propensity to evil itself, in the subjective ground for the adoption of his maxim, in his supersensible
moral character.

Now insofar as a man observes himself to do evil, he recognizes in his moral character a propensity to evil, a common
ground or principle of evil which makes possible all particular
evil maxims as *his* acts, and from which all such maxims proceed. He cannot conclude from this, of course, that his character is irremediably evil, incapable of any good, but he can
conclude that in order to be morally good or to become so, he
must *break* with the evil he observes in himself by an "incessant counteraction" against the evil propensity in his nature.
The subjective possibility of this break with evil and counteraction against it can as little be *explained* as could the propensity to evil itself. Kant does suggest that divine cooperation
might be necessary for this break with evil to occur; [62] but
here, as in the case of evil, the responsibility for it is, from a
moral point of view, the agent's own. The break with evil and
the development of man's predisposition to good must, however, be presupposed as *possible*, because the law commands it
of us. [63]

Kant now inquires into the subjective conditions for the
possibility of the development of moral good in man. He asks,
as he did in the case of the evil in human action, what must be
true of a man's supersensible moral character if he does in fact
break with evil and develop the predisposition to good within
him? Virtue's empirical character, as we have seen, is always a
gradual reform, a slow progress from bad to better. But goodness of will as it must be found in man's highest maxim, his supersensible moral character, requires not a "change of practices (*Sitten*)," but rather a "change of heart" establishing a

good disposition (*Gesinnung*) as the supreme ground of our maxims.[64] The condition for the possibility of genuine moral progress is therefore not a gradual reform but a "revolution" or "conversion" of our disposition to good.[65] This "conversion" is described by Kant in biblical terms as "a kind of rebirth, as it were a new creation." [66]

Kant's language at this point is both picturesque and inspirational; but if we are not cautious, we may easily be misled by it. Kant is *not* concerned here with giving an account of the manner in which men, in time, *become* good (he has already stated that we do this by "endless progress" and "gradual reform"); he is concerned rather with the character which the supersensible disposition of a man must exhibit, irrespective of time, if he is to *be* a good man. Phrases like "change of heart," "revolution," "conversion," the "transformation of one's cast of mind," all carry with them the strong suggestion of a sudden *temporal* change, as though the break with evil were a conspicuous *moment* in a man's life. This impression is reinforced by Kant's use of biblical phrases such as "old man" and "new man," and by other passages in which Kant definitely appears to be saying that the adoption of a good disposition, the "reversal of the highest ground of a man's maxims," is an event in time.[67] In spite of these passages, however, we should not confuse this "change of heart" with an actual "change" of any kind in time. Kant, indeed, contrasts the gradual moral progress of man in time with the change of heart which is the condition for its possibility. He notes that, because this change of heart can be known only through a gradual temporal reform, we can never be sure that it has taken place.[68] And he emphasizes the "permanence" and "unchangeableness" of this disposition, in contrast to the mutability of the empirical character which human virtue assumes in time.[69] This "unchangeableness," as he makes clear elsewhere,

is due to the fact that the good disposition "is not mutable like
the progression of a phenomenon but is rather something supersensible, and is, consequently, not fluctuating in time." [70]

Kant speaks of this disposition to progress as a "holiness of
maxims," and "establishment of the purity of the law as the
supreme ground of all our maxims." And yet, he points out,
"The man who adopts this purity into his maxim is indeed not
yet holy by reason of this (for there is a great gap between
the maxim and the deed [*That*])." [71] A good disposition, let
us remember, is the subjective condition for the possibility of
the *pursuit* of moral perfection. But man, who has brought on
himself a propensity to evil, can only pursue moral perfection
through moral *progress*, can only seek holiness through a
maxim of steady progress toward it. Thus when Kant speaks
of the good man's highest maxim as "the maxim of holiness
of the disposition," [72] he is not referring to the maxim of a
will which is itself holy, but to a maxim of progress toward
holiness, the maxim of "incessant counteracton" against man's
propensity to evil. So long as man continues to possess a propensity to evil which renders him liable to moral transgression, it is beyond his power to perform the *deed* whereby he
might actually become a holy being. "The maxim of holiness
of the disposition" is therefore only the maxim of constant
moral progress, the principle of adopting particular maxims
ever and ever closer to holiness. A good disposition does not
make a man *holy*, but only makes him *good*. Regarded as the
supersensible ground for a life of moral progress, a good disposition is a kind of "revolution," eternally counteracting and
overcoming the innate propensity to evil through constant
and morally motivated limitation and discipine of those inclinations through which this propensity manifests itself. But
even the best disposition cannot *extirpate* the propensity to

evil, and end man's self-incurred liability to transgression of the moral law.

Thus even the man whose disposition is good, even the best of men, in Kant's view, cannot attain the moral perfection of holiness. And it is this discovery, based on the thesis of radical evil, which gives rise to the first antinomy of practical reason, which we discussed in Chapter 4. The complete moral perfection of the holy will is the unconditioned component of the highest good. If I cannot conceive the attainment of this perfection as a practical possibility, then I commit myself not to make it my end. Hence, if I cannot conceive the practical possibility of such complete moral perfection, I am committed not to obey the moral law. This conclusion, as we have seen, is an *absurdum practicum*, an antinomy of practical reason.

In Chapter 4 we gave some attention to Kant's attempt to resolve this antinomy through the postulate of immortality. We saw that this attempt rested on Kant's assertion that holiness of will is somehow to be "met with" in the endless progress toward it, or in the disposition which is the supersensible ground for such progress. But we saw also that the postulate of immortality could not, by itself, resolve the antinomy facing Kant. This postulate does not explain how it is that, although holiness itself is never attained by man, he may still regard himself as having reached moral perfection through a good disposition or an endless progress toward holiness. The gap between the *disposition* and the *deed* has not been bridged. Kant has not even asked how the disposition to progress toward holiness can substitute for holiness itself. It is not until the *Religion* that Kant asks this question, and attempts in his response to it to complete his account of the dialectic of practical reason and the content of moral faith.

The Postulate of Divine Grace

Kant begins Section One of the second book of the *Religion* with a discussion of the unconditioned component of the highest good, and of man's duty to pursue it. It is our duty, says Kant, to seek the realization of "the ideal of man well-pleasing to God," or of "mankind in its complete moral perfection." [73] And since it is our duty to seek the attainment of this ideal, we must presuppose the possibility of its attainment if we are to avoid an *absurdum practicum:*

We *ought* to conform to it; consequently, we must be *able* to do so. Did we have to prove in advance the possibility of man's conforming to this archetype, as is absolutely essential in the case of concepts of nature . . . we should have to hesitate before allowing even to the moral law the authority of an unconditioned and yet sufficient determining ground of the will.[74]

But, as the thesis of radical evil has shown, the realization of the ideal of moral perfection in an entire course of life is not possible for man. Such a course of life, says Kant, cannot even be put before us as an *example* for our emulation, since the most we can attain is a *progress* toward it.[75]

Moral perfection, says Kant, must therefore be "posited" (*gesetzt*) in the holiness of a man's *disposition*.[76] A disposition to constant progress *toward* holiness in this sense "accords" (*übereinstimmt*) with the ideal of holiness.[77] But even this moral ideal of a holy disposition is not identical with the supreme righteousness (*Gerechtigkeit*) of moral perfection in *deed*, since the latter "would have to consist in a course of life completely and faultlessly harmonious with that disposition." [78] Hence, says Kant, when we posit moral perfection in the goodness of man's disposition, we must recognize that the righteousness thereby attained is "a righteousness not our own."

And yet an appropriation [*Zueignung*] of this righteousness for the sake of our own disposition must be possible when our own disposition is made at one with that of the archetype, although the greatest difficulties will stand in the way of our rendering this appropriation comprehensible [*begreiflich*].[79]

Kant next considers three such "difficulties" and attempts through their solution to produce a "deduction of the idea of a *justification* [*Rechtfertigung*] of an individual who is indeed guilty, but who has changed his disposition into one well-pleasing to God." [80] This attempt, however, is far from satisfactory, and Kant's inquiry seems to be directed largely toward matters not directly relevant to the question at hand. The question before us, it would seem, concerns the nature and possibility of an "appropriation of a righteousness not our own" which may in some manner compensate for the moral deficiencies due to the radical evil in man's nature. Kant holds that this appropriation can occur when a man's disposition accords with the ideal of holiness, and indeed that it *must* be presupposed to occur if an *absurdum practicum* is to be avoided. But *how* are we to form a conception of it, and hence to conceive the practical possibility of the unconditioned component of the highest good? This is the question which we must answer. That Kant's discussion of the three "difficulties" at this point does *not* answer it can be seen by briefly examining this discussion itself.

Kant states the first difficulty thus: "How can a disposition count for the deed itself, when the deed is *always* (not in general, but at each instant of time) defective?" At first glance, this seems to be just the question we want Kant to answer for us. But on closer examination, it is apparent that neither this question nor Kant's answer to it show any advance over his treatment of the first antinomy in the second critique. For, as closer inspection of the question itself shows, Kant has already *assumed* that, on account of man's good disposition, his deed is *not* defective *"überhaupt,"* but is only defective "at each instant of time." He has already assumed, that is to say, that the disposition counts for the deed and justifies it, but does not tell us how this is to be conceived of. His answer to this difficulty consists only in repeating the claim of the second critique that God, "who knows the heart, through a purely intellectual intuition," regards man as justified on account of his supersensible disposition.

Kant's second difficulty concerns "moral happiness" (*moralische Glückseligkeit*), our assurance of "the reality and constancy of a disposition which ever progresses in goodness." It is indeed difficult even to see how this discussion is relevant to the problem of the "appropriation of righteousness" by the man of good disposition. It has been assumed already that the individual in question has effected a change of heart in himself, broken with evil and set himself on the road toward good. His disposition is *assumed* to be good. To inquire into the manner and degree of assurance a man may have that his disposition is in fact a good one can in no way help us to understand how this disposition effects an "appropriation of righteousness not his own" for the purpose of conceiving the practical possibility of moral perfection.

The third and "apparently greatest" difficulty, says Kant, is this: "Whatever a man may have done in the way of adopting a good disposition, . . . *he nevertheless started from evil*, and this guilt he may by no possibility wipe out." Once again, Kant seems to be asking the right question. But he does not ask, as we would expect and hope, how the guilty individual becomes *justified*, but rather asks how his justification can be reconciled with the fact that "before Supreme Justice . . . no one who is deserving of punishment may ever go unpunished." This question, in spite of Kant's ingenious discussion of it, is not to the point. For we are concerned here not with whether evil is punished but with whether and how men may be *justified*. The criminal remains just as blameworthy for his crime *after* he has been punished for it as he was before. Justice may, indeed, have been satisfied by his punishment, but this punishment has not in the least lessened his guilt for the crime he has committed. In the same say, when Kant shows that man's justification does not violate the demand of justice that evil should always be punished, this does nothing to show how this justification itself takes place.

In treating of this third difficulty, however, Kant does not in fact restrict himself to the (essentially irrelevant) question of punishment for man's guilt. Or, more precisely, he does not restrict his theory of "vicarious atonement" (*stellvertretende Genugthuung*) to the solution of this difficulty, but applies it also in another way which *is* crucial for his solution to the problem of man's justification and in the highest degree relevant to it. Alongside Kant's statements that the "new man" (the disposition to progress) takes upon himself the sufferings and punishments due to the "old man" (the propensity to evil) and bears his guilt vicariously, we find also the statement that this disposition *"takes the place of the deed* in its perfection (vertritt . . . *die Stelle der That in ihrer Vollendung*)," and that the "new man" as *advocate* makes it possible for men to hope to appear before their judge as justified (*gerechtfertigt*).[81] "Holy Scripture," says Kant,

sets forth this intelligible moral relationship in the form of a narrative, in which two principles in man, as opposed to one another as heaven and hell, are represented as persons outside him; who

not only pit their strength against each other but also seek (the
one as man's accuser, the other as his advocate) to establish their
claims *legally* as though before a supreme judge.[82]

After speaking of man's holy disposition as his "advocate,"
and as "standing in the place" of his imperfect deed, Kant
goes on to make the following remarkable observation:

Here, then, is that surplus,—the need for which was noted pre-
viously—over the merit from good works, and it is itself a merit
reckoned to us *by grace*. That what in our earthly life . . . is
ever only a *becoming* (namely, becoming a man well-pleasing to
God) should be reckoned to us as if we were already in full possession of it—to this we really have no legal claim
[*Rechtanspruch*] . . . and so the accuser in us would be more
likely to propose a judgment of condemnation. Thus the verdict
[*Urtheilspruch*] is always one of grace alone, but fully in accord
with eternal righteousness, if we are released from all liability [for
the sake of this goodness in faith]; for this verdict is based upon
an atonement (an atonement which consists for us only in the
idea of an improved disposition, known only to God).[83]

Man's appropriation of righteousness, therefore, is in Kant's
view a merit (*Verdienst*) which God reckons to us *by grace*
for the sake of the disposition to good which man himself has
adopted. To this verdict, says Kant, man has no legal claim
"but only a receptivity [*Empfänglichkeit*] . . . ; and a supe-
rior's decree [*Rathschluss*] conferring a good for which the
subordinate possesses nothing but the (moral) receptivity is
called *grace* [*Gnade*]." [84] Thus it is only through faith in divine grace that it is possible for man to conceive of an appropriation of "a righteousness not his own," and of the practical
possibility of moral perfection. God's grace must be presupposed if an *absurdum practicum* is to be avoided as regards the
unconditioned component of the highest good.

It has been formidably argued by Silber, however, that the

supposition of grace is not open to Kant and that it contradicts the most fundamental tenets of his moral theory.[85] Kant holds, according to Silber, that man's freedom is "absolute," that "the moral individual makes himself into whatever he is from a moral standpoint. . . . If his acts can be imputed to him, they must follow from the exercise of his own freedom." "It follows from this conception of freedom," says Silber, that

no man can be good for another. Kant rejected the doctrine of vicarious atonement because it runs counter to the nature of freedom. No matter how good another person is, his excess of goodness (were such an excess possible) would in no way remove another person's lack of goodness or redeem his evil.[86]

Kant does say, it is true, that no man's guilt "may be discharged by another person, so far as we can judge according to our human reason," and that "as far as reason can see, . . . this contradicts spontaneity"; but he was nonetheless very far from rejecting the doctrine of vicarious atonement.[87] Indeed, he says that it is "a mystery revealed to us through our reason" that God must have some means of "supplementing, out of the fullness of his own holiness, man's lack of requisite qualifications therefor." This doctrine, he admits, is

hard to reconcile with reason, since that which is to be accredited to us . . . must take place not through foreign influence but solely through the best use of our own powers. And yet the impossibility thereof . . . cannot really be proved, because freedom itself . . . remains, as regards its possibility, just as incomprehensible to us as is the supernatural factor which we would like to regard as a supplement to the spontaneous but deficient determination of freedom.[88]

Silber's objection at this point is similar in many way to the difficulty raised by Hegel in connection with faith in God as

a moral world-ruler. Kant could not, as we saw above, reconcile God's creation of a good world with man's free purposive
volition in pursuit of the highest good. But since *both* God's
creative production of the world and man's freedom are transcendent ideas, it is idle speculation to ask how, or even
whether, they can be compatible with each other. Atonement,
like "the creation of man to a free use of his powers," involves a relation between two transcendent ideas, a relation
that is unknown, unknowable, and even incomprehensible to
us. "Of this," says Kant, "God has revealed to us nothing and
can reveal nothing since we would not *understand* it." [89]

This dismissal of the speculative problem involved in divine
grace, however, does not really serve to answer Silber's
strongest objections, which are not theoretical but moral in
nature. For whether we take divine grace to consist in God's
cooperation with man's efforts, or merely in a justifying "verdict" (which, since they are both said to be done for the sake
of his disposition to good, might in fact be regarded as two
ways of describing one and the same thing), we still must
consider the *justice* of God's act of cooperation and of his justifying verdict. "Even God," says Silber, "cannot help the
guilty individual without violating the moral law." [90] To
offer grace, God would have to "decide to qualify the moral
requirements of the law, or fail to hold the absolutely free
being responsible for his freedom." Since his propensity to
evil is brought upon man by his own free act, not even a disposition to good can justify him so long as this propensity remains. "Kant tries to reassure himself," Silber notes, by saying
that grace "of course implies that the individual has done all
he can. But if the individual has done all he can, he does not
need grace. And if he has not, even Kant agrees he should not
get it." [91]

Silber sees no solution to the problem facing Kant at this

point short of a complete revision of his ethics, and in particular an elimination of the "absolute" conception of freedom, to which Silber expresses an especial aversion. It might be worth while, however, to see whether a less radical solution to Kant's problem might be discovered, one more in keeping with his own doctrines and with the spirit of the critical philosophy as a whole. It certainly must be conceded that there is much in Kant's own writings which seems to support Silber's conclusions, and that Kant's attempt to resolve the problem of justification in the *Religion* is not nearly as decisive or as clear as we would like it to be. Still, I believe that a solution to Kant's problem can be found within the scope of the critical philosophy, and that it does consist in precisely the doctrine of grace enunciated—albeit unclearly—in the *Religion.*

Throughout his writings, Kant lays emphasis on the strictness of the moral law, and its independence of private human wishes and weaknesses; in several places, he remarks that a "pardoning" or "beneficent" judge, one who judges leniently and not according to the law, is a contradiction in terms.[92] Kant is always wary of the tendency in men to rely on God's mercy, and to use this as an excuse for not doing what they can to improve themselves.[93] In the *Religion,* he takes special pains to dissociate himself from doctrines of grace which "reduce man to a state of sighing moral passivity in which nothing great or good is undertaken and everything expected from the mere wishing for it." [94] Kant's *rhetoric* concerning the "sternness" of the law and the "inexorability" of divine justice is strong indeed, but the philosophical implications of this rhetoric are not at all clear. Silber says that "Kant could see clearly the incompatability of forgiveness" with his moral philosophy.[95] But this is precisely what Kant did not "see." Throughout the *Religion* he maintains *both* that the man of good disposition may put his trust in God's grace, *and* that this grace is "fully in accord with eternal justice," that man may receive grace only if he possesses the moral "receptivity" for it.[96]

What *is* clear from Kant's rhetoric about the strictness and inexorability of divine justice is that for him God's grace must be something *rational*, something in which we trust rationally, and for the sake of rational morality. Forgiveness cannot be something "outside" morality, or something "higher than" it. No theory of divine grace can be adequate which, like that of Kierkegaard, represents our faith in forgiveness as *irrational*, as an "offense" to reason, or a "placing of the individual higher than the universal." [97] Even less could Kant accept the sentimental moral confusion of Feuerbach, when he says:

Only the love which has flesh and blood can absolve from the sins which flesh and blood commit. A merely moral being cannot forgive what is contrary to the law of morality. . . . The moral judge, who does not infuse human blood into his judgment judges the sinner relentlessly, inexorably. . . . The negation or annulling of sin is the negation of abstract moral rectitude,—the positing of love, mercy, sensibility. Mercy is the *Rechtsgefühl der Sinnlichkeit*.[98]

Feuerbach's view, of course, is immediately more attractive than Kant's apparently stern moralism; Feuerbach appeals to the vague and noble humane sentiments which all of us feel, to our compassion, our love of man, our common human reasonableness. But Kant does not reject humanity, sympathy, compassion, or mercy any more than Feuerbach does. He regards a forgiving disposition, along with beneficence and righteousness, as a morally good quality in man's nature and holds that a "conciliatory spirit" (*Versöhnlichkeit*) is a duty of virtue for all men.[99] Kant rejects this sentimentalist view of forgiveness because it fails to give forgiveness any rational or moral foundation, because in spite of its immediate moral appeal to us, this view is unable to distinguish forgiveness from simple immorality and inhumanity, from avarice, murder, or deceit. But the mercy, humanity, and compassion to which Feuerbach appeals in us only have their appeal because we recognize that it is altogether *right* and *good* that men should be forgiven, that forgiveness accords with true morality, and that reason itself is on the side of mercy rather than of "abstract moral rectitude." It is only because an unforgiving morality is a *false* morality that we accord to mercy the respect we do. And it is only a forgiveness which is compatible with the moral law which can command this respect.

Divine grace, then, cannot be just *any* verdict of acquittal, but must be a verdict rendered in accordance with a definite moral standard or rule. Kant's task, then, must be that of distinguishing divine grace from an immoral leniency by exhibiting its moral structure. If the discussions of grace in the *Religion* are approached with this task in mind, it is not difficult to discern a moral account of God's justifying verdict. "With all our strength," says Kant,

we must strive after the holy disposition of a course of life well-pleasing to God, in order to believe that the love of God toward man (already assured us through reason), so far as man does endeavor with all his power to do the will of God, will make good, in consideration of his upright disposition, the deficiency of the deed, whatever this deficiency may be.[100]

From this passage, along with what we have already noted about grace, it is evident that man makes himself morally "receptive" to grace by becoming good "insofar as it is in his power" to do so (*so viel in seinem Vermögen ist*).[101] No man, of course, can himself ever be certain that he has done all in his power, but this will be known to God, who intuits the supersensible *disposition* which grounds his sensible deed. For the sake of this disposition (*um jenes Guten im Glauben willen*), God complements man's moral efforts with His justifying verdict of grace.[102] Man has no "legal claim" to this justifying verdict, but it is nonetheless a moral and a just verdict, since it is based on his disposition, on "something *real* which is of itself well-pleasing to God." [103] Man justifies *himself* insofar as he does everything in his power to become good; but God, for the sake of man's disposition to holiness, forgives him the evil which it is not in his power to undo, and by His justifying verdict renders this disposition equivalent to that moral perfection which is the unconditioned component of the highest good.

It is just this sort of account, however, which fails to satisfy Silber. He argues that since for Kant human freedom is "absolute," man is responsible for *all* the evil he does. Moral good and evil are equally in man's power to do or not to do, since both are equally products of his "absolute" freedom. If man truly did everything in his power to avoid evil, he would not commit it at all, and would not need grace. But if he has not done all in his power, even Kant agrees that he ought not to receive God's aid or forgiveness. "Following Kantian principles," says Silber, "forgiveness is a moral outrage." [104]

Silber is certainly correct in maintaining that for Kant all of man's guilt follows from the exercise of freedom, and that man is responsible for every use he makes of his freedom. But from this alone it certainly does not follow that no human guilt may be forgiven. Indeed, if man were not *responsible* for his misdeeds, they would not even be in need of *forgiveness*. Silber seems, at points, to confuse the *forgiveness* of a deed with the giving and accepting of an *excuse* for it, or even with declining the *responsibility* for it.[105] But these concepts are very different. If someone offered to "forgive"

me for something for which I am not responsible, I would not
be thankful but indignant. For in offering me "forgiveness"
such a person would imply that I *am* responsible for the thing
in question, and imply also that I am *blameworthy* for it. In
asking for forgiveness, I *admit* my responsibility and my guilt
for the deed in question, but *ask* that this guilt be lifted from
me, that the evil I have done not be held against me. Forgiveness does not excuse evil; it justifies the agent in spite of his
evil.

Neither does it follow that because man's guilt is due to his
exercise of freedom it is within his power, absolutely and in
every respect, to avoid guilt. No matter how "absolute" our
conception of freedom, for example, we cannot reasonably
say of our *past* misdeeds that it is now within our power to
avoid having done them. If yesterday I gave my dog a mali-
cious kick, I am certainly responsible for it, since it was a
product of my free volition. But though it is true to say that
yesterday I *could have* avoided kicking the dog, it is *not* true
to say that I *can* (today) avoid having kicked him, or that it
is (now) *within my power* to avoid having kicked him.
Hence in this case it is certainly true to say that I am guilty
for having kicked the dog, that I am responsible for what I
did, but that it is not (today) within my power to avoid this
guilt.

Let us see how this simple observation applies to Kant's
theory. We see in fact from men's actions that all men do evil,
become guilty, and we infer that there is in all of us a propensity to evil as part of our supersensible moral character,
which constitutes the condition for the possibility of these evil
acts as products of our free volition. This propensity, since it
belongs to our supersensible character, is not a deed in time,
and therefore is not itself a *past* deed. But it has many relevant features in common with a past deed in time. Since it is a

condition for the possibility of our evil acts in time, the propensity to evil is "antecedent to every use of freedom in experience . . . and is thus conceived of as present in man at birth." [106] Like a past deed, this propensity was adopted by free volition, and it is something for which we can be held responsible; and yet, also like a past deed, it is not something which we can *now* undo, for it is "inextirpable by human powers." [107] We may say, if we like, that since this propensity was brought upon us by our own free volition, we *could have* avoided it. But, as Kant and Kierkegaard have told us, a remark of this kind can serve as nothing more than an idle evasion of the inescapable fact that we *have* brought this evil upon ourselves and that we cannot now rid ourselves of it. The thesis of radical evil, as we have seen, conditions our very pursuit of moral perfection, and tells us that in this pursuit "we cannot start from an innocence natural to us but must begin with the assumption of a wickedness of the will in adopting maxims contrary to" the law.[108] Once we recognize the thesis of radical evil, we must recognize too that this thesis defines the conditions for our pursuit of moral perfection, and we must not yearn nostaligically for the innocence we have lost, or dwell despairingly on the conjecture that it might at some point have been within our power to avoid it. We must accept responsibility for this evil, and turn to the task of making better men of ourselves. In this respect, says Kant,

the courage to stand on one's own feet is itself strengthened by the ethical doctrine of reconciliation, in that this doctrine represents as wiped out [*abgetan*] what cannot be altered, and opens up to man the path to a new mode of life.[109]

Kant clearly does *not* hold, then, that it is within man's power as a free being to be rid of the propensity to evil for which he is responsible, and which he has brought upon himself by his free action.* Rather, this propensity is shown by his evil deeds themselves to be an inseparable part of his moral character, as a condition for the possibility of his own free performance of these deeds. What *is* within his power is the *counteraction* of this propensity, the adoption of a disposition to good and the leading of a life of progress from bad to better. And, Kant maintains, the good man may trust that for the sake of this good which is in his power to do, God will complete by His verdict of forgiving grace these imperfect efforts to attain complete moral perfection. Indeed, the good man must hold to this faith in divine grace, for only in this way can he conceive the practical possibility of moral perfection, and avoid the moral despair of an *absurdum practicum*.

It might still be wondered, however, how God is to be justified morally in granting forgiveness to man for the sake of his disposition to good. This disposition may be "something real which is well-pleasing to God," but this does not show that it is a *sufficient* condition for a genuine moral "receptivity" to grace. To be sure, the adoption of this disposition is all that lies within man's power in becoming morally better, but the lofty requirements of the law cannot take our self-imposed weaknesses into account, or "reduce the requirements of the law to our measure." [110] How can Kant justify his claim that the disposition to good is a sufficient condition for a morally justified verdict of grace?

The answer to this question is simpler than we might at first imagine. Kant distinguishes, as we have noted already, between "narrow" or "perfect" duties (what we must do or accomplish) and duties which are "wide" or "imperfect" (what we must strive for, or make our end). Now Kant holds, as we have already had the opportunity to remark, that moral

* Whether, in view of this, Kant really holds an "absolute" conception of freedom, I will leave for Silber to decide.

perfection, holiness of will, is a duty of the second kind, a "wide" or "imperfect" duty, something we are obliged to *seek;* but it is not a duty of the first kind, something which we are obliged to *attain.*[111]

It is man's duty to *strive* for this perfection, but not to *achieve* it (in this life), and his pursuit of perfection, accordingly, is only a continual progress. Hence while this duty is indeed narrow and perfect with regard to the object (the Idea which one should make it one's end to realize), in relation to the subject it is only a wide and imperfect duty to oneself.[112]

Is this a "compromise" with the sternness of the law, a "reduction" of its requirements to suit human weaknesses? If so, it is one to which Kant held consistently throughout his works and thoroughly incorporated into his moral theory. For, indeed, only when the duty to seek moral perfection is seen in this way can the moral law address itself rationally to any *but* a holy being, who would not need the constraint of the law in any case.

Thus when a man adopts a disposition to good, and follows a course of life of constant moral progress and striving after moral perfection, he has already done what the moral law *requires* him to do.* By fulfilling this requirement, of course,

---

* Whether this requirement itself can be fulfilled without the aid of divine grace is a question which Kant leaves open. The impossibility of a divine *election* (*Erwählung*) can as little be demonstrated as can the impossibility of vicarious atonement or the creation of free beings (*Rel* 143g 134e). Thus Kant can *accommodate* an Augustinian or even a Calvinist view of the total depravity of man in the absence of divine aid. But against the implications of such a view, Kant would urge the following considerations: Whether or not man would be incapable of good apart from divine aid, the fact remains that man, as we know him, does possess a predisposition to good in the form of an *awareness* of the moral law through reason. He knows that he *ought* to become good. Hence, in Kant's view, we must *presuppose* that this aid is available to us in some way or other, and we may

man is still far from moral perfection, but he has become "a subject receptive [*empfängliches*] to goodness." [113] A disposition to good is thus seen by Kant as a sufficient condition for man's moral receptivity to grace, and the moral agent may put his rational trust in God's grace in completing his efforts and fulfilling his unconditional moral purpose.

In view of the great importance attached to "repentance" in the Christian doctrine of grace, it might be asked whether it is included in any way in Kant's theory of divine grace. It is clear for Kant that the attitude of a disposition well-pleasing to God, the "firm resolve to do better in the future" is not genuinely possible without some sober reflection on one's misdeeds and a sincere repentance for them: "To repent (*bereuen*) of a past transgression when we recall it is inevitable and, in fact, we even have a duty not to let this recollection atrophy." [114] But Kant contrasts true moral repentance, done with "an intention to do better" with a monastic "penance" (*büssen*) "which, out of superstitious fear or hypocritical self-loathing goes to work with self-torture and crucifixion of the flesh, does not aim at virtue but rather at fantastic atonement [*schwärmerische Entsündigung*]." [115] And Kant is highly skeptical of "the self-inflicted torment of the repentant sinner (a very ambiguous state of mind, which ordinarily is nothing but inward regret at having infringed the rules of

adopt this presupposition simply on moral considerations, without needing in any way to have the availability of this aid or its means *revealed* to us. Thus in Kant's view whether or not we accept a doctrine of "total depravity," our moral situation remains the same. "Granted that some supernatural cooperation may be necessary to his becoming good," says Kant, "man must . . . *lay hold* of this aid (which is no small matter)—that is, he must adopt this positive increase of power into his maxim" (*Rel* 44g 40e). And of course the view that man can *obtain* God's cooperation through cultic devotions and rites is condemned by Kant as "religious illusion" and "pseudo-service [*Afterdienst*] of God" (*Rel* 168ffg 156ffe).

prudence)." [116] That repentance which is necessarily bound up with "a departure from evil and an entrance into good, the laying off of the old man and putting on of the new," the repentance bound up with this "rebirth," is by no means foreign to Kant's thought, and is certainly an inseparable part of the disposition which is receptive to God's grace and forgiveness. But for Kant repentance must not be separated from that "love of the good" which gives it true moral worth.[117]

Trust in God's forgiving grace, then, is an important aspect of moral faith, and is itself justified in the *Religion* by an *absurdum practicum* argument. Assume that I deny the existence of a loving and forgiving God. If I deny this, I must deny that I can conceive the possibility of moral perfection. But since moral perfection is the unconditioned component of the highest good, I must deny that I can conceive the possibility of the highest good. But if I deny that I can conceive the possibility of the highest good, I commit myself not to obey the moral law. And this is an *absurdum practicum*. The doctrine of divine grace is necessary to Kant's resolution of the first antinomy of practical reason, and it must therefore be accorded, along with freedom, immortality, and God's moral governance of the world, the status of a *postulate of practical reason*. Faith in divine grace is part of the moral attitude toward our past evils and our moral aspirations. In faith the moral agent places his rational trust not only in God's beneficence as world-creator and wise providence as world-ruler, but also in God's just forgiveness as the moral judge and the loving and merciful Father of mankind.

Conclusion

In the preceding chapters we have studied Kant's conception and rational defense of religious faith, seeking the sources
for this doctrine in the principles of the critical philosophy,
and we have attempted to rethink Kant's philosophy of moral
faith from its foundation in those principles. Through an examination of Kant's *absurdum practicum* arguments, his doctrine of the highest good, and his resolution of the dialectic of
practical reason, we have seen in detail that Kant's rational defense of faith in God, in immortality, and in divine grace
forms an integral part of the critical philosophy, and is a necessary consequence of Kant's best thinking and most mature
philosophical insights. Moral faith, in fact, is the outlook, the
Weltanschauung of the critical philosophy itself, and in gaining an understanding of it we have made it possible to grasp
most clearly the critical conception of man's condition, and
the rational response to that condition dictated by the principles of the critical philosophy. If Kant's critical philosophy is
accorded proper recognition as one of the truly great achievements of the human intellect, then his philosophical defense of
religious faith must also share in this greatness.

Kant's doctrine of moral faith is grounded in his conception
of the dialectical nature of man—man as a being both finite
and rational, encumbered with inescapable limitations and yet

possessed of a rational capacity which points beyond these limitations. Human reason defines for man a final end, a single highest purpose for his existence, an ideal inseparably related to his finite rationality itself. The rational pursuit of this end in the face of man's own necessary limitations, in the face of the failure and uncertainty which surround his efforts, demands a *moral faith*, an outlook which he cannot renounce without at the same time renouncing his reason and his rational destination themselves.

As simple and profound as it is, there is nothing original or extraordinary in the outlook of moral faith as it is presented by Kant. This faith is, finally, no more than the courage to struggle toward the attainment of one's moral ends, sustained through hardship and apparent failure by a loving trust in God as the wise and beneficent Providence in whose hands all will be well. Moral faith is the choice of finite rationality to remain rational while confronted by its finitude, the choice of sober hope rather than wild despair. Its outlook is little more than the stoic virtues of courage and resignation combined with the three "theological" virtues of Christianity, faith, hope, and love. Yet it was not here that Kant sought the "original" or the "extraordinary." The common fate of mankind does not change with time, its problems are never original ones. The fundamental riddles of human life are not decipherable by an extraordinary revelation, but demand of us that difficult and completely ordinary courage and wisdom through which alone we are capable of seeing human life for what it is. If, in the final analysis, Kant tells us no more than that we must face our condition with moral courage and trust, he does not pretend philosophically to solve the problems of our existence for us. The outlook of moral faith is not in any sense a *solution* to the dialectic of man's situation, but is only a rational means of *facing* the inescapable tension and perplexity which belongs essentially to us as finite rational beings. We know already that the road we travel is a dark and a difficult one; we should not expect philosophy to tell us otherwise. In Kant's view, philosophy has succeeded if it has given clarity and rationality to the difficult wisdom and hard-won virtue whose validity we recognize already.

The moral arguments, says Kant, are not "newly discovered," but only their "basis is newly set forth." [1] Kant's originality is not to be found in the outlook of moral faith itself, but in his recognition and formulation of its rational defense. This originality can best be seen if we compare Kant's doctrine of moral faith to the solutions to the problem of the relation between philosophy and faith offered by other great modern thinkers. Many great thinkers of the modern period, among them Descartes, Spinoza, Leibniz, Locke, Berkeley, and Hegel, attempted to find a place for religious belief within the structure of a comprehensive system of philosophical knowledge. Each of these philosophers included his religious convictions within such a system by attempting to give them the status of speculative truths, knowable by empirical evidence or by rational demonstration. This speculative solution to the problem of philosophy and faith was challenged, however, by another strain of modern thought—a strain best exemplified by Pascal and Kierkegaard. They denied the abstract "God of the philosophers" in the name of the God of a personal faith whose emotional meaning could not be pigeonholed in a metaphysical system or reduced to the barren truths of impersonal rational demonstration. They insisted instead on a living God encountered through a living faith, a faith which does not hesitate to acknowledge the danger and uncertainty of its situation and recognizes itself as a "wager," a "leap," which must be undertaken in the absence of rational defense and to which the abstract certitude of speculative argumentation is entirely irrelevant.

Kant must look upon this dispute between the "philosophers" and the "men of faith" with divided loyalties. His deepest convictions lie with Pascal and Kierkegaard. With them, he must deny the speculative solution to the problem of philosophy and faith. The inadequacy of this solution does not show itself—as Pascal and Kierkegaard themselves thought—in its conflict with biblical faith, since biblical faith as such, with its positive and historical basis, might simply be wrong. The speculative solution is inadequate because it conflicts with the genuine and valid conception of man's condition which biblical faith contains. The men of faith have perceived, as the philosophers have not, that man's finite rationality is a problematic condition, a condition of inescapable tension and conflict. Man's response to this condition cannot take the form of the complacent detachment of objective and theoretical cognition, but must engage his will and his emotions also. The human condition is a *problem;* the ultimate response to it, therefore, is not contemplation but *decision.* Speculative philosophy confuses the finite and problematic standpoint of human reason with the infinite, disinterested standpoint of divine contemplation. Its dogmatism, like the sophistical objections of the complacent critics of religious faith, must be answered "in Socratic fashion, by the clearest proof of the ignorance of the objectors." [2] When Kant "denies *knowledge,* in order to make room for *faith,*" he denies the dogmatism of a philosophy which ignores the problematic character of man's condition and reduces his response to this condition from a personal choice and commitment to a merely abstract and disinterested theoretical assertion.

Yet, although Kant agrees with Pascal and Kierkegaard that

the speculative solution to the problem of philosophy and faith is inadequate, he can as little accept their own solution as he could the solution of the dogmatists. For in their zeal to maintain the distinctive character of faith, Pascal and Kierkegaard denied not only theoretical knowledge but even rationality itself. For them, the object of faith is a "paradox," something "absolutely different" from reason, and the encounter with this object can take place only at the "limit" of reason, in a decision which reason does not and cannot pretend to explain or justify.³ Hence it becomes necessary, even "rational," that reason itself should be disavowed in the response of faith.⁴ But in this way faith, the response of man to his problematic condition, ceases even to be *his* response, loses the character even of a *decision*.⁵ Kant denies speculative dogmatism, but he must deny this irrationalism with equal force. Man does not possess reason as his highest faculty only to forsake and disavow it in the face of the most important questions which confront him. His ability to communicate autonomously and universally with other men was not given him only to be denied where matters are most crucial. If the "philosophers" had ignored the problematic character of man's finite rationality by failing to recognize the limits of reason, the "men of faith" lack the courage to use a limited reason, and attempt to flee the problematic condition of finite rationality by a renunciation of reason in the face of human finitude and a blind submission to the irrational.

Along with the "philosophers," then, Kant demands a rational account of religious convictions, and demands that these convictions be justified by inclusion in a rational system of philosophy. If the "men of faith" are correct in pointing to the necessity that man respond to his existence by a leap of faith, this necessity and the outlook of faith themselves require rational justification through a critical self-examination

of the human condition. In Kant's *absurdum practicum* arguments, the human self-knowledge obtained in the critical philosophy is used to formulate and justify this decision, this leap
of faith. Thus critical self-knowledge reveals not only that
faith and reason are *compatible* with each other, but that for a
being both finite and rational, faith and reason *require* each
other. It is this unification of faith and reason, this attempt to
preserve both the personal character of religious conviction
and the universal communicability of reason, which constitutes the true originality and lasting value of Kant's moral defense of faith.

Notes

See page xi for a list of abbreviations used in citing works by Kant.

Introduction

1. A xii.
2. *WA* 35g 3e.
3. Kroner, *Kant's Weltanschauung,* 30ff; Greene, "The Historical Context and Religious Significance of Kant's *Religion,*" lxii.
4. Greene, lxii.
5. Heidegger, *Kant and the Problem of Metaphysics,* 24g 31e.
6. *KpV* 9ng 9ne; *Anthro* 231.
7. *KpV* 25g 24e.
8. *TL* 382g 41e; *G* 454g 122e.
9. A 302 = B 359.
10. A 332 = B 379.
11. A 642 = B 670.
12. A 339 = B 397.

Chapter 1: Kant's Moral Arguments

1. *VE* 98ffg 78ffe; A 795 = B 823ff; *VpR* 8–11, 31–34, 138–42, 158–62; *KpV* 107ffg 111ffe; *Wh* 136ff; *KU* 442ffg 292ffe; *Rel* 3ffg 3ffe; *EaD* 332ffg 74ffe; *TL* 480ffg 153ffe; *NVT* 396nff; *Log* 65ff.

2. Beck, *A Commentary on Kant's Critique of Practical Reason,* Chs. XIII, XIV; Cousin, *Leçons sur la Philosophie de Kant,* 304ff.

3. Adickes, *Kants Opus Postumum, dargestellt und beurteilt,* 720ff, 769–885.

4. Schrader, "Kant's Presumed Repudiation of the Moral Arguments in the *Opus Postumum,*" 228ff; Silber, "The Ethical Significance of Kant's *Religion,*" cxlff.

5. Adickes, 846.

6. Schrader, 236; cf. *OP* XXII 125f.

7. Kemp Smith, *Commentary to Kant's Critique of Pure Reason,* 638; Beck, 276.

8. Adickes, 846; cf. 776ff.

9. A 822 = B 850; *KU* 470g 322e.

10. A 820 = B 848; A 823 = B 851.

11. A 820 = B 848; *Log* 66f.

12. *KpV* 134g 139e; *Wh* 139n.

13. A 822 = B 850.

14. A 821 = B 849; A 822 = B 850; *Log* 66.

15. A 823 = B 851.

16. A 823 = B 851.

17. *Wh* 141; *Log* 66.

18. *Wh* 141.

19. Kierkegaard, *Concluding Unscientific Postscript,* 182.

20. A 829 = B 857.

21. *KpV* 142g 147e.

22. Ewing, *The Fundamental Questions of Philosophy,* 236.

23. *Wh* 140; B xxix.

24. *KU* 427g 324e.

25. A 824 = B 852.

26. A 824 = B 852.

27. Cf. Canfield, "Knowing About Future Decisions," 129.

28. *KpV* 143g 149fe; *Rel* 189g 177e.

29. A 823 = B 851f.

30. *KpV* 114g 118e.

31. *KpV* 114g 118e.

32. Beck, 261.

33. *KpV* 64g 67e.
34. Cohen, *Kants Begründung der Ethik*, 254n.
35. *KpV* 142fg 148e.
36. *KU* 450fg 302e.
37. Beck, 241.
38. A 828 = B 856.
39. *G* 405g 73e.
40. *VpR* 160.
41. *VE* 107g 86e; *VpR* 31; *KU* 472g 325e.
42. A 830 = B 858.
43. *KpV* 142g 148e.
44. *VpR* 32; *KpV* 146g 151e.
45. Tillich, *Systematic Theology* II, 116.
46. *Rel* 190g 178e.
47. Wittgenstein, *Philosophical Investigations*, 187f.
48. Webb, *Kant's Philosophy of Religion*, 65f.
49. *KpV* 146g 151e; *KU* 451ng 301ne.
50. *KpV* 3fg 3fe.
51. Adickes, 846.
52. *OP* XXI, 30.
53. Adickes, 811.
54. *KpV* 31g 31e, 42g 43e; *RL* 252g 60e; *OP* XXI, 21.
55. *KpV* 42g 43e; *KU* 468g 320fe.
56. *KpV* 28g 29e.
57. *KpV* 29g 29e, 4ng 4ne.
58. *KpV* 28g 28e, 27g 26e.
59. A 533 = B 561.

Chapter 2: Finite Rational Volition

1. Adickes, 846.
2. Cohen, 353.
3. Paulsen, *Kant's Life and Doctrine*, 318g 321e.
4. Greene, lxii; Teale, *Kantian Ethics*, 218; see also Döring, "Kant's Lehre vom höchsten Gut," 94ff.

5. Schopenhauer, *The World as Will and Representation*, 621g 524e.

6. *KpV* 108g 112e; *Rel* 5g 5e.

7. *KpV* 108g 112e.

8. *Rel* 23g 19e; *TL* 225g 25e.

9. See Paton, *The Categorical Imperative*, 43, 166.

10. *KU* 196fg 33fe; *KpV* 58g 61e.

11. *VpR* 129, 137; *TP* 279n.

12. *G* 414g 81e.

13. *VpR* 127, 129.

14. *VpR* 114.

15. *Rel* 36g 31e.

16. *KpV* 25g 24e.

17. *Rel* 36g 31e.

18. *VpR* 127.

19. *G* 420nfg 88ne.

20. *Rel* 6ng 6ne.

21. *TL* 225g 25e.

22. *Anthro* 265.

23. *G* 427g 95e.

24. *KpV* 21g 19e.

25. *KU* 197g 34e; *KpV* 117g 122e; *VpR* 157f.

26. See Paton, *The Modern Predicament*, 325.

27. Greene, lxiif.

28. *TP* 279.

29. *TP* 280f.

30. *TP* 281.

31. *TP* 278.

32. *G* 399g 67e.

33. *G* 393g 61e.

34. *KpV* 25g 24e.

35. *KU* 182g 18e.

36. *KpV* 61g 63fe.

37. *TP* 280.

38. *TL* 385g 44e; *Rel* 6ng 6ne.

39. *TL* 385g 44e.

40. *G* 399g 67e.
41. *KpV* 34fg 35e.
42. *TL* 450g 118e.
43. *G* 393g 61e.
44. *KpV* 60g 62e.
45. *KpV* 64g 67e.
46. *G* 393g 61e, 396g 64e; See Paton, *The Categorical Imperative,* 35ff, 43.
47. Beck, 245.
48. *G* 394g 62e.
49. Beck, 134.
50. *KpV* 60g 62e.
51. *KpV* 25g 24e.
52. Beck, 134f.
53. Beck, 130.
54. *KpV* 58g 60e.
55. *KpV* 60g 62e.
56. *KpV* 60g 62e.
57. *KpV* 62g 64e, italics added.
58. *KpV* 64g 66e.
59. *KpV* 65g 67e.
60. *KpV* 64g 67e.

Chapter 3: The Highest Good

1. *G* 428g 95e.
2. *Anthro* 227.
3. *KpV* 60g 62e.
4. *KpV* 60g 62e.
5. *TL* 223g 22e, 394g 54e, 405g 66e.
6. *Rel* 51g 47e; *TL* 445g 113e.
7. *Rel* 46ffg 42fe; *VpR* 146; *TL* 484ffg 158ffe.
8. *TL* 399g 59e.
9. *TL* 385g 44fe.
10. *TL* 393g 53e, 446fg 113fe; See Dietrichson, "What Does Kant Mean By 'Acting from Duty'?" 314ff.

11. *KpV* 151g 155e.

12. *VE* 318g 252e.

13. *P* 443g 6e, 445g 10e.

14. *P* 486ffg 95ffe.

15. *Rel* 98g 90e.

16. *VE* 317g 252e.

17. *G* 393g 61e.

18. *G* 393g 61e; *KpV* 110g 115e; *TL* 481g 155e.

19. *VE* 18fg 15e.

20. *KpV* 59fg 61fe.

21. *Anthro* 227.

22. *KpV* 111g 115e.

23. A 814 = B 842.

24. *KU* 450g.

25. *VE* 97g 77e.

26. *Rel* 5g 4e.

27. *VE* 97g 77e; cf. *KpV* 112g 117e and Silber, "The Copernican Revolution in Ethics: The Good Reexamined," 278.

28. *KpV* 112g 116e.

29. *KpV* 35g 36e.

30. *TL* 390g 49e.

31. *Anthro* 277.

32. *KpV* 111g 115e.

33. *Anthro* 277.

34. *VE* 8g 7e; *KpV* 64fg 66fe, 111ffg 115ffe.

35. *KpV* 108g 112e.

36. *KpV* 108g 112e.

37. A 322 = B 379.

38. *Rel* 5g; *KU* 442g 293e, 434g 284e.

39. *KpV* 122g 126e.

40. *Rel* 64g 57e.

41. *VE* 102g 82e; *VpR* 33; A 805 = B 833ff.

42. *KpV* 110fg 115e, italics added.

43. *Rel* 97g 89e.

44. Silber, "Kant's Conception of the Highest Good as Immanent and Transcendent," 472ff, 491ff.

45. *TL* 391ffg 51ffe.
46. Silber, "Kant's Conception of the Highest Good," 492.
47. Beck, 244f.
48. *Rel* 5g 5e.
49. Beck, 244f.
50. Schilpp, *Kant's Pre-Critical Ethics*, 137f.
51. *KU* 434g 284e.

Chapter 4: The Practical Postulates

1. *KpV* 107g 111e.
2. *KpV* 122g 126e.
3. *VE* 310g 246e; *G* 414g 81e; *KpV* 32g 33e, 128g 133e.
4. *G.* 414g 81e; *KpV* 32g 33e; *Rel* 64g 57e; *TL* 377g 36fe.
5. *VpR* 146; *Rel* 47g 43e.
6. *VpR* 146.
7. *VE* 308g 244e.
8. *KpV* 118g 122fe; *G* 428g 95fe.
9. *VE* 96g 77e.
10. Cf. *VpR* 149ff and *Rel* 43g 38e.
11. *TL* 485g 159e.
12. *TL* 393g 53e.
13. *Rel* 28g 23e, 58g 51e.
14. *Rel* 57g 50e.
15. *Rel* 64g 57e.
16. *Rel* 36g 31fe.
17. *Rel* 57g 50e.
18. *Rel* 20fg 16fe.
19. *Rel* 35g 30e.
20. *Rel* 37g 32e.
21. *Rel* 37g 32e.
22. *Rel* 27g 22fe.
23. *Rel* 28g 23e.
24. *Rel* 44g 40e.
25. *Rel* 37g 32e.
26. *Rel* 51g 46e.

27. *Rel* 67ng 61ne; *TL* 446g 113e.

28. *Rel* 47g 43e, 51g 47e.

29. *KpV* 122fg 127e.

30. *Rel* 51g 47e.

31. *KpV* 122g 126fe.

32. *KpV* 122g 127e.

33. *KpV* 123g 127e.

34. *EaD* 334g 73fe; *Rel* 66g 60e.

35. *Rel* 67g 60e.

36. *VE* 104g 84e; *VpR* 201; *EaD* 337g 81e; *Rel* 44g 40e.

37. *Rel* 66ffg 60ffe.

38. *KpV* 122g 127e.

39. Greene, lix.

40. Caird, *The Critical Philosophy of Immanuel Kant*, II, 303.

41. *KpV* 145g 151e.

42. *EaD* 334g 77e.

43. *Rel* 69g 62e.

44. *EaD* 334g 77e.

45. B 411ff, A 413 = B 440, A 819 = B 847, A 337n = B 395n.

46. *Rel* 161ng 148ne.

47. *EaD* 335g 79e.

48. *KpV* 139g 144e.

49. *KpV* 111g 115e.

50. *KpV* 111g 115e.

51. *KpV* 113g 117e.

52. *G* 438g 106e, italics added.

53. *G* 438g 106e; A 810= B 838.

54. *KU* 452g 303e.

55. *G* 438g 106e.

56. *KU* 452g 303e.

57. *KU* 452g 303e.

58. *TL* 454g 122e.

59. *KpV* 113g 118e.

60. *KU* 452g 303e.

61. *KpV* 114g 119e.

62. A 812 = B 840, A 814 = B 842.

63. A 811 = B 839.

64. *VpR* 6; *KpV* 128fg 133e; *Rel* 69ffng 63ffne, 161g 149e; *EaD* 339g 83e.

65. *KpV* 115g 119e.

66. Cf. *KpV* 115g 199e, 125fg 129fe with *KpV* 123ng 128ne, 136fg 142e; and compare *Rel* 5g 5e with *Rel* 69ffng 63ffne, 161g 149e.

67. Greene, lxiv.

68. *KpV* 123ng 128ne.

69. *KpV* 125g 130e.

70. *Vpr* 15.

71. *KpV* 125g 130e.

72. Beck, 275. This view is also expressed by Whittemore, "The Metaphysics of the Seven Formulations of the Moral Argument," 161.

73. Beck, 275.

74. *KpV* 145g 151e.

75. *KU* 454g 305e.

76. Beck, 275.

77. Hegel, *Phänomenologie des Geistes*, 436.

78. Hegel, 436f.

79. Hegel, 277.

80. *VpR* 13f, 36; A 571 = B 599ff.

81. *VpR* 109, 127, 130.

82. *VpR* 181.

83. Hegel, 277f, 437.

84. A 811 = B 839; *KpV* 125g 130e.

85. *Anthro* 251.

86. *VpR* 205ff; *EaD* 337g 81e.

87. *MT* 263f.

88. *VpR* 207.

89. *MT* 264.

90. *Rel* 142g 133e.

91. Hegel, 437.

92. Beck, 275.

93. *KU* 450ng 301ne.

94. *Rel* 139g 130e.

95. Hegel, 18.

96. Schweitzer, *The Essence of Faith,* 10g 26fe.

97. B 395n; Schweitzer, 23g 35e.

98. *KpV* 145g 151e; *KU* 455g 306fe.

99. *KpV* 134g 139e; A 805 = B 834.

100. *KpV* 136g 141e.

101. A 328 = B 384; A 644 = B 672.

102. Vaihinger, *The Philosophy of As-If,* 621g 272e.

103. A 641 = B 669, A 742 = B 770, A 830 = B 858; *VpR* 10f; *KpV* 120g 125e.

104. B xxvin.

105. A 303 = B 359, A 310 = B 366.

106. A 323 = B 379.

107. A 328 = B 384.

108. *KpV* 134g 140e.

109. *VpR* 53ff; A 696 = B 724; *Prol* 355ffg 104ffe; *KU* 456g 307e, 464ng 315fne; *Rel* 65fng 58fne; cf. also *VpR* 47ff; A 578 = B 606, A 640 = B 668.

110. *VE* 102g 82e.

111. *Rel* 139g 130fe.

112. *KpV* 133g 138e, 135g 140e; *KU* 456g 307e.

113. *KpV* 135g 140e; A 819 = B 847; *KU* 457g 308fe.

114. *KpV* 143g 148e.

Chapter 5: Moral Faith and Rational Religion

1. Adler, 282.

2. *KU* 458g 309e.

3. *KU* 471g 324e.

4. A 829 = B 857; cf. *KU* 446g 296e, 452g 303e, 481g 335e; *Rel* 115g 106e.

5. *KU* 197g 31e.

6. *KpV* 117g 122e.

7. *KU* 452g 303e.

8. *VpR* 140.

9. *VpR* 140.

10. A 814 = B 842.

11. *KU* 472g 324e.

12. *VE* 119g 95e; cf. *VE* 100g 80e; *Log* 69; *VpR* 211f; *KU* 471fg 324e; *Rel* 171g 159e; *SF* 47f; *RR* 618.

13. *Rel* 139g 130e.

14. *KU* 418g 335e.

15. *VE* 121g 97e.

16. *VpR* 211.

17. *KU* 481g 335e.

18. P 495g 114e.

19. *VpR* 96.

20. *VpR* 16.

21. *VpR* 15; cf. *VpR* 31.

22. *KpV* 131ng 136ne.

23. A 697 = B 725, A 700 = B 728; *Prol* 356fg 105fe.

24. *VpR* 93ff; *KU* 459ng 311ne; *Rel* 65fng 58fne, 168g 156fe, 183g 171e.

25. *Prol* 357g 106e.

26. *Prol* 357g 106e.

27. *Prol* 356fg 105e; *VpR* 123.

28. *KU* 353g 198e.

29. *VE* 119g 95e.

30. Greene, lxiv.

31. See Paton, *The Modern Predicament*, 325.

32. *Rel* 29ffg 24ffe.

33. *Rel* 168ffg 156ffe.

34. *Rel* 5fg 5e.

35. *VE* 119g 96e; cf. *KU* 482g 335e; *VpR* 212.

36. *VE* 119g 95fe.

37. *VpR* 212.

38. *VE* 117ffg 94fe.

39. *KU* 449ng 300ne.

40. *KU* 449ng 300ne.

41. Beck, 275f.

42. *KU* 466g 318e.
43. *Rel* 97fg 89e, 139fg 130fe.
44. *Rel* 6ffng 5ffne.
45. *TL* 482fg 155fe.
46. Beck, 276.
47. B xxxiii.
48. B xxxiii.
49. *TL* 484g 157e.
50. *KU* 476g 329e.
51. *KU* 440fg 291e.
52. *TL* 483g 156e.
53. *KU* 441g 292e.
54. *KU* 477fg 330e.
55. *KU* 482ng 335ne.
56. Hare, "Theology and Falsification, B," 100ff.
57. *KU* 452g 303e.
58. Heidegger, *Being and Time*, 301g 348e.
59. *Rel* 66g 60e, 74g 68e.
60. *Rel* 44g 40e.
61. *EaD* 335g 79e; *EaD* 334g 77e; *Rel* 67g 61e; *RR* 644.
62. *KpV* 143g 149e.
63. Freud, *Future of an Illusion*, 354g 49e.
64. Freud, *Future of an Illusion*, 356g 52fe.
65. Freud, *Future of an Illusion*, 355g 48fe; *Civilization and Its Discontents*, 440g 28e, 439ffg 27ffe.
66. Freud, *Civilization and Its Discontents*, 443g 31e.
67. Freud, *Future of an Illusion*, 377g 87e.
68. Cf. Freud, *Future of an Illusion*, 349ffg 41ffe and *WA* 35ffg 3ffe.
69. *IKU* 230fng 35ne.
70. *KpV* 143fng 149ne.
71. *KpV* 143g 149e.
72. *KpV* 129g 134e; *KU* 481g 334e; *Rel* 154g 142e; cf. *TL* 487g 162e; *SF* 36.
73. A 819 = B 847; *G* 443g 110fe; *KpV* 41g 41fe; *KU* 481fg 335e; *Rel* 3fg 3fe; *TL* 443fg 110e.

74. *Kpv* 129g 134e.
75. *Rel* 97fg 89e; *G* 433g 101e.
76. *Rel* 98g 89e.
77. *Rel* 100g 92e.
78. *Rel* 94g 86e.
79. *Rel* 98g 90e.
80. *Rel* 95g 87e.
81. *Rel* 98g 90e.
82. *Rel* 98g 90e.
83. *Rel* 96g 88e.
84. *Rel* 99g 90fe.
85. *G* 433g 101e.
86. *RL* 227g 28e.
87. *Rel* 99fg 91e.
88. *Rel* 96g 88e.
89. *Rel* 102g 93e.
90. *Rel* 105g 96e; cf. *Rel* 103g 94e.
91. Hoekstra, *Immanente Kritik zur Kantischen Religionsphilosophie*, 93.
92. *SF* 37, 45, 51; *Rel* 107g 98e, 123ng 113ne, 135ng 126ne; Barth, *Protestant Thought from Rousseau to Ritschl*, 169n.
93. *Rel* 12g 11e.
94. *Rel* 102fg 94e.
95. *SF* 49f; *Rel* 104g 95e.
96. *Rel* 168g 156e.
97. *Rel* 103g 94e.
98. *Rel* 174g 162e.
99. *Rel* 106g 97e, 135ng 126ne.
100. *RL* 355g 129e; *Rel* 102g 113e.
101. *Rel* 179g 167e.
102. *SF* 50; *Rel* 122g 113e; *WA* 35g 3e.
103. *Rel* 175g 163e.
104. *Rel* 121g 112e.
105. *Rel* 51g 47e; Pünjer, *Die Religionslehre Kants*, 2f; Hoekstra, 92.
106. *Rel* 167g 155e.

107. *Rel* 130g 121e.

108. Barth, 175f; cf. *Rel* 102g 93e.

109. *Rel* 79g 74e, 111g 102e, 136ng 127ne, 140ng 131ne, 184ng 172ne, 194ng 182ne; *VpR* 144f.

110. Cf. *Rel* 156fg 144fe.

111. Ritschl, *The Christian Doctrine of Justification and Reconciliation,* 10f.

112. Greene, lxxvif; Dakin, "Kant and Religion," 418f.

113. Lösment, *Zur Religionsphilosophie Kants,* 43.

114. Otto, *The Idea of the Holy,* 5g 19e.

115. *Rel* 113fg 104fe; *SF* 54ff.

116. *KU* 238g 75e; *Rel* 109g 100e.

117. *KpV* 71ffg 74ffe; *Wh* 139.

118. *Rel* 175g 163e.

119. Lösment, 43; Greene, lxxvi; Otto, 136g 131e.

120. Otto, 136g 131e.

121. Otto, 171ffg 160ffe.

122. Cf. Otto, 161g 153e.

123. *Rel* 114g 105e.

124. Otto, 13e, 167g 153e.

125. Freud, *Future of an Illusion,* 350g 43e; *SF* 33.

126. *Rel* 155g 143e.

127. *Rel* 136ng 127ne; *RR* 621.

128. *SF* 63.

129. *VpR* 220.

130. *VpR* 220ff; *Rel* 122g 113e; *SF* 48.

131. *Rel* 107g 97fe.

132. *SF* 23ff, 36ff.

133. Barth, 171.

134. *VpR* 220, 222.

135. *VpR* 220, 222.

136. *SF* 48.

Chapter 6: Radical Evil and Divine Grace

1. Cf. *VE* 104g 84e, 134fg 107fe; *VpR* 224ff.
2. *VpR* 149ff; cf. *Anthro* 324f, which may have postdated the *Religion,* according to the dating information supplied by Arnoldt, *Anthro* 354.
3. *Rel* 26g 21e.
4. *Rel* 28g 23e, 58g 51e, 44g 40e.
5. *Rel* 44g 40e.
6. *Rel* 21g 17e.
7. *Rel* 36g 31e.
8. *Rel* 36g 31e.
9. *Rel* 36g 31e.
10. *Rel* 35g 30e.
11. See Silber, "Ethical Significance," cxxixff.
12. *Rel* 37g 32e.
13. *Rel* 32g 27e.
14. *Rel* 21g 16e.
15. *Rel* 25g 21e.
16. *Rel* 21ng 17ne.
17. *Rel* 29g 24e.
18. *Rel* 21g 16e.
19. *Rel* 28fg 23fe.
20. *Anthro,* 251, 265.
21. *Rel* 29g 24e, italics added.
22. *Rel* 22g 17e.
23. *Rel* 29g 24e.
24. *Rel* 20g 16e.
25. *Rel* 19g 15e.
26. *Rel* 32g 27e.
27. *Rel* 30g 25e.
28. *Rel* 37g 32e.
29. *Rel* 29ffg 24ffe.
30. *Rel* 20g 16e.
31. *Anthro* 266.

32. *Anthro* 251, 265.

33. *Anthro* 251; *Rel* 29ng 24ne.

34. *Rel* 28g 23e.

35. *Rel* 35g 30e.

36. Hume, *A Treatise of Human Nature*, 411.

37. *Rel* 39g 28e.

38. *G* 407g 74fe.

39. *Rel* 20g 16e.

40. *Rel* 25g 20fe, 37g 32e.

41. *Rel* 50g 46e.

42. *Rel* 37g 32e, 73g 67e.

43. *Rel* 41g 36e.

44. *Rel* 68fg 62e.

45. *Rel* 64g 57e.

46. *Rel* 32g 27e, 30g 25e.

47. *Rel* 41g 36e.

48. Kierkegaard, *The Concept of Dread*, 28.

49. *Rel* 43g 38e.

50. *Rel* 43g 38e.

51. Kierkegaard, *The Concept of Dread*, 33.

52. *Rel* 32g 28e.

53. *Rel* 33g 28e.

54. *Rel* 33fg 29e; *EF* 355g 99e, 358ffg 103ffe, 374ffg 121ffe, 375fng 123ne.

55. *Rel* 39g 34e.

56. *Rel* 50fg 46e.

57. *Rel* 51g 46e.

58. *Rel* 47g 43e, 48g 43e, 50g 46e.

59. *Rel* 47g 42e.

60. *Rel* 47g 42e.

61. *Rel* 46g 42e.

62. *Rel* 44g 40e, 143g 134e; *VpR* 207ff.

63. *Rel* 45g 40e, 47g 43e, 50g 46e.

64. *Rel* 46g 42e.

65. *Rel* 48g 43e, 51g 46e.

66. *Rel* 47g 43e.

67. *Rel* 47g 43e, 48g 43e, 73g 68e, 75g 69e.
68. *Rel* 48g 43e, 68g 62e.
69. *Rel* 48g 43e, 51g 46e, 71g 65e.
70. *EaD* 334g 78e.
71. *Rel* 46g 42e.
72. *Rel* 47g 43e.
73. *Rel* 60g 54e.
74. *Rel* 62g 56e.
75. *Rel* 64g 57e.
76. *Rel* 66g 60e.
77. *Rel* 66g 60e.
78. *Rel* 66g 59e.
79. *Rel* 66g 60e.
80. *Rel* 66–76g 60–70e.
81. *Rel* 75g 69e, 75ng 69ne.
82. *Rel* 78g 73e.
83. *Rel* 75fg 70e.
84. *Rel* 75ng 70ne.
85. Cf. Porter, 225.
86. Silber, "Ethical Significance," cxxxi.
87. *Rel* 72g 66e, 143g 134e.
88. *Rel* 191g 170e.
89. *Rel* 143g 134e.
90. Silber, "Ethical Significance," cxxxi.
91. Silber, "Ethical Significance," cxxxii.
92. *VE* 79g 66e, 134g 107e; *KpV* 123g 127e, 127ng 132ne; *VpR* 167; *Rel* 141g 132e, 146ng 137ne.
93. *Rel* 200g 188e.
94. *Rel* 184g 172e.
95. Silber, "Ethical Significance," cxxxii.
96. *Rel* 75ng 70ne, 76g 70e, 178g 166e.
97. Kierkegaard, *Repetition*, 132ff; *Fear and Trembling*, 80; *Sickness Unto Death*, 244ff.
98. Feuerbach, *The Essence of Christianity*, 60g 48fe.
99. *TL* 461g 130e; *VE* 38g 31e.
100. *Rel* 120g 110e.

101. *Rel* 117g 107e.
102. *Rel* 78g 70e.
103. *Rel* 173g 161e.
104. Silber, "Ethical Significance," cxxxiii.
105. Silber, "Ethical Significance," cxxxiif.
106. *Rel* 22g 17e.
107. *Rel* 37g 32e.
108. *Rel* 51g 46e.
109. *Rel* 184g 172e.
110. Silber, "Ethical Significance," cxxxiii.
111. Cf. Clark, *Introduction to Kant's Philosophy*, 279.
112. *TL* 446g 113e.
113. *Rel* 48g 43e.
114. *TL* 486g 160e; cf. *Rel* 24ng 19ne.
115. *TL* 485g 159e.
116. *Rel* 24g 19e.
117. *Rel* 24ng 19ne, 47g 43e, 73g 68e.

Conclusion

1. *KU* 458g 309e.
2. B xxxi.
3. Kierkegaard, *Philosophical Fragments*, 55, 61ff.
4. Pascal, *Pensées*, pars. 233, 268, 273.
5. Pascal, *Pensées*, pars. 279, 284; Kierkegaard, *Philosophical Fragments*, 77.

Bibliography of Works Cited

Works by Kant

Unless otherwise noted, citations of Kant in German refer to *Kants Gesammelte Schriften, Königlich Preussischen Akadamie der Wissenschaften*, Berlin.

Kritik der reinen Vernunft [A . . . = B . . .], Bd. 3–4. (*Immanuel Kant's Critique of Pure Reason*, tr. Norman Kemp Smith. London: Macmillan & Co., 1963.)

Prolegomena zu einer jeden künftigen Metaphysik, die als Wissenschaft wird auftreten können [*Prol*], Bd. 4. (*Prolegomena to Any Future Metaphysics*, ed. Lewis White Beck. New York: Bobbs-Merrill, Inc., 1950.)

Grundlegung zur Metaphysik der Sitten [*G*], Bd. 4. (*The Moral Law: Kant's Groundwork of the Metaphysic of Morals*, tr. H. J. Paton. New York: Barnes & Noble, Inc., 1963.)

Kritik der praktischen Vernunft [*KpV*], Bd. 5. (*Critique of Practical Reason*, tr. Lewis White Beck. New York: Bobbs-Merrill, Inc., 1956.)

Kritik der Urtheilskraft [*KU*], Bd. 5. (*Critique of Judgment*, tr. J. H. Bernard. New York: Hafner Publishing Co., 1951.)

Die Religion innerhalb der Grenzen der blossen Vernunft [*Rel*], Bd. 6. (*Religion within the Limits of Reason Alone*, tr. Theodore M. Greene and Hoyt H. Hudson. New York: Harper and Row, 1960.)

Die Metaphysik der Sitten: Vorrede, Einleitung und Erster Theil: Metaphysiche Anfangsgrunde der Rechtslehre, [RL], Bd. 6. (*The Metaphysical Elements of Justice,* tr. John Ladd. New York: Bobbs-Merrill, Inc., 1965.)

Die Metaphysik der Sitten: Zweiter Theil: Metaphysische Anfangsgründe der Tugendlehre [TL], Bd. 6. (*The Doctrine of Virtue,* tr. Mary J. Gregor. New York: Harper and Row, 1964.)

Der Streit der Fakultäten [SF], Bd. 7.

Anthropologie in pragmatischer Hinsicht [Anthro], Bd. 7.

Beantwortung der Frage: Was ist Aufklärung? [WA], Bd. 8. ("What is Enlightenment?" *Kant on History,* tr. Lewis White Beck, Robert E. Anchor, and Emil L. Fackenheim. New York: Bobbs-Merrill, Inc., 1963.)

Idee zu einer allgemeinen Geschichte in weltbürgerlicher Absicht [IAG], Bd. 8. ("Idea for a Universal History from a Cosmopolitan Point of View," *Kant on History.*)

Was heisst: Sich im Denken orientieren? [Wh], Bd. 8.

Über das Misslingen aller philosophische Versuche in der Theodicee [MT], Bd. 8.

Über den Gemeinspruch: Das mag in der Theorie richtig sein, taugt aber nicht für die Praxis [TP], Bd. 8.

Das Ende aller Dinge [EaD], Bd. 8. ("The End of All Things," *Kant on History.*)

Zum Ewigen Frieden [EF], Bd. 8. ("Perpetual Peace," *Kant on History.*)

Von einem neuerdings erhobenen vornehmen Ton in der Philosophie [NVT], Bd. 8.

Logik [Log], Bd. 9.

Pädagogik [P], Bd. 9. (*Education,* tr. Annette Churton. Ann Arbor: University of Michigan Press, 1960.)

Reflexionen zur Religionsphilosophie [RR], Bd. 19.

Erster Einleitung zur Kritik der Urtheilskraft [IKU], Bd. 20. (*First Introduction to the Critique of Judgment,* tr. James Haden. Bobbs-Merrill, Inc., 1965.)

Opus Postumum [OP], Bd. 21–22.

Vorlesungen über die philosophische Religionslehre [*VpR*], hrg. Karl Heinrich Ludwig Pölitz. Leipzig: Verlag der Taubert-'schen Buchhandlung, 1830.
Eine Vorlesung Kants über Ethik [*VE*], hrg. Paul Menzer. Berlin: Pan Verlag Rolf Heise, 1924. (*Lectures on Ethics,* tr. Louis Infield. New York: Harper and Row, 1963.)

Secondary Sources on Kant

Adickes, Erich. *Kants Opus Postumum, dargestellt und beurteilt, Kant-Studien* Ergänzungsheft 50, 1920.

Adler, Max. *Das Soziologische in Kants Erkenntniskritik.* Wien: Verlag der Wiener Volksbuchhandlung, 1924.

Barth, Karl, *Protestant Thought from Rousseau to Ritschl,* tr. Brian Cozens. New York: Harper and Row, 1959. Ch. IV.

Bauch, Bruno. "Luther und Kant," *Kant-Studien,* Bd. 9, 1904.

Beck, Lewis White. *A Commentary on Kant's Critique of Practical Reason.* Chicago: University of Chicago Press, 1960.

Caird, Edward. *The Critical Philosophy of Immanuel Kant.* New York: Macmillan Co., 1889.

Clark, Norman. *Introduction to Kant's Philosophy.* London: Methuen & Co., 1925.

Cohen, Hermann. *Kants Begründung der Ethik.* Berlin: Bruno Cassirer Verlag, 1910.

Cousin, Victor. *Leçons sur la Philosophie de Kant.* Paris: Librarie Philosophique de Ladrange, 1844.

Dakin, A. Hazard. "Kant and Religion," Whitney and Bowers, eds., *The Heritage of Kant.* Princeton: Princeton University Press, 1939.

Delekat, Friedrich. *Immanuel Kant: Historisch-Kritische Interpretation der Hauptschriften.* Heidelberg: Quelle & Meyer, 1963.

Dietrichson, Paul. "What Does Kant Mean by 'Acting from Duty'?" Wolff, ed., *Kant: A Collection of Critical Essays.* Garden City: Doubleday & Co., 1967.

Döring, A. "Kants Lehre vom höchsten Gut," *Kant-Studien*, Bd. 4, 1900.

England, F. E. *Kant's Conception of God*. London: Allen & Unwin, 1925.

Ewing, A. C. *The Fundamental Questions of Philosophy*. London: Routledge and Kegan Paul, 1951.

Gauchwal, Balbir Singh. "The Moral Religion of Kant and the Karmayoga of the Gita," *Kant-Studien*, Bd. 55, 1964.

Greene, Theodore M. "The Historical Context and Religious Significance of Kant's *Religion*," *Religion within the Limits of Reason Alone*, tr. Theodore M. Greene and Hoyt H. Hudson. New York: Harper and Row, 1960.

Hägerstrom, Axel. *Kants Ethik*. Upsala: Almqvist & Wiksell Buchdrückerei, 1902.

Heidegger, Martin. *Kant und das Problem der Metaphysik*. Bonn: 1929. (*Kant and the Problem of Metaphysics*, tr. James S. Churchill. Bloomington: Indiana University Press, 1962.)

Hoekstra, Tjeerd. *Immanente Kritik zur Kantischen Religions-Philosophie*. Kampen: J. H. Kok, 1906.

Kroner, Richard. *Kant's Weltanschauung*, tr. John E. Smith, Chicago: University of Chicago Press, 1956.

Lösment, Max. *Zur Religionsphilosophie Kants*. Königsberg: Otto Kümmel, 1907.

Matson, W. I. "Kant as Casuist," Wolff, ed., *Kant: A Collection of Critical Essays*.

Miller, E. Morris. *The Moral Law and the Highest Good*. Melbourne: Melbourne University Press, 1928.

Paton, H. J. *The Categorical Imperative*. New York: Harper and Row, 1965.

——. *The Modern Predicament*. London: Allen & Unwin, 1955.

Paulsen, Friedrich. *Immanuel Kant: Sein Leben und seine Lehre*. Stuttgart: Fr. Frommanns Verlag, 1898. (*Immanuel Kant: His Life and Doctrine*, tr. J. E. Creighton and Albert Lefebvre. New York: Charles Scribner's Sons, 1902.)

——. "Kant der Philosoph des Protestantismus," *Kant-Studien*, Bd. 4, 1900.

Porter, Noah. *Kant's Ethics*. Chicago: S. C. Griggs & Co., 1886.

Pünjer, G. Ch. Bernard. *Die Religionslehre Kants*. Jena: Verlag von Herrmann Dufft, 1874.

Schrader, George A. "Kant's Presumed Repudiation of the Moral Arguments in the *Opus Postumum:* An Examination of Adickes' Interpretation," *Philosophy*, 1951.

Schweitzer, Albert. *Die Religionsphilosophische Skizze der Kritik d. r. V.* Freiburg im Breisgau: C. A. Wagner's Universitäts Buchdrückerei, 1899. (*The Essence of Faith*, tr. K. F. Leidecker. New York: Philosophical Library, 1966.)

Silber, John R. "The Copernican Revolution in Ethics: The Good Reexamined," *Kant: A Collection of Critical Essays*.

———. "Kant's Conception of the Highest Good as Immanent and Transcendent," *Philosophical Review*, LXVIII (1959).

———. "The Ethical Significance of Kant's *Religion*," *Religion within the Limits of Reason Alone*.

Smith, Norman Kemp. *Commentary to Kant's Critique of Pure Reason*. New York: Humanities Press, 1962.

Staeps, H. "Das Christusbild bei Kant," *Kant-Studien*, Bd. 12, 1907.

Teale, A. E. *Kantian Ethics*. New York: Oxford University Press, 1951.

Webb, C. C. J. *Kant's Philosophy of Religion*. Oxford: Clarendon Press, 1926.

Whittemore, Robert. "The Metaphysics of the Seven Formulations of the Moral Argument," *Tulane Studies in Philosophy*, III, 1954.

Other Sources

Canfield, John V. "Knowing About Future Decisions," *Analysis*, Vol. II, No. 6 (1962), pp. 117–129.

Feuerbach, Ludwig. *Sämtliche Werke*, Bd. 6. Stuttgart: Fr. Frommanns Verlag, 1960.

———. *The Essence of Christianity*, tr. George Eliot. New York: Harper and Row, 1957.

Freud, Sigmund. *Gesammelte Werke*, Bd. 14. London: Imago Pub. Co., 1948.

——. *The Future of an Illusion*, tr. W. D. Robson-Scott and James Strachey. Garden City: Doubleday & Co., 1961.

——. *Civilization and Its Discontents*, tr. James Strachey. New York: W. W. Norton & Co., 1961.

Hare, R. M. "Theology and Falsification, B," Flew and MacIntyre, eds., *New Essays in Philosophical Theology*. London: SCM Press, 1961.

Hegel, Georg Wilhelm Friedrich. *Phänomenologie des Geistes*. Hamburg: Felix Meiner Verlag, 1952.

Heidegger, Martin. *Sein und Zeit*. Tübigen: Max Niemeyer Verlag, 1963. (*Being and Time*, tr. John Macquarrie and Edward Robinson. New York: Harper and Row, 1962.)

Hume, David. *A Treatise of Human Nature*. Oxford: Clarendon Press, 1967.

Kierkegaard, Søren Aabye. *Fear and Trembling*, tr. Walter Lowrie. Garden City: Doubleday & Co., 1954.

——. *Repetition: An Essay in Experimental Psychology*, tr. Lowrie. New York: Harper and Row, 1964.

——. *The Concept of Dread*, tr. Lowrie. Princeton: Princeton University Press, 1957.

——. *Philosophical Fragments*, tr. David F. Swenson and Howard V. Hong. Princeton: Princeton University Press, 1962.

——. *Concluding Unscientific Postscript*, tr. Lowrie. Princeton: Princeton University Press, 1941.

——. *The Sickness unto Death*, tr. Lowrie. Garden City: Doubleday & Co., 1954.

Nietzsche, Friedrich. *Gesammelte Werke*. München: Musarion Verlag, 1926. Bd. 17.

——. *The Portable Nietzsche*, ed. Walter Kaufmann, New York: The Viking Press, 1954.

Otto, Rudolf. *Das Heilige*. Breslau: Trewendt & Granier, 1920. (*The Idea of the Holy*, tr. John W. Harvey. London: Pelican Books, 1959.)

Pascal, Blaise. *Pensées*, French and tr. H. F. Stewart. New York: Random House, 1965.

Ritschl, Albrecht. *The Christian Doctrine of Justification and Reconciliation*, tr. McIntosh and Macaulay. Edinburgh: T. & T. Clark, 1900.

Schopenhauer, Arthur. *Sämtliche Werke*, Bd. 2. Wiesbaden: Eberhard Brockhaus Verlag, 1949.

———. *The World as Will and Representation*, tr. E. F. J. Payne. New York: Dover Publications, 1958. Vol. I.

Tillich, Paul. *Systematic Theology*. Chicago: University of Chicago Press, 1963.

Vaihinger, Hans. *Dans Philosophie des Als-Ob*. Berlin: Reuther & Reichard, 1911. (*The Philosophy of As-If*, tr. C. K. Ogden. New York: Harcourt, Brace & Co., 1935.)

Wittgenstein, Ludwig. *Philosophical Investigations*, German and tr. G. E. M. Anscombe. New York: Macmillan Co., 1953.

Index